The EU and crisis response

Manchester University Press

The EU and crisis response

Edited by

Roger Mac Ginty, Sandra Pogodda
and Oliver P. Richmond

MANCHESTER UNIVERSITY PRESS

Copyright © Manchester University Press 2021

While copyright in the volume as a whole is vested in Manchester University Press, copyright in individual chapters belongs to their respective authors.

An electronic version of this book is also available under a Creative Commons (CC-BY-NC-ND) licence, thanks to the support of the European Union's Horizon 2020 research and innovation programme (EUNPACK – A conflict sensitive unpacking of the EU comprehensive approach to conflict and crises mechanism), under grant agreement no.: 693337. This licence permits non-commercial use, distribution and reproduction provided the editor(s), chapter author(s) and Manchester University Press are fully cited and no modifications or adaptations are made. Details of the licence can be viewed at https://creativecommons.org/licenses/by-nc-nd/4.0/

Published by Manchester University Press
Oxford Road, Manchester M13 9PL

www.manchesteruniversitypress.co.uk

British Library Cataloguing-in-Publication Data
A catalogue record for this book is available from the British Library

ISBN 978 1 5261 6479 7 hardback
ISBN 978 1 5261 4835 3 paperback

First published 2021

The publisher has no responsibility for the persistence or accuracy of URLs for any external or third-party internet websites referred to in this book, and does not guarantee that any content on such websites is, or will remain, accurate or appropriate.

Typeset
by Sunrise Setting Ltd, Brixham

Contents

List of figures	vii
List of tables	viii
Notes on contributors	ix
Acknowledgements	xv
List of abbreviations	xvi

1 Introduction: controversies over gaps within EU crisis management policy 1
Roger Mac Ginty, Sandra Pogodda and Oliver P. Richmond

2 Critical crisis transformation: a framework for understanding EU crisis response 26
Oliver P. Richmond, Sandra Pogodda and Roger Mac Ginty

3 The potential and limits of EU crisis response 60
Pernille Rieker and Kristian L. Gjerde

4 The EU's integrated approach to crisis response: learning from the UN, NATO and OSCE 86
Loes Debuysere and Steven Blockmans

5 Securitisation of the EU approach to the Western Balkans: from conflict transformation to crisis management 115
Kari M. Osland and Mateja Peter

6 The paradoxes of EU crisis response in Afghanistan, Iraq and Mali 139
Morten Bøås, Bård Drange, Dlawer Ala'Aldeen, Abdoul Wahab Cissé and Qayoom Suroush

7 The effectiveness of EU crisis response in
  Afghanistan, Iraq and Mali   166
  *Ingo Peters, Enver Ferhatovic, Rabea Heinemann
  and Sofia Sturm*

8 Dissecting the EU response to the 'migration crisis'   201
  Luca Raineri and Francesco Strazzari

Index   227

Figures

2.1	Critical crisis	49
3.1	Serbia/Kosovo 2000–16: terms reflecting different EU agendas	67
3.2	Ukraine 2000–16: terms reflecting different EU agendas	71
3.3	Libya 2000–16: terms reflecting different EU agendas	75
3.4	Afghanistan 2000–16: terms reflecting different EU agendas	77
3.5	Iraq 2000–16: terms reflecting different EU agendas	78
3.6	Mali 2000–16: terms reflecting different EU agendas	80
7.1	Categorising effectiveness: the example of CFSP	168

Tables

2.1	Critical crisis transformation	51
3.1	Selected 'category words'	64
7.1	Classification of peacebuilding frameworks	170

Contributors

Dlawer Ala'Aldeen is the Founding President of the Middle East Research Institute. Formerly, he served as Minister of Higher Education and Scientific Research in the Kurdistan Regional Government and as Professor of Medicine at Nottingham University. He has long been engaged in capacity-building and nation-building projects in Iraq, and has published extensively on political and security dynamics, governance systems and democratisation in the Middle East. His recent books include: *Nation-Building and the System of Governance in the Kurdistan Region* (2013, in Kurdish) and *State-Building: A Roadmap for the Rule-of-Law and Institutionalisation in the Kurdistan Region* (2018, in Kurdish).

Steven Blockmans is Director *a.i.* of the Brussels-based think tank Centre for European Policy Studies and Professor of EU External Relations Law and Governance at the University of Amsterdam. He is the author of *The Obsolescence of the European Neighbourhood Policy* (2017) and *Tough Love: The EU's relations with the Western Balkans* (2007), and he has published widely on the EU's integrated approach to external action. Steven is a frequent media commentator and regularly advises governments of countries in wider Europe and in Asia on their relations with the EU. He is a member of the EU's track 1.5 process with Russia.

Morten Bøås is Research Professor at the Norwegian Institute of International Affairs (NUPI). He is the author of numerous articles, and his books include *The Politics of Conflict Economies: Miners, Merchants and Warriors in the African Borderland* (2015), *Africa's Insurgents: Navigating an Evolving Landscape* (2017, co-edited with Kevin Dunn) and *Doing Fieldwork in Areas of International Intervention: A Guide to Research in Violent and Closed Contexts* (2020, co-edited with Berit Bliesemann de Guevara). From 2016 to 2019, Bøås was the Principal Investigator of the European Commission Horizon 2020-funded EUNPACK.

Loes Debuysere is a Researcher in the CEPS's Foreign Policy Unit. Her expertise and publications are situated at the intersections of gender politics, democratisation and micro-level dynamics of conflict. Her geographic area of expertise is North Africa and the Maghreb. Loes holds a PhD in Conflict and Development Studies from the University of Ghent and an MA in Middle Eastern Studies from SOAS, University of London. She is affiliated as a Researcher with the Middle East and North Africa Research Group (MENARG) of Ghent University.

Bård Drange is a Doctoral Researcher in Political Science at the Peace Research Institute Oslo (PRIO) and the University of Oslo. His doctoral research is on issues of peace and justice coupled with conflict management and conflict dynamics in Colombia. Drange holds an MA in Peace and Conflict Studies from the University of Oslo. Previously, he worked as a Junior Research Fellow at NUPI on the role of external actors in statebuilding, with a geographic focus on the Sahel.

Enver Ferhatovic studied Political Science/Law (MA, 1999) at Freie Universität Berlin. Between 2000 and 2013 he worked for the UN, Organization for Security and Co-operation in Europe (OSCE) and the EU in New York, Sarajevo, Khartoum, Kabul, Nairobi, Brussels and Berlin. Between 2016 and 2019 he was the Research Fellow for EUNPACK. His teaching and research areas are European Security and Foreign Policy, International Relations (IR) Theory and Peacebuilding. He is currently writing his PhD on the effectiveness of Common Security and Defence Policy (CSDP) policing missions.

Rabea Heinemann holds a BA in European Studies from the University of Magdeburg and an MA in IR from Freie Universität Berlin, Humboldt-Universität zu Berlin and University of Potsdam. She has studied in St Petersburg and worked in Brussels and Vienna in EU-related foreign policy institutions. Currently, she works at Deutsche Gesellschaft für Internationale Zusammenarbeit (GIZ) and advises the Federal Ministry for Economic Cooperation and Development (BMZ) regarding the German Presidency of the Council of the European Union.

Kristian L. Gjerde is a Research Fellow at the NUPI and a PhD candidate in Political Science at the University of Oslo. He is co-editor of the Nordic area studies journal *Nordisk Østforum*. His publications include articles on Russian domestic and foreign policy in the journals *East European Politics* and *European Security*. He has a keen interest in the use of programming as a tool in Social Science and Area Studies research, and has developed software for visual exploration of text collections (peer-reviewed in the *Journal of Open Source Software*).

Roger Mac Ginty is Professor at the School of Government and International Affairs, and Director of the Durham Global Security Institute, both at Durham University. He edits the journal *Peacebuilding* and co-directs the Everyday Peace Indicators project.

Kari M. Osland is Senior Research Fellow and Head of the Research Group on Peace, Conflict and Development. Her research fields include international assistance to police reform, including security sector reform, peace operations, peace- and statebuilding, political analysis of the Balkans, war crimes (especially genocide and questions related to international tribunals) and comparative methodology.

Mateja Peter is a Lecturer (Assistant Professor) in IR at the University of St Andrews and a Senior Research Fellow at NUPI. Previously she was a Postdoctoral Fellow at the United States Institute of Peace (USIP), the German Institute for International and Security Affairs (SWP) and the Norwegian Institute for Defence Studies (IFS). She holds a PhD and an MPhil from the University of Cambridge and a BA from the University of Ljubljana. She is pursuing research on global governance and international organisations, peace operations and statebuilding, questions of international authority and broader politics of international interventions in (post-)conflict territories.

Ingo Peters studied Political Science at Freie Universität Berlin (PhD, 1987) and at the University of Lancaster (MA in IR and Strategic Studies, 1983). He is currently Associate Professor at the Otto-Suhr-Institute for Political Science, Freie Universität Berlin, and Executive Director of the Center for Transnational Studies, Foreign and Security Policy. His teaching and research areas are German foreign policy, European security and EU foreign policy, transatlantic relations and IR theory.

Sandra Pogodda is a Lecturer in Peace and Conflict Studies in the Politics Department at the University of Manchester. Sandra completed her PhD in IR at the University of Cambridge as a Marie Curie Fellow before joining the Johns Hopkins School of Advanced International Studies, the United States Institute of Peace and the University of St Andrews as a Postdoctoral Research Fellow. Her research focuses on contemporary revolutions in the Arab region and their impacts on Peace and Conflict Studies. Among her publications are two co-edited volumes: *Post-Liberal Peace Transitions* (2016) and the *Palgrave Handbook of Disciplinary and Regional Approaches to Peace* (2016).

Luca Raineri is Researcher in Security Studies at the Scuola Superiore Sant'Anna of Pisa. His research investigates the security implications of transnational phenomena, focusing in particular on the Sahara-Sahel region.

Oliver P. Richmond is a Research Professor in IR, Peace and Conflict Studies in the Department of Politics at the University of Manchester. He is also an International Professor at Dublin City University. His publications include *Peace Formation and Political Order in Conflict Affected Societies* (2016) and *Failed Statebuilding* (2014). He is the editor of the Palgrave book series *Rethinking Peace and Conflict Studies* and co-editor of the journal *Peacebuilding*.

Pernille Rieker is a Research Professor at NUPI and full Professor at Inland University College. She holds a PhD from the University of

Oslo (2004). Her research interests are European foreign and security policy, with a special focus on the EU, France and the Nordic countries. Her latest publications include the article 'Plugging the capability–expectations gap: Towards effective, comprehensive and conflict-sensitive EU crisis response?', in *European Security* (2019, 28:1, 1–21, with Steven Blockmans), and the monograph *French Foreign Policy in a Changing World: Practising Grandeur* (2017).

Francesco Strazzari is Professor in IR at the Scuola Superiore Sant'Anna of Pisa, and Adjunct Professor at NUPI (Oslo) and at the School of Advanced International Studies (SAIS) Europe, Johns Hopkins University (Bologna). He works on the complex interlinkages between organised crime and armed conflict, with a focus on the European neighbourhood.

Sofia Sturm holds a BA in Political Science from the University of Vienna and an MA in IR from Freie Universität Berlin, Humboldt-Universität zu Berlin and University of Potsdam. She has studied in Jerusalem and worked in foreign policy institutions in New York and the Occupied Palestinian Territories. Currently, she works at GIZ and advises the BMZ regarding the design of future-fit development policies and strategies, focusing on African–European relations and the German EU Presidency 2020.

Qayoom Suroush has an MA in Politics and Security from OSCE Academy in Bishkek. He has worked as a researcher with different leading research organisations, including Afghanistan Analysts Network (AAN), Human Rights Watch (HRW) and Afghanistan Research and Evaluation Unit (AREU). He has published on a variety of subjects, including Afghanistan's police reform and the programme of the EU's Police Mission in Afghanistan. Suroush is currently working as a Researcher with the Centre for Civilians in Conflict (CIVIC). Suroush's general research and academic interests are security, conflict, history and Islamic studies.

Abdoul Wahab Cissé is a Researcher at the Resource Centre of the Alliance for Rebuilding Governance in Africa (ARGA), an African think tank based in Dakar. He was also for ten years an Associate Professor of Political Science at IMES (Catholic University of West

Africa), Dakar. His expertise and publications relate to migration issues, governance in general and issues of security and social cohesion. His priority research area is West Africa. Cissé holds a PhD in Political Science from Sciences Po Bordeaux, and a DEA in African Studies and a DEA in Sociology from the University of Bordeaux. He holds also an MA in Philosophy from the Cheikh Anta Diop University in Dakar.

Acknowledgements

The research underpinning this book was funded by the EU's Horizon 2020 research and innovation programme (EUNPACK – A Conflict-Sensitive Unpacking of the EU Comprehensive Approach to Conflict and Crises Mechanism), under grant agreement number: 693337. The editors and chapter authors are grateful to all those who contributed to the research through participation in interviews, focus groups and questionnaires.

Abbreviations

AREU	Afghanistan Research and Evaluation Unit
ARGA	Alliance for Rebuilding Governance in Africa
CCT	Critical Crisis Transformation
CFSP	(EU) Common Foreign and Security Policy
CM	Conflict Management
CMR	Central Mediterranean Route
CR	Conflict Resolution
CSDP	(EU) Common Security and Defence Policy
CT	Conflict Transformation
DDR	Disarmament, Demobilisation and Reintegration
DPA	(UN) Department of Political Affairs
DPKO	(UN) Department of Peacekeeping Operations
EaP	Eastern Partnership
EASO	(EU) European Asylum Support Office
EC	European Commission
ECHO	European Civil Protection and Humanitarian Aid Operations
ECOWAS	Economic Community of West African States
EEAS	European External Action Service
ENP	European Neighbourhood Policy
ESS	European Security Strategy
EU	European Union
EUAM	EU Advisory Mission
EUBAM	EU Border Assistance Mission

EUCAP	EU Capacity Building Mission
EUFOR	EU Force
EUGS	EU Global Strategy on Foreign and Security Policy
EUJUST LEX	EU Rule of Law Mission in Iraq
EULEX	EU Rule of Law Mission in Kosovo
EUNAVFOR MED	EU Naval Force – Mediterranean
EUPOL	EU Police Mission
EUROJUST	EU Agency for Criminal Justice Cooperation
EUROPOL	EU Agency for Law Enforcement Cooperation
EUSR	EU Special Representative
EUTF	EU Emergency Trust Fund (for Africa)
EUTM	EU Training Mission
FAMa / MAF	*Forces armées maliennes* / Malian Armed Forces
GAMM	(EU) Global Approach to Migration and Mobility
HIPPO	(UN) High-Level Independent Panel on Peace Operations
HR/VP	(EU) High Representative/Vice President
INGO	International Non-Governmental Organisation
IPCB	International Police Coordination Board (Afghanistan)
IR	International Relations
LOTFA	Law and Order Trust Fund for Afghanistan
MENA	Middle East and North Africa
MINUSMA	(UN) Multidimensional Integrated Stabilization Mission in Mali
NATO	North Atlantic Treaty Organization
NGO	Non-Governmental Organisation
NTM-A	NATO Training Mission-Afghanistan
NUPI	Norwegian Institute of International Affairs
OECD	Organisation for Economic Co-operation and Development
OHCHR	Office of the High Commissioner for Human Rights

OSCE	Organization for Security and Co-operation in Europe
PARSEC	Programme d'Appui au reforcement de la Sécurité
PFCA	(EEAS) Political Framework for a Crisis Approach
SAR	Search and Rescue
SGUA	Support Group for Ukraine
SSR	Security Sector Reform
UNHCR	United Nations High Commissioner for Refugees
UNMIK	United Nations Interim Administration Mission in Kosovo
UNSMIL	United Nations Support Mission in Libya

1

Introduction: controversies over gaps within EU crisis management policy

Roger Mac Ginty, Sandra Pogodda and Oliver P. Richmond

Introduction

Just as the United Nations (UN) was not established with peacekeeping missions in mind, the European Union (EU) was not established with external security, crisis intervention, or peacebuilding on the agendas of its founders. They were initially focused on using trade to overcome nineteenth- and early-twentieth-century regional geopolitics, opening up a federal path for formerly warring states, as well as fitting into a jigsaw of regional and global ordering mechanisms. In its later iteration, the EU developed external facing orientations, policies and capabilities over an extended period, often reactively and in the face of emergencies, while developing its own problematic governmentalities for peacebuilding (Pogodda et al., 2014). A gap soon emerged in that it had little viable capacity for crisis management. As this book will reveal, there has been considerable tension between the notion and practice of conflict management as a stand-alone and often technical intervention, and arguments in favour of more expansive interventions that take into account human rights, democracy, development, trade and a vibrant civil society. Either approach, and all points in between, comes with a series of ethical and practical challenges that occupy much of this book.

This led to a controversial dance around the classic problem of whether conflict management strategies might be adequate as freestanding strategies of engagement, and whether peacebuilding responses might be retracted if they were, not to mention the 'outmoded' conditionalities that were previously attached to EU involvement in regional crises and conflicts (such as human rights, democracy, development, trade and a vibrant civil society).

Crises pose extraordinary challenges since they constitute events that have 'the potential to cause a large detrimental change to the social system and in which there is a lack of proportionality between cause and consequence' (Walby, 2015: 14). While the EU has been involved in a series of continuously morphing and deepening internal crises (Habermas, 2012; Giddens, 2014; Offe, 2015), this book focuses on the Union's capacity to respond to crises outside of the internal market.

The EU's recent development of a distinct interventionary practice for external crisis responses (Bátora *et al.*, 2016) inspired this book to investigate its underlying rationales, its effects and how the new practice fits into the EU's portfolio of foreign policy interventions. *Crisis management* as the best-known type of crisis response conceptually separates intervention from the EU's normative and institutional goals, foregrounding the interests of the originating actor. Consequently, it risks a loss of local legitimacy and conflict sensitivity among the recipients of such practices. At the same time, there has been a policy-driven interest in developing more effective conflict responses approaches on behalf of the EU (Tocci, 2017) and making sure they were conflict-sensitive. This book investigates whether, and if, this paradoxical circle of norms, interests and ambitions can be squared. Is the EU's crisis response approach conflict-sensitive, does it support or undermine local agency, or more substantive peacebuilding strategies, and does it prioritise organisational dynamics and EU stability and security or conflict-affected populations?

In its effort to evaluate EU crisis interventions, this book puts forward an innovative typology for crisis response, which goes beyond the limited ambitions of stabilising a region and containing the spill-over effects of conflicts that characterise *crisis management* (this typology is explained in detail in Chapter 2). By drawing on different generations of Peace and Conflict scholarship, the book assumes that crises can also be resolved (*crisis resolution*), transformed (*crisis transformation*) or tackled through critical transformative approaches (*critical crisis transformation*). Crisis resolution addresses the needs of crisis-affected populations and considers economic marginalisation, conflicts and 'bad governance' as root causes of crises. By contrast, crisis transformation deals with the structural drivers of conflict and builds a framework for emancipation from crisis conflict dynamics. In critical crisis intervention, our framework imagines an approach in which the EU jointly designs its interventions with local networks of elite and non-elite actors at the epicentre of the crises, connected with regional and international organisations with the aim of sharing resources and coordinating crisis response strategies.

The following chapters explore different elements of the problem of how to connect state and EU approaches to crisis response, and mitigate causal factors of violence in war-zones, while also attempting to accommodate local political claims for emancipation. Geographically, it examines EU engagements in the MENA, Mali, Afghanistan and Eastern European regions. It does so via different perspectives: ethnographic, institutionalist, security oriented and case-study oriented. It explores the gap between critical intentions and pragmatic politics aimed at averting crisis and conflicts. It rejects the notion that a crisis can be separated from the deeper causal factors of a longer-term conflict, and acknowledges that crisis management is thus closely related to peacebuilding. In doing so it critically demonstrates the acute problems of maintaining critical ethnography, preventing the tendency to shift analysis from the local to elite, emancipation to security and interests, substituting institutionalist priorities for human rights and needs. Performatively, this book collectively illustrates chapter by chapter the risks and difficulties inherent in the attempt to separate crisis from conflict, the constant defaulting to elite and institutional prerogatives even when engaged with ethnographic or institutionalist methods, and the 'counter-insurgency' style methodological tendency to equate and reduce critical intent to hegemony or interests.

Thus, the subsequent chapters are framed by a critical issue: how far is there a gap between crisis management theory, the EU's institutionalised understanding of it and conflict sensitivity or local legitimacy on the ground? This introductory chapter outlines the structure and key findings of the book and introduces the typology that lies at the heart of the book. This typology is discussed in more detail in Chapter 2. It draws on critical Peace and Conflict Studies theory, a crisis management–crisis resolution–crisis transformation–framework through which to critically evaluate EU policy and practice. Most of the chapters point to a major gap between local legitimacy and EU practice, even if EU doctrines tend to be more critically aligned. A number of chapters (e.g., those by Raineri and Strazzari, and Osland and Peter) help outline the EU's evolution as a foreign policy, regional and global actor. They show that this evolution was not linear, not without missteps, was often reactive, and was subject to distraction by internal politics and concerns. All of this applies to the EU's crisis response mechanisms and stances.

While a substantial literature exists on the EU as a regional and global actor (see, e.g., Tonra and Christiansen, 2018; Schumacher *et al.*, 2018), this book investigates the Union's crisis responses simultaneously from an Organisational Studies and Peace and Conflict Studies perspective. Research on EU-sponsored peacebuilding is well advanced, but much of it concentrates on single case studies, reports on specific projects and neglects to examine EU mechanisms. This sustained examination of crisis response is comparative and looks at EU discourse and mechanisms, as well as the actual on-the-ground responses and their local reception. The research into the formation of crisis response at the EU level provides a detailed analysis of the evolution of the crisis intervention apparatus, its ambitions, repertoires and strategies. Moreover, it contrasts EU crisis interventions with the responses of other international organisations. These dimensions of the research examine the nature of organisations, how they respond to challenges and crises and how they can marshal capacities and project their power and resources. In the case of the EU, we are interested in how the EU constructs narratives for its actions, and how its policies are forged and orientated for the challenges the EU faces and the actions it takes. We are interested in how the organisation has navigated between constructing and maintaining a comprehensive approach to its external actions, the divergent interests of its member states and the peculiarities of different crises and locations. Important in this is the fact that the EU has adopted an 'integrated approach' to crisis management and has put in place considerable architecture and machinery to respond to crises in a measured and coordinated way. Yet questions remain about the EU's actorness – or the extent to which it constitutes, and is perceived to constitute, a coherent foreign policy actor (McDonagh, 2015).

The book's Peace and Conflict Studies components, on the other hand, locate crisis response conceptually and examine how EU intervention is perceived on the ground. This analysis of local reception of the EU as a crisis response actor contributes to the 'local turn' in the study and practice of peace interventions (Schierenbeck, 2015): to what extent are international interventions sensitive to local needs and aspirations or driven by institutional and/or geopolitical considerations? Who initiates and sets the agenda of the intervention? Who decides on an exit strategy? And how legitimate are EU crisis interventions within the crisis-affected population? In large part this book is about power, or the power of a large international organisation to affect its will in crisis situations on its doorstep and further afield, and the power of local actors (national or sub-states) to utilise, co-opt, resist, subvert and delay EU interventions.

In order to examine these issues of crises, intervention and international organisation we have developed a comprehensive and comparative approach through a large multipartner research project entitled EUNPACK (Bøås and Rieker, 2019). The project was comprised of a consortium of thirteen institutions (one each from Afghanistan, Belgium, Germany, Iraq, Italy, Kosovo, Mali, Norway, Serbia, Slovakia, Tunisia, Ukraine and the UK) and was able to combine desk-based study with field research in a number of conflict-affected countries – as well as Brussels. Through the research of our locally embedded partner institutions, this project has – to some extent at least – been able to avoid the dilemmas encountered by external researchers (Maschietto, 2015). The result is a state-of-the-art investigation into how the EU mobilises and projects its crisis response policies. Uniquely, this research project and book have been able to move towards a dialogue between two sub-disciplines that are often siloed and rarely benefit from intellectual cross-fertilisation: Peace and Conflict Studies and Organisational Studies. Both fit within the larger discipline of International Relations (IR), and both draw on a range of other disciplines such as Gender Studies, Anthropology, Psychology, Sociology and History. Yet they rarely 'speak' to each other in a sustained way. This book can be read as an attempt to spark a cross-disciplinary conversation and to assess the utility of lending and borrowing between concepts, theories and vernacular that often remain in siloes.

Fundamentally, the book is also interested in the highly problematic and often glossed-over interface between international organisations' institutionalist and geopolitical goals and their tensions with the political claims made by local populations in crisis situations. It is about the projection and reception of international intervention, and its general failure to be related to local political claims for security, human security and conflict transformation. It prompts us to interrogate apparently discrete and binary concepts like local and international, and encourages us to be mindful of the multiscalar and complex nature of conflict systems. As the chapters in this book reveal, there is considerable connectivity at work in relation to all scales involved in conflict and attempts to address it.

What does EU Crisis Management seek to address?

Clearly, the EU's internal integrity was at the heart of developments, representing a further underlying substantial controversy about the EU as a peace project (Manners and Murray, 2016) and its ability to translate and disseminate the historical lessons its very existence represented for the newer conflict zones of the late twentieth century and beyond. Indeed, its responses to regional wars, and its contributions to peacekeeping and peacebuilding have long been controversial, consistently indicating a substantial gap between policy doctrine and interests, often oscillating between a normative and humanitarian vision or a geopolitical approach, and worse, placing the stability of EU policy, doctrines and institutions over the situations of the conflict-affected citizens in its near abroad (Richmond, 2000; Richmond *et al.*, 2011). They have also been undermined by a lack of consensus among its members and the occasional unilateral action (as with Germany's role in the breakup of the former Yugoslavia, or the divisions between member states over the US invasion of Iraq). Its engagement with peacebuilding and development, though impressive in scale and ambition, has also been bedevilled by the same gaps, which might be described as an implementation–expectation gap which has also been transferred to what might be understood as a retrogressive interest in crisis management.

Since its legal inception in the Maastricht Treaty of 1992, any efforts to establish a joint security, foreign and defence policy were the result of a dilemma, rather than a conscious political choice. Member states' fear of losing their sovereignty through integration has been pitched against the inevitable erosion of sovereignty that would result from the *lack of* integration, regionalisation, consolidation and optimisation of national military capacities (Giddens, 2014: 202). To make matters more complicated, the intervening years have seen many turning points in international relations: from the liberal hubris of the 1990s, to the War on Terror and its devastating consequences, Russia's annexation of Eastern European territory and NATO's first and last Responsibility to Protect (R2P) intervention in Libya. In this tumultuous political environment, the EU's foreign policy continues to be the outcome of 'creeping devolution' rather than a decision to join forces against shared external challenges (Habermas, 2009: 88).

It is important to note that the conceptualisation and theorisation of 'crisis management' has always tended to represent a very preliminary intellectual and policy strategy in the face of an emerging threat or risk for any political system. Crisis management has implied, since the nineteenth century, and certainly during the Cold War, an attempt to dampen and mitigate war and conflict as a first step, perhaps providing a platform for political agreements to be reached later on. It represents a very distant attempt to enable emancipatory and transformatory forms of political settlement in conflict-affected societies. Academics have tended to argue that crisis-oriented epistemologies tend to be unable to move beyond pacification towards dealing with underlying causal factors, whereas policy-driven usages highlight the necessity and immediacy of a response to a dangerous threat even at the expense of peace agreements, political reforms and longer-term remedies, resolutions or transformations. Thus, there has always been a gap or blockage between crisis management and peacemaking. In general, a mistaken but convenient conflation of crisis response with transformatory political policies (such as peacebuilding) persists in scholarly literatures and policy doctrines, especially in the context of the EU. By contrast the UN has a much clearer picture of the gradations of praxis involved in sequenced approaches to crisis management and diplomacy, peacekeeping, mediation, peacebuilding and more recently towards 'sustaining peace' (Ponzio, 2018). Whereas in the past, it seemed that the EU followed (with some time lag) the epistemological approaches to war, violence, reform and peace that were being pioneered in the UN system, more recently, the EU seems to have struck out in its own direction, with a problematic lack of clarity about the intellectual history of the frameworks it was seeking to deploy.

Among the various institutions and policies of EU foreign policy, crisis response – as a mechanism – has only emerged as the result of Baroness Ashton's institutional reforms since 2010 (Tercovich, 2014). The ideological basis as well as the conceptual and strategic framework of this new mechanism have remained poorly defined (Pavlov, 2015) though there is a tendency to regard it as more transformatory rather than geopolitical in the EU's context. In practice, it was more geopolitical than transformational. Despite these 'teething problems', the new EU crisis response mechanism was slated to become the EU's overarching security and emergency approach (Tercovich, 2014: 151). Hence, this book is a sustained examination of the EU's crisis response mechanisms in conflicts in its neighbourhood, extended neighbourhood and further afield. It investigates the factors that have shaped EU crisis response, local perceptions of its interventions abroad and ultimately resulted in the failure of the new mechanism to become a paradigm-changing innovation within European foreign policy.

Ultimately, EU Crisis Management is aimed at preserving the integrity of the core Union at a primary level, patrolling its external boundaries and contributing to rather than initiating, stabilisation measures where crises on its peripheries threaten both. However, given the EU's normative self-identity, and given the demands of conflict-affected societies drawn into this process, crisis management has inevitably morphed into something approaching peacebuilding, and a longer term more rights-based framework, which the EU has found even harder to perform in a convincing manner. Awkwardly, the result has been something more akin to counterinsurgency than peacebuilding, and certainly more like early conceptions of crisis and conflict management, rather than transformation. The latter would involve a far more longer-term, structural engagement on behalf of the EU, and the focus to move from the integrity of the EU to the human security of conflict-affected citizens. By using a framework that modifies the usual palate of conflict responses (conflict management, conflict resolution, conflict transformation and critical conflict transformation) into crisis responses (crisis management, crisis resolution, crisis transformation and critical crisis transformation) we are able to see the extent to which EU mechanisms and responses engage with security, rights and development. We are also able to use the framework to assess the geographical and temporal ambition of EU responses: the near neighbourhood or further afield, and short-term or long-term.

Key findings

A key finding ties the book together: there is an increased emphasis on security in the EU's crisis responses (Raineri and Strazzari, 2019), which is often at the expense of strategies designed to be conflict-sensitive and critically engaged with local political claims. This trend contains much nuance and we must be careful to guard against over-generalisation. In their chapter, Debuysere and Blockmans highlight that the EU has not officially given up on the engagement with the root causes of crises as proclaimed by its integrated approach. Yet, institutionalised perspectives rarely managed to move beyond elite, state and institutional level prerogatives, goals and constraints. Moreover, EU crisis intervention is characterised by contradictory trends according to the chapter by Peters, Ferhatovic, Heinemann and Sturm, resulting from turf wars between the different EU foreign and security policy institutions. This means that there is an acute tension between critical crisis transformation discourses on the part of the EU, the short-term nature of crisis management thinking, and conflict sensitivity on the ground in practice (as Chapter 2 suggests).

At the same time, we should be in no doubt that creeping, but accelerating, securitisation is observable in EU stances, strategies and statements in relation to what it identifies as threats on and beyond its borders. As will be discussed in the chapters in this book, this does not only have implications for how the EU is perceived; it also has implications for the nature of the Union. One of the key assumptions that guided this research project is that we should judge the EU, and other international organisations, according to what they do and do not do, not just according to declarations, statements and ambitions. Case studies from the former Yugoslavia, Libya, Afghanistan, Mali and elsewhere, along with detailed study of EU statements, reveal a complex picture of an organisation that is attempting to navigate a path through a difficult and dynamic external environment while also maintaining normative standards. While the EU by no means is able to act unilaterally (it must contend with other external actors, strong states and many exogenous factors, as well as internal nationalisms) it has considerable capabilities. It has convening power in the sense of bringing multiple states under one umbrella, has significant material power, and seeks to project a normative or collective power through its statements and declared ambitions. As seen over an extended period, the EU – in some of its interventions – was aware of the complexities of contemporary conflict and particularly of the links between development, rights and conflict. Thus, in some cases, the EU was at the forefront of promoting rights and development in its conflict and crisis response initiatives. The EU – at least discursively – seemed more comfortable with emancipatory and people-focused approaches to peace than many other institutions. However, its practices are more opaque, either due to conceptual confusion or the sheer scale of the problems caused by limited political legitimacy on the ground.

As this book demonstrates, the space for interventions that championed peace and rights (two very political concepts) seems to have shrunk. In its place has been a narrow focus on security and stabilisation, which has also played out in the related epistemological framing of EU foreign policy, peacebuilding and crisis management. Crucial here too is to ask: What is being secured and stabilised? The withdrawal of focus on rights, people and development has meant that often the focus is on securing institutions and regimes overseas. These institutions and regimes may have questionable effectiveness and respect for rights and minorities (Pogodda et al., 2014). Yet they are seen as the most viable contact point for the EU and are to be shored up. Alex de Waal's (2015) concept of the 'political marketplace' comes into play here, with regimes and institutions able to offer the EU the promise of security, stability and sometimes service delivery in return for material support and the symbolic affirmation that goes along with it. The danger for the EU, however, and this danger applies to other donors, is that they become captured by the regime or institution. As Raineri and Strazzari's chapter reminds us, if an external crisis spirals into an EU-internal crisis, crisis response might become beholden to unaccountable rulers, militias and warlords. Chapter 2's typology, drawing on older debates about the pros and cons of conflict management versus resolution and transformation theory, confirms this deficiency.

An introspective and self-serving streak of EU crisis response has become increasingly visible. There is much more awareness in the EU of the possibility of overseas crises impacting on the EU itself. This has especially been the case in relation to inward migration to the EU – with conflict and the associated economic and social dislocation being major contributory factors. For many observers, these conflicts gained and maintained the attention of EU member states not primarily because of the casualty figures in the conflict, but because it was thought that they helped generate migration towards the EU. With migration and the perception of migration fuelling populism within EU member states, external crisis response turned into a mechanism to deal with domestic political issues (see Chapter 7, this volume). Hence, from the migration crisis in the Balkans that opened the possibility for a normative EU foreign policy to the migration crisis of 2015 that closed this window, the EU has come full circle (see Chapter 8, this volume). Thus, it is no accident that 'crisis' discourses have supplanted peacebuilding, rights, democratisation and development frameworks, lending themselves to neo-trusteeship, counter-insurgency, stabilisation and resilience agendas. Since the beginning of the twenty-first century, the emancipatory content of these agendas has remained unproven, not to say implausible.

The same applies to the rise of militant groups in Syria, Iraq, Libya and Mali. Many of these groups are covered by the 'terrorism' and radicalisation narratives favoured by some politicians and policy-makers. A key feature of some of these narratives is that 'terrorism' and radicalisation are transnational and have implications in the centre as much as the periphery. In other words, narratives about militancy in Libya (the periphery) can be quickly related to the 'home front' (the centre) in the form of the 2017 suicide bomb attack on the Manchester Arena in the UK. Thus for the EU and the member states that construct its policies, seemingly far-away events can constitute, or be perceived to constitute, a real and present danger to citizens within the EU. Again, similar arguments were made and phenomena observed in earlier debates on conflict and crisis management, which necessitated a move away from security and interest-oriented framing towards what became known in the 1990s as liberal peacebuilding praxis, which was multidimensional and longer term.

As will be explained throughout this book, the EU's slide away from rights and more optimistic views of peace has not been consistent. A key nuance in this picture has been a spatial differentiation between the near and extended neighbourhoods. The fact that the EU has an extended neighbourhood is, in itself, worthy of comment. It shows, on the one hand that the organisation has (or perhaps had) ambitions to be a global development and pro-peace player. It equipped itself institutionally and programmatically to have a global reach and project its material and symbolic resources. On the other hand, the notion of an extended neighbourhood shows an understanding of the extended nature of conflict and crises. Thus, crises were unlikely to be contained: they had the potential to have spill-over effects and unintended consequences that were likely to reach the EU itself.

To interpret this shift between different types of crisis response, the project developed an analytical framework that drew on a key conceptualisation from Peace and Conflict Studies in Chapter 2. The widely accepted framework of conflict responses (Richmond, 2010) – conflict management, conflict resolution, conflict transformation and critical conflict transformation – has been useful in helping to conceptualise, categorise and understand how states and other institutions have attempted to deal with conflict. The framework has been useful as a way of thinking through the actions involved, the extent of those actions and the motivations behind them. Under this framework, conflict management is the least ambitious response and is respectful of the institutions (often states) and structures (often sovereignty and political economies) that contribute to conflict. It aims to manage the cost of conflict rather than directly confront the conflict. Conflict transformation is regarded as a more ambitious conflict response, and one that is people-focused and willing to address the underlying drivers of conflict such as the construction of identity. As part of the EUNPACK project, the conflict management–conflict resolution–conflict transformation analytical framework was extended to crisis response as a way of stimulating and ordering our thinking on how the EU responds to crises. Throughout this book, we can see how crisis response has been shaped by different ideological forces, moving interventions between different levels: from the potential of a comprehensive approach to crisis transformation to the limited ambition of crisis management.

Other arguments and findings

One issue that recurs in this book is the extent to which crises are constructed, maintained, narrated, minimised and time-limited. The definition of a crisis and the design of its response are seen as exercises of power (Hay, 1996; Gamble, 2014; Walby, 2015). Part of this is connected to the 'naming power' of political and social actors to designate, formally or informally, a certain phenomenon as a crisis. The concept of 'crisis' maintains a short-term epistemological frame for any response, and confines it to negative peace methods, heavily constrained by interests and power relations. It offers a conservative response to risk and systemic destabilisation, rather than the human rights framing the EU gloss tends to assume is to be delivered. Ironically, it appears to have been misapplied in EU policy and academic circles, or alternatively has been used to constrain the political substance of peacemaking and peacebuilding, leaving EU norms somewhat undermined. In relation to perceptions of inward migration to Europe in particular, it was interesting to see the co-constitution of the crisis. On the one hand, there were the conflict-related drivers of migration such as the wars in Afghanistan and Syria. On the other hand, there were the public discourses and political mobilisations in a number of European states that emphasised nativist sentiments. These discourses and mobilisations often became manifest in anti-incumbency and anti-institutional political movements and so threatened sitting governments and existing institutions. In short, the plight of the refugees was constructed as a threat to member state governments and the EU itself. So, in the case of migration, it is worth noting that it was the complex interplay between the risk of incomplete agreements (Scipioni, 2015), an actual phenomenon (inward migration to and through the EU) and the perception and political utilisation of that phenomenon that led to a tipping point in the evolution of the EU's crisis response in some of our cases. While crises can provide windows of opportunity for wide-ranging political change (Gamble, 2014), the migration crisis of 2015 has constrained the transformative potential of EU crisis intervention. It should be noted, of course, that non-EU member states (e.g., Turkey, Lebanon, Jordan) have been, by far, most impacted by migrant and refugee flows.

Another finding that runs through this book is that many of the categories that we routinely use to explain the social and political world are worthy of interrogation. On the one hand, it is understandable that we have a 'short-hand' of phrases and categories that we use to explain social phenomenon in an efficient and comprehensible way. Yet, on the other hand, many of these categories do not bear scrutiny. Consider, for example, the notion of 'the local': it is not immediately clear if the term relates to the national government (and elites within it) or any of a number of sub-state levels. When we further interrogate the term 'local', then more problems appear. In a networked and transnational world, and one in which commerce – not to mention peacebuilding and development programmes – mean a mobility of ideas, people and capital, then it is difficult to conceive of a hermetically sealed local, but such issues are also present within the categories of 'international', 'regional' and 'state' (Richmond and Mac Ginty, 2019). The point of engaging with the local, the everyday, as well as with subsequent frameworks such as hybridity in critical genealogical terms, is to lay bare the workings of power relations from a subaltern perspective in order to produce sustainable, rights-oriented and justice-based systems of political order (which one would assume for the UN and EU, for example). Such systems, by their very nature, face challenges in their crisis transformation and peacemaking capacities, whose legitimacy depends on the way they reorder power relations and respond to subaltern claims.

A key finding from across the project related to data and information, or the extent to which local and international actors were able to understand each other with any sense of accuracy in the light of such imbalances and challenges. The EU, in keeping with many international and transnational actors, faced challenges of gathering and collating information from national settings. At times, this was constrained by the security situation and 'compound living'. At other times, there was information overload and capacity issues (Read *et al.*, 2016). These problems extended to within the EU itself where there was not always adequate lesson-learning within the institution, a factor often relating to the 'churn' or turnover of mission and headquarters staff. At the local level, there was often confusion as to who or what constituted the EU. In a number of cases, local actors tended to conflate the EU with other international actors or its member states. Nuances in EU strategy that may have been the result of pained negotiations and trade-offs in Brussels were not readily perceived by local 'beneficiaries'. In Mali, for instance, over half of respondents who had contact with the EU did not know if it was the EU or another organisation who was operational. All of this points to the value of transparency and communication within and between institutions and other actors. It also illustrates the importance of communication through actions. While local and external actors can invest considerable energy into messaging and declarations, it is action and inaction (e.g., delivery of programmes or follow-through by local actors) that are often most noticeable.

In all of the cases, the complexity of intervention and crisis response is apparent. Intervention is not a discrete exercise that is limited in terms of time, space and impact. Instead, it is part of a set of wider political, social, economic and cultural interventions – many of which have unanticipated outcomes. Actors – whether local or international – are not standalone. Instead they will have complicated and intersectional hinterlands and relationalities that are not always easily observable by others. Crucially, there will be unanticipated outcomes. For example, EU outsourcing of the management of migration in Libya resulted in the empowerment of non-state armed actors and the further development of a political economy around migration. Clearly, this was not the aim of EU policy but it is one that is likely to have long-term effects.

A recurring theme in the book is temporality or timing. The notion of a crisis suggests urgency and the need for a fast response. As already noted, there is a sense that crises are socially constructed, maintained and de-escalated with some actors having greater agency than others. In other words, temporality is a social construction (Read and Mac Ginty, 2017). What was very noticeable from a number of the case studies was that the EU and various sites of intervention operate according to different timeframes. For the EU, there are a mix of technocratic timeframes (connected with budgetary cycles, programmatic log-frames and the tenure of staff) and political timeframes (connected with political machinations within the EU and electoral cycles within member states). Yet these timeframes may have little resonance or meaning at the site of intervention. Here national and local political machinations are likely to matter more and they may not always synchronise with those of external actors. In some cases, external actors arrived, delivered programmes and left with an almost robotic disconnection with the local rhythms of life. The breadth of the EUNPACK project has meant that it has been possible to capture a range of EU crisis interventions and responses – at inception, planning, implementation, monitoring and post-implementation evaluation. Indeed, such a timeline suggests a linearity that does not always seem consistent with events in Brussels or in the receiving country. In virtually all of the EUNPACK case studies, it was clear that there were tensions between the urgency of crises and the longer term timeframes required for development and peacebuilding.

Fieldwork

It is worth bearing in mind that fieldwork in conflict-affected contexts requires considerable sensitivity. The safety of the researched and researcher need to be considered and all EUNPACK fieldwork was conducted in accordance with a strict ethical framework. Fieldwork in conflict-affected contexts faces multiple problems (in addition to any physical dangers faced by the researcher and the researched): gatekeeping by those who want to promote an institutional or party narrative, surveillance by states or neighbours, the sometimes invisibility of women and minorities, the risk of re-traumatising victims of violence and the risk of using concepts and language that might betray bias or offend. Fundamentally, it is not always clear that social science researchers are well equipped to access the opinions and thoughts of people living through crisis situations and who may have a very different cultural and social ethos. Attempts to have 'partnerships' with scholars and practitioners in the Global South are often unable to escape North–South structural imbalances and political economies associated with research, publishing and dissemination.

With these points in mind, the EUNPACK project engaged in extensive fieldwork in a meta context in which there is a doctrinal and policy confusion over terms and concepts like crisis management and peacebuilding, and a blurring of the line between the sensitive engagement of external actors with local elites and social movements and responding to subaltern political claims. We sought to investigate the emancipatory agenda that the EU claims through approximately thirteen hundred interviews, perception surveys and documentary analysis in Afghanistan, Mali, Iraq, Libya, Kosovo and Ukraine. There was an attempt to access 'bottom-up' voices – the very voices that are often difficult to access and easy to overlook (Spivak, 1988; Lederach, 1997; Firchow and Mac Ginty, 2017) – although such attempts must come with caveats. The fieldwork was conducted by local organisations (sometimes partnered with others from the EUNPACK team). The premise behind using local researchers was that local actors are usually best-placed to access and understand local institutions and narratives. Of course, we were aware of the opportunities and challenges associated with insider and outsider statuses but, on balance, calculated that local researchers would have many advantages in relation to gatekeeping, access and context. While EUNPACK sought to have an overarching analytical framework (as outlined in the next chapter) this could not be too rigid given local circumstances. Thus, in consultation with local project partners some methods were modified (e.g., the terminology used in questionnaires) to suit particular cases.

Structure of the book

All of the chapters touch on conceptual issues (many discussed above) and draw on original primary material.

The book starts by presenting its analytical and conceptual framework in Chapter 2. Here, the authors are investigating the possibilities inherent in crisis response. By developing a framework that identifies, explains and illustrates four potential levels of crisis intervention, Pogodda, Richmond and Mac Ginty demonstrate the limitations of the pervasive concept of crisis management. Indeed, it is seen as the least advanced of all levels of intervention, as its ambitions are limited to containing the crisis. Instead, the authors argue, crisis resolution, crisis transformation and its critical variant would be better suited to accommodate the normative ambitions of EU foreign policy, while also providing more useful approaches to the crisis. This means that crises needed to be seen as a long-term dynamic requiring strategies more normally associated with peacebuilding, because conflict management cannot be maintained after the short term without political progress. After all, crisis management is limited to shielding the EU from the effects of a crisis, but does not engage with the root causes of instability, conflict or other man-made disasters. While different chapters show how the complex interaction of member states' interests, external interference and the tensions between different EU institutions ultimately limit the standard EU response to mere containment, Bøås, Drange, Ala'Aldeen, Cissé and Suroush (Chapter 6, this volume) agree that crisis management has ultimately failed and needs to be replaced with a transformatory approach in order to avoid further erosion of the EU's legitimacy.

Crucial to understanding the EU's crisis response mechanisms and actions is the fact that the EU does not act unilaterally. Instead, it is merely one of a number of multilateral and transnational actors that are often at work in conflict-affected and humanitarian settings. As Debuysere and Blockmans observe in their chapter, the EU strives towards a comprehensive approach, covering all cycles of a crisis and coordinating the response of all EU institutions (as set out in the 2016 EU Global Strategy on Foreign and Security Policy). Yet attempts to integrate all aspects of the EU crisis response system into a comprehensive approach seems complicated by there being a crowded field of actors, and the fact that formal, elite, state-level and regional actors are favoured over social movements, citizens and local frameworks of legitimacy. Moreover, the attentions and resources of member states are divided between their own national strategies, the EU, the UN and other international organisations (e.g. NATO or OSCE). This has implications for policy coherence.

In this forcefield of coordination, the integration of local partners is normally deprioritised. Debuysere and Blockmans show a range of challenges facing the EU in its attempts to construct and maintain a coherent stance. These include the sheer variety of crises facing the EU, varying understandings of conflict sensitivity by EU personnel and the difficulty of including national stakeholders in most phases of the policy cycle. Their chapter points to the limitations of determining conflict sensitivity via the perspective of elites, states and institutional viewpoints. It offers an organisational and institutional logic that places the EU in relation to 'conflict sensitivity' rather than conflict-affected societies. This presents a historical and political problem for the EU's aim to become more conflict-sensitive.

Raineri and Strazzari (Chapter 8, this volume) investigate the crisis which has proven to be at the heart of recent EU crisis response in its neighbourhood and extended neighbourhood: the migration crisis of 2015. Here, the intertwining of external and internal crises has limited the ambitions of crisis response abroad. 'Constructive ambiguity', that diplomatic tool derived from the geopolitical balance of power, they argue has helped the EU to bridge consensus gaps across different configurations of interests and fears. However, the resulting realist approach to the crises in the EU's neighbourhood was focused predominantly on the containment of irregular migration. Moreover, they show how the 'othering' that emerged from the discursive construction of the migration crisis overrides the relationship between proximity and normativity, which had traditionally characterised EU engagement outside of the internal market.

The chapter by Osland and Peter examines EU activities in the Western Balkans over a two-decade period and thus is able to show the evolution of EU strategy over time. It shows, with particular reference to the EU's rule-of-law support programme in Kosovo (EULEX), how the often benign intentions of the EU to move towards a conflict transformation agenda were thwarted by short-termism (see also Davis, 2015, on short-termism in a different context). The result was that policies and actions usually fell within the conflict management paradigm. Indeed, the case study bears out much of the wider story of the book. The case is one of a slide towards securitisation over the longer term aimed more at preserving the core than assisting the periphery, perpetuating negative forms of peace. There is also evidence of miscommunication between local and external parties with all sides harbouring suspicions of the other, or narratives developing about the other based on a lack of complete information, and problems of coordination within the EU itself. The proximity of the Western Balkans to the EU also makes this a controversial case and explains the tendency towards conflict transformation approaches, at least in the earlier part of the period (Shepherd, 2010).

The study by Peters, Ferhatovic, Heinemann and Sturm on EU crisis response in Afghanistan, Iraq and Mali reflects upon the effectiveness of the EU as a crisis response actor and raises questions about the nature of effectiveness and how we might go about measuring it. The chapter focuses on Security Sector Reform (SSR) and its comparative approach – across three cases – allowing a broad view of EU responses. The chapter is able to draw on EU and organisational studies and thus covers key topics like the actorness of the EU (what sort of actor is it) and the perceptions of international organisations (see also Rieker and Blockmans, 2019). One factor that shines through from the chapter are the disparities between strategy as set out in EU documents, and on-the-ground realities of how those strategies are manifest and perceptions of those strategies in case study countries. The chapter shows that mission mandates and core EU documents show a consistency from the EU in relation to SSR strategy. While core documents might show that the EU remains 'on message' in terms of key principles, there is not always institutional coherence across EU institutions, within EU institutions and with member states. This becomes manifest in attempts to translate policy into tasks especially when beholden to a claim to be producing comprehensive responses. Programmes and projects do not always reflect the original intentions of those who designed them. What becomes clear from the chapter, and in keeping with the overall argument of the book, is that EU crisis response has seen an increasing emphasis on stabilisation and securitisation – something that is not lost on host populations.

This stakeholder analysis is also found in the chapter by Rieker and Gjerde who examined more than seventy thousand press releases from the European Commission (EC) and the Council of the European Union to produce an official narrative on EU crisis response. They then compared this official narrative with perceptions in target countries, breaking this down in terms of proximity to the EU: the enlargement area (Kosovo/Serbia), the neighbourhood area (Ukraine, Syria, Libya) and the extended neighbourhood (Afghanistan, Iraq, Mali). They place their examination in the context of the EU's foreign policy repertoire, or the total sum of foreign policy instruments at its disposal at any given point. Rieker and Gjerde's mix of qualitative and quantitative work shows a spatial differentiation in EU crisis response stances and actions. They find a shift towards a greater focus on security rather than integration in the enlargement area and in the neighbourhood area; and an increase in a harder security agenda in the 'extended neighbourhood' region – especially in the Mali crisis, which is closest to the EU; but also to some extent in Afghanistan and to a lesser extent in Iraq. Another key finding is the general lack of understanding of the local situation, and poor conflict sensitivity, both of which are likely to limit the impact of EU crisis response. This indicates that the EU has not yet implemented a crisis response approach that can be characterised by crisis transformation.

Concluding thoughts

The EU was formed partly in view of the post-war logic of delegating conflict management – and later peacebuilding – to regional actors, as in the UN Charter's Chapter VIII. During the 1990s and into the 2000s as the UN's peacebuilding agendas became more multidimensional and were applied across the Global South and the Balkans, it was apparent that the EU was following suit in its near abroad (Kappler, 2014). It was for the first time now able to fulfil its role in this respect. The peacebuilding framework was a logical outgrowth of the EU's place in the UN and international system, its normative identity and its needs to address political instability, violence and war on its periphery.

The frameworks that it developed initially followed the UN's paradigm of liberal peacebuilding, adopting a more active stance not just on issues of democratisation and human rights, but on development, the rule of law and civil society. In other words, it moved from a limited conflict management towards the more expansive conflict resolution or conflict transformation stances.

The EU became a major diplomatic, donor and peacebuilding actor around the world, with all of the engagements this entailed. This rapid expansion, however, drew it into serious external conflicts and underlined its deep limitations, which where both material and normative, and reflected the growing gap between the development of sophisticated policy (Tocci, 2014) and Eurocentric self-interest (which also has led to tensions within the internal process of integration). The EU's presence had a powerful appeal, despite its security deficiencies because of its normative alignment that was appreciated among conflict-affected societies as being anti-war, in support of democracy, human rights and civil society, as an ambitious donor and because its diplomacy appeared to check predatory political elites.

Criticism of the deficiencies of EU policy engagement and their alignment with its internal normative framework, but most notable in their security dimensions, soon appeared. They perhaps spurred the EU's interest in the obvious lacuna of crisis management (previously a prerogative of great powers and the UN Security Council). Thus began a journey into a conceptual and policy dead-end, one well known in European, Cold War history. Crisis management was to become a retraction in practice (though not on paper) of the democracy, rights and civil society elements of EU engagement, in favour of its even more limited security capacity. As many of the chapters in this book show, the retreat into more securitised and limited foreign policy activities meant a reduction of the organisation's normative ambitions to make peace. These were already under criticism for a tendency to revert to Eurocentric understandings of political order and geopolitics over a more detailed understanding of the political claims of subalterns outside of the EU and indeed the West. The EU fell into a trap, partly of its own making, this suggests.

A longstanding lesson of international history has been that the rationality of political order and the crises state-like organisations face tends to make crisis management incompatible with the social and political advances the EU was mainly associated with. An interest in conflict sensitivity, local data and political claims in conflict-affected societies around the EU's periphery has followed a similar path. The chapters in this study show that, through its different logics of securitisation, institutionalism, supranationalism, integration, liberalism and ethnography, it remains trapped in a near-nineteenth-century, Eurocentric logic of geopolitical balancing, underestimating the risks of peripheral wars via short-termism and self-interest.

Strategies of conflict sensitivity thus appear expedient, much like UN policies for local ownership. The EU crisis management framework cannot bridge the gap between geopolitics and the preservation of core institutions, states and their borders, with inequalities, human rights, democratisation and development in conflict-affected countries. The attempt to produce a more critical understanding of crisis engagement the EU has implicitly engaged in in order to provide a platform for peace and security, has muddied the waters between peacebuilding and crisis management, and been deflected towards inwards concerns about preserving integration. This study has shown how this move, rather than filling the gap between peace and crisis, co-opted more sophisticated EU peacebuilding, development and association ambitions, returning them to short-term stabilisation measures, themselves barely successful and rarely locally legitimate. This has produced a political void to some degree in many of our case studies, in which crisis management actually means stabilisation before withdrawal (in line with first-generation UN peacekeeping doctrine, which had to be abandoned in the 1960s because wars tended to restart upon withdrawal). It risks becoming a prelude to further conflict.

References

Bátora, J., S. Blockmans, E. Ferhatovic, I. Peters, P. Rieker and E. Stambøl (2016) *Understanding the EU's Crisis Response Toolbox and Decision-Making Processes*, EUNPACK Report (WP D4.1) (Brussels: NUPI).

Bøås, M. and P. Rieker (2019) *EUNPACK Executive Summary of the Final Report & Selected Policy Recommendations: A Conflict-Sensitive Unpacking of the EU Comprehensive Approach to Conflict and Crisis Mechanisms* (Brussels: Centre for European Policy Studies).

Davis, L. (2015) 'Make do, or mend? EU security provision in complex conflicts: The Democratic Republic of Congo', *European Security*, 24(1): 101–119.

de Waal, A. (2015) *The Real Politics of the Horn of Africa: Money, War, and the Business of Power* (Cambridge: Polity).

Firchow, P. and R. Mac Ginty (2017) 'Including hard-to-access populations using mobile phone surveys and participatory indicators', *Sociological Methods & Review*, 49(1): 133–160.

Gamble, A. (2014) *Crisis Without End? The Unravelling of Western Prosperity* (New York: Palgrave Macmillan).

Giddens, A. (2014) *Turbulent and Mighty Continent: What Future for Europe?* (Cambridge: Polity).

Habermas, J. (2009) *Europe: The Faltering Project* (Cambridge: Polity).

Habermas, J. (2012) *The Crisis of the European Union: A Response* (Cambridge: Polity).

Hay, H. (1996) 'Narrating crisis: The discursive construction of the "winter of discontent"', *Sociology*, 30(2): 253–277.

Kappler, S. (2014) *Local Agency and Peacebuilding: EU and International Engagement in Bosnia-Herzegovina, Cyprus and South Africa* (Basingstoke: Palgrave Macmillan).

Lederach, J.P. (1997) *Building Peace* (Washington D.C.: United States Institute of Peace).

Manners, I.R. and P. Murray (2016) 'The end of a Nobel narrative? European integration narratives after the Nobel Peace Prize', *JCMS: Journal of Common Market Studies*, 54(1): 185–202.

Maschietto, R.H. (2015) 'Dilemmas of Peace Studies fieldwork with emancipatory concerns. Fieldwork report', *Journal of Peace, Conflict & Development*, 21: 167–179.

McDonagh, K. (2015) '"Talking the talk or walking the walk": Understanding the EU's security identity', *JCMS: Journal of Common Market Studies*, 53(3): 627–641.

Offe, C. (2015) *Europe Entrapped* (Cambridge: Polity).

Pavlov, N. (2015) 'Conceptualizing EU crisis management', *European Foreign Affairs Review*, 20(1): 23–42.

Pogodda, S., O.P. Richmond, N. Tocci, R. Mac Ginty and B. Vogel (2014) 'Assessing the impact of EU governmentality in post-conflict countries: Pacification or reconciliation?', *European Security*, 23(3): 227–249.

Ponzio, R. (2018) 'The UN's new "sustaining peace" agenda: A policy breakthrough in the making', Stimson Center, Commentary, 23 February, www.stimson.org/2018/un-new-sustaining-peace-agenda-policy-breakthrough-making/ (accessed 28 May 2020).

Raineri, L. and F. Strazzari (2019) '(B)ordering hybrid security: EU stabilisation practices in the Sahara-Sahel region', *Ethnopolitics*, 18(5): 544–559.

Read, R. and R. Mac Ginty (2017) 'The temporal dimension in accounts of violent conflict: A case study from Darfur', *Journal of Intervention and Statebuilding*, 11(2): 147–165.

Read, R., B. Taithe and R. Mac Ginty (2016) 'Data hubris? Humanitarian information systems and the mirage of technology', *Third World Quarterly*, 37(8): 1314–1331.

Richmond, O.P. (2000) 'Emerging concepts of security in the European order: Implications for "zones of conflict" at the fringes of the EU', *European Security*, 9(1): 41–67.

Richmond, O.P. (2010) 'Genealogy of peace and conflict theory', in O.P. Richmond (ed.), *Palgrave Advances in Peacebuilding: Critical Developments and Approaches* (Basingstoke: Palgrave Macmillan), 14–38.

Richmond, O.P. and R. Mac Ginty (2019) 'Mobilities and peace', *Globalizations*, 16(5): 606–624.

Richmond, O.P., A. Björkdahl and S. Kappler (2011) 'The emerging EU peacebuilding framework: Confirming or transcending liberal peacebuilding?', *Cambridge Review of International Affairs*, 24(3): 449–469.

Rieker, P. and S. Blockmans (2019) 'Plugging the capability–expectations gap: Towards effective, comprehensive and conflict-sensitive EU crisis response?', *European Security*, 28(1): 1–21.

Schierenbeck, I. (2015) 'Beyond the local turn divide: Lessons learnt, relearnt, unlearnt', *Third World Quarterly*, 36(5): 1023–1032.

Schumacher, T., A. Marchetti and T. Demmelhuber (eds) (2018) *The Routledge Handbook on the European Neighbourhood Policy* (Abingdon: Routledge).

Scipioni, M. (2018) 'Failing forward in EU migration policy? EU integration after the 2015 asylum and migration crisis', *Journal of European Public Policy*, 25(9): 1357–1375.

Shepherd, A.J.K. (2010) '"A milestone in the history of the EU": Kosovo and the EU's international role', *International Affairs*, 85(3): 513–530.

Spivak, G. (1988) 'Can the subaltern speak?', in C. Nelson and L. Grossberg (eds), *Marxism and the Interpretation of Culture* (Urbana, IL: University of Illinois Press), 271–313.

Tercovich, G. (2014) 'The EEAS Crisis Response System', *Journal of Contingencies and Crisis Management*, 22(3): 150–157.

Tocci, N. (2017) 'From the European Security Strategy to the EU Global Strategy: Explaining the journey', *International Politics*, 54(4): 487–502.

Tonra, B. and T. Christiansen (eds) (2018) *Rethinking European Union Foreign Policy* (Manchester: Manchester University Press).

Walby, S. (2015) *Crisis* (Cambridge: Polity).

2

Critical crisis transformation: a framework for understanding EU crisis response

Oliver P. Richmond, Sandra Pogodda and Roger Mac Ginty

Introduction

This chapter seeks to provide a conceptual and theoretical underpinning to the book, and the themes explored in it are found in subsequent chapters. The EUNPACK project represented a mix of conceptual and case study work, with the conceptual work providing a common set of understandings that could be applied to the case study work. Drawing from theories of Peace and Conflict, the work was particularly interested in the extent to which a commonly accepted framework for understanding responses to conflict could be applied to how the EU responds to crises. The conflict response framework stretches from conflict management to conflict resolution and to conflict transformation, with conflict management the most conservative and conflict transformation the most ambitious. As part of the EUNPACK project, and as reflected in this book, our intellectual project has been to gauge the extent to which the conflict response framework can be extended to EU crisis responses (thus becoming crisis management, crisis resolution and crisis transformation). Moreover, our intention has been to go further and have a critical reading of the framework and introduce the notion of critical crisis transformation.

The purpose behind this approach has been to interrogate EU crisis response in a structured way, and to allow us to categorise these responses in terms of how they sought to deal with crises. In particular, and mirroring the conflict management, conflict resolution and conflict transformation frameworks, our aim was to ascertain to what extent EU crisis response was conservative and constrained (crisis management) or emancipatory and ambitious (crisis transformation).

Academic and policy research on the emergence of crises, and how to respond to them, has received significant attention over the first two decades of the twenty-first century (Callinicos, 2010; Calhoun and Derlugian, 2011; European Commission, 2012; Gamble, 2014; Walby, 2015; Kjaer and Olsen, 2016). Since then, the EU has found itself involved in a series of continuously morphing and deepening crises (Habermas, 2009, 2012; Giddens, 2014; Offe, 2016), and thus has had multiple opportunities for developing a sound understanding of effective crisis response. In keeping with the core–periphery aspect of EU policy, key concepts used in EU institutions represent an attempt to shape politics in crisis and conflict areas. The EU's perspective of conflict tends to be of reduced severity and risk as the distance between the knowledge–power–language nexus of the EU framework of institutions and policies (i.e., the EU's 'normative' and strategic power) and crisis locations increases (EEAS, 2016). A crisis is not measured by the severity of its damage to the affected society in the periphery but by its potential to affect the EU's interests and objectives.

This spatial weakening of EU perceptions and policy has received increasingly sophisticated theorisation (Ferguson and Gupta, 1992: 6–23): policies designed for distant crises tend to be based on the perceptions and interests of the core *habitus* (Bourdieu, 1977) as well as the organisation's capacities and goals, rather than on the dynamics or political claims of the peripheral conflict. Policy is discursively powerful in the core, practically weak where it is actually applied in the periphery, and often mismatched against local political claims. This undermines the legitimacy of EU engagement even as it becomes discursively more sophisticated. Much of the academic and policy literature focuses on security-related technical or bureaucratic issues, often without looking at wider issues of history, culture, epistemology, or methodological issues – all of which offer contextualised explanations of conflicts and the posture of responding institutions.

The EU crisis response (EEAS, 2016) shows evidence of different strategies depending on the geographical and political distance of the crisis context. Remote crises afford EU policy-makers the opportunity to avoid a 'crisis of crisis management', in which the very forces that could help to overcome a crisis are paralysed by the complexity and severity of the crisis itself (Offe, 2016).

This chapter investigates whether EU crisis management frameworks represent a weakening of the aims of EU peacebuilding as distance increases from its policy-making cores. In theoretical terms this is a reversal of what amassed empirical evidence suggests: that a shift from conflict management practices to critical forms of crisis transformation are required if the EU is to have a normative and legitimate foreign policy in conflict-affected societies around the world.

The EU crisis response approach could learn from conflict theory and its typology of conflict responses: conflict management, conflict resolution and conflict transformation. This latter approach, conflict transformation (and specifically a critical reading of it), holds the possibility of addressing the structural drivers of conflict and their networked, relational, local to globally scaled dynamics, and of the emancipation of individuals, communities and institutions. Accordingly, this chapter begins with a theoretical background that conceptualises crises and postulates that the EU currently has four related crisis response attitudes. This section suggests that a fifth crisis response stance, critical crisis transformation, which draws on critical theories of peace and conflict, would actually be in keeping with the stated normative ambitions of the EU. However, it would require an engagement with new, context-sensitive and relational phenomena in international relations, increasingly understood to be crucial in peace and war. The next section of the chapter unpacks the conflict response models – conflict management, conflict resolution, conflict transformation and critical approaches to peace – in order to pave the way for a discussion of more advanced possibilities. We then look at a series of contemporary cases studies, including cases where the EU has contemporary strategic engagements in crises within its different circles of influence, such as Libya, Ukraine and Mali in order to examine the empirical nature of EU crisis management. We conclude the chapter by evaluating our conceptualisation of a critical version of this concept and policy framework.

Theory and concepts

Conflicts and crises are intrinsically linked but differentiated, among other factors, by positionality, subjectivity and politics.

While its material conditions (scale, duration, nature and intensity of violence) allow *conflict* to be assessed or categorised even to the unaffected outsider, *crises* tend to lie in the eye of the beholder (a specific group, the state, the EU, NATO, the UN, and so on). Defined as events with the 'potential to cause large detrimental change to the social system' (Walby, 2015: 14), crises differ from conflicts in so far as only actors within the social system under threat are likely to identify those events as a crisis. Hence, war constitutes a crisis for conflict-affected populations, but not for countries that are far removed, unless crucial security or economic networks are affected. Given the high probability that conflicts will not be contained within national borders, regional or international actors tend to identify large-scale or persistent conflicts as crises if large-scale spill-over effects from a conflict occur or have to be expected. This de facto overlap between crisis and conflict implies that a distinction between the two concepts has to be based on an analysis of EU discourse and of the deployed interventionary toolbox. Within the EU, crisis response involves a distinct set of decision-making processes and institutions as well as access to specific resources (Bátora *et al.*, 2016; Pietz, 2017).

Crises provide windows of opportunity (Gamble, 2014: 30) as the imminent threat tends to remove political, economic or democratic constraints on policy-makers. Defining a crisis and designing responses to it thus bestows power on policy-makers (Hay, 1996: 255). Once a crisis has been defined, a lack of constraints often precipitates a lack of proportionality between cause and consequence (Walby, 2015: 14), rendering crisis a make-or-break point for the legitimate authority of leadership (Gamble, 2014: 32). In the case of EU crisis response, the window of opportunity could be twofold: externally, the EU's position in crisis response is relatively strengthened in comparison to a crisis-affected government. Hence, the onset of a crisis could facilitate previously blocked policies, if linked to offers of support. Internally, if distinct crisis protocols are established, response policies may be able to bypass the complex structures of the EU's Common Security and Defence Policy (CSDP) and its drawn-out process of mission deployment. This has recently come to pass in the form of Art. 28 (1) stabilisation actions, which may enable more flexible and effective approaches to crisis response under the authority of the High Representative for Foreign Affairs and Security Policy as well as the European External Action Service (EEAS) (Pietz, 2017).

Crises can be categorised by the sphere in which they emerge (e.g., economic, fiscal, financial, political, social, etc.) or their gravity (e.g., existential, structural, acute, contained, etc.). The former analytical approach might stress the interdependence of different types of crisis, describing one type of crisis as the consequence of another. By contrast, the latter approach hints at the level at which crises can be addressed. If a crisis is able to cascade through different spheres, its underlying causes might be of a structural nature. In politics, however, crises are often treated as isolated shocks, whose causes are narratively reduced to a containable and ultimately manageable threat often through political or security tools. However, intervention is based upon previous concepts, drawn of other events, carrying a range of biases which then create a blindspot for the analysis of the new problem (Roitman, 2016: 17–34).

In EU foreign policy, tensions between power, knowledge, and local claims have been dealt with in four main ways in the past:

1. A realist strategy with its emphasis on maintaining centralised states with hard boundaries and a focus on security issues has been applied to the EU's *extended neighbourhood and beyond* (e.g., in response to regime change in Libya) (Goldgeier and McFaul, 2001: 1–26). Here, European interests rather than norms and rights have been prevalent in the design of a crisis response strategy. Intervention in a crisis only occurs when threats or opportunities emerge within this international system (Burton and Dukes, 1990: introduction). In addition, humanitarian crises can prompt short-term crisis responses in the form of humanitarian assistance.
2. A structuralist approach to material needs, equality, and the distribution of resources has been applied to the *neighbourhood countries*. This was based on the recognition that stark welfare and economic differences between the EU and its neighbourhood had fuelled migration towards the internal market and its promises of welfare and income opportunities. Structuralist intervention included the promotion of trade creation and assistance for governance reforms in order to stimulate development, as well as a half-hearted element of democracy promotion (mainly within

the framework of trade relations), pointing to matters of structural violence (Article 2 in Galtung, 1969: 167–191). The EU European Neighbourhood Policy (ENP) was constructed to help deliver stability and integration (in all but institutions) in order to create a security community of friendly, and reformist states on its periphery, but largely failed to do so. Its latest revision tones down integration and shifts its focus further towards stability, while progressive and emancipatory goals have never been part of the policy. Given that the EU's neighbourhood is large and troubled – stretching from Ukraine to Syria and Libya – spillover effects of conflicts in the neighbourhood may prompt crisis intervention. Crisis response in those cases would be limited to containment and stabilisation.

3. As soon as countries were recognised as *accession countries*, they become subject to the liberal strategy of building democratic representation, implementing institutional reform, extending rights and development beyond the state, reflecting what Manners has described as the EU's 'normative power' (e.g., Cyprus and its 'europeanisation'). EU membership can only be achieved through a process of unilateral institutional assimilation as accession countries have to adapt to the Copenhagen criteria and the *acquis communitaire*. During the accession process, the EU engages through diplomacy, adjustment programmes and association agreements. Intervention in crises occurs when institutions and trade are significantly threatened or if crises spread towards the EU's borders, threatening European stability (Manners, 2002: 235–258). At this stage, the EU rejects any responsibility beyond assistance for the stabilisation of crisis contexts.

4. The critical, welfarist and social democratic approach is reserved solely for *EU member countries*. Within its geographical and political core, the EU's institutional framework and its evolution reflects its Monnetist foundations in a system designed to promote solidarity between states, aiming at regional convergence and the extension of shared security, extended rights and material well-being. Crisis intervention is vital here, not only as a principle of solidarity[1] but due to the interdependence of all economies within the internal market. Hence, any conflict, instability or large-scale disaster on EU territory is bound to trigger a crisis response. Interventionary practices are cemented

by a broad range of public goods at the regional and intergovernmental level, which are closely linked to internal stability and external security (Whitman, 1998). This follows closely on from the experience of the evolution of UN peacebuilding from the 1990s onwards and more expansive forms of intervention and programming, which emerged as a consequence of its normative goals (Richmond *et al.*, 2011).

These four options might not be mutually exclusive as the intensity of the crisis – or political interests – could trump the political and geographical distance to the EU. A very severe crisis within the extended or immediate neighbourhood, for instance, might require interventions traditionally reserved for inner-European crises. Normative stances within the European Council could equally overcome a clear determination of crisis responses. The case of Syria suggests that neither geopolitical nor normative concerns can push the EU towards decisive crisis response, however. A similar pattern was observed with the breakup of Yugoslavia. The more member states are of the opinion that the realist approach to crises is unacceptable, and that preference should be given to a liberal or social democratic approach, the more pressure builds for stronger EU crisis intervention outside the borders of the EU (especially once internal irregularities are settled). Hitherto however, the EU has not sufficiently developed institutions able to do much more than work with the UN and donor system, except in a few cases so far. It often claims to be pushing towards the fourth approach (above) in policy documents, but practice rarely has reflected this outside of its core states.

The limitations of these four key approaches has prompted interest in local ownership, micropolitics, resilience, and indigenous or traditional practices: in other words, the 'local turn', which is an attempt to engage with local political claims, to understand local politics better, and to establish more 'authentic' and just forms of peace (Mac Ginty and Richmond, 2013). As a result of the EU's continuous confrontation with crises since 2009, a similar reconsideration of political strategies may occur at the European level.[2] We argue that its crisis response approach could be usefully informed by critical theories in an interdisciplinary framework. Thus, our proposed fifth approach, critical crisis transformation, would draw in the latest critical arguments and evidence and involve:

5. A blending of liberal-progressive and welfarist, feminist, post-colonial, post-structuralist critiques and approaches to the above four categories; a hybrid form of crisis response, predicated on the legitimacy that arises in localised politics, also connected (via relationality, networks, and mobility) to matters of historical and distributive justice (e.g. global justice) (Comaroff and Comaroff, 2012).

This critical crisis transformation position draws from the Peace and Conflict literature and the consensus reached therein that 'desecuritisation' can only occur through more subtle diplomatic approaches (mediation, negotiation, conflict transformation). This position recognises the pacific value of a multiplicity of factors (peacebuilding, democratisation, human rights, justice, gendered and environmentally sensitive responses) and points to the importance and salience of hybrid political orders (Boege *et al.*, 2008; Albrecht and Wiuff Moe, 2015: 1–16).

Conflict response framework

The academic study of peace and conflict has – over a number of decades – developed a framework for understanding conflict and responses to conflict. The framework – consisting of conflict management, conflict resolution, conflict transformation and critical conflict transformation – provides a means of classifying responses to conflict (from conservative to emancipatory), the language used to justify the responses, and the types of actions employed. This section sketches the different traditions in the framework and finishes with critical conflict transformation, bearing in mind that we will develop the idea of critical crisis transformation later in the chapter.

Conflict management

Conflict management constitutes the first-generation approach to ending conflict, commonly equated with political realism. Conflict management has emerged from the realist tradition of statecraft and realpolitik (Kissinger, 1954). It rests on the assumption that conflict is somehow a natural or inevitable state of affairs and has a limited state-centric discourse that excludes non-state actors and issues. Relationships between disputants are to be balanced, controlled, or modified by the insertion and presence of third parties. This modifies the classic friend–enemy distinction in favour of an externally managed balance between disputants. This provides third parties with a significant resource (and can allow third parties to cast themselves as neutral and disinterested arbiters who do not have responsibility for the cause or maintenance of conflict) (Bercovitch and Rubin, 1992; James, 1994; Bercovitch, 1996).

Conflict management approaches aim at the production of a basic minimum order without overt violence, or at least an 'acceptable' level of violence minimally disruptive to the state and international system. The related literature is concerned with issues like neutrality and impartiality, trust, the timing and form of intervention (whether it is diplomatic, in the form of mediation, or coercive, in the form of military intervention). Indicative of conflict management approaches and their underlying ontological, epistemological and methodological frameworks is the literature on hurting stalemates and ripe moments (Princen, 1992; Zartman, 1982). This argues that there are windows of opportunity where conflicts can be settled through the production of a basic, negative peace (Galtung, 1998; Diehl, 2016). In this worldview, violent conflict is acceptable as long as it is contained, and sometimes calculations are made to enable violent conflict so as to change 'facts on the ground'. See, for example, western ambivalence (if not support) for Croat and Bosnian military offensives in the run up to the Dayton Accords negotiations in 1995, or for Israeli actions against Hezbollah – and Lebanon more generally – during the 2006 'summer war'. Conflict management responses, and a tolerance of hurting stalemates, allow mediators, diplomats, and peacekeeping operations to mobilise (Zartman, 2003: 19; James, 1994).

Much of this literature focuses on the different generations of peacekeeping, and mediation as a diplomatic or quasi-diplomatic activity (Hammarskjold, 1958). The limited engagement via peacekeeping is usually based upon the fragile equation of state interests, issues, and resources, and often depends upon external guarantors, though it also recognised that elements of the liberal agenda – the capacity of international alliances, institutions and organisations – bring a semblance of order through international cooperation over coercion.

Conflict resolution

A second generation of debates and stances crystallised around the concept of conflict resolution (partly as a critique of conflict management's limitations) (Dunn, 2004). This took a more ambitious stance on peace, leading to the notion of a 'win-win' or a positive peace, as opposed to conflict management's negative peace approach (Galtung, 1998; Diehl, 2016). This approach perceived conflict to be psychological, sociobiological, or as a product of political, economic and social structures that deny or impede human needs (Isard, 1992: chapter 2). As such, it moved many thinkers away from notions of inevitable forms of conflict. It was specifically focused on an understanding of the root causes of conflict. From this perspective conflict arises out of a repression of human needs, and is a social (Azar and Burton, 1986: 29; Gurr, 1970) as well as a psychological phenomenon.

This was revolutionary in terms of conflict analysis theory in that it broke away from purely state-centric notions of conflict, pointing to its relational nature. Relative deprivation theory, for example, identifies a sense of injustice as a source of social unrest, and the frustration-aggression approach sees frustration as a necessary or sufficient condition for aggression (Dollard *et al.*, 1939; Runciman, 1972: chapter 2; Berkowitz, 1993). Human needs theory offered a framework for understanding what caused conflict and how it might be resolved, derived from a civil society oriented discourse and aimed at constructing a positive peace in the context of transnational relations. This approach prioritised human needs over state security, structural violence, and the need for alternative forms of communication to be developed, pointing to engagement with local civil society organisations and a cobweb model of global order in order to negotiate a civil or social peace which would then trickle up to political elites to be implemented.

Human needs – identity, political participation, and security – are viewed as non-negotiable because they are founded on a universal ontological drive (Azar and Burton, 1986). From this assertion, it was a short step to the realisation that the repression and deprivation of human needs is the root of protracted conflicts (Azar, 1990: 9–12), along with structural factors, such as underdevelopment. This equated both development and civil society discourse with peace. Debates about conflict resolution evolved towards 'multi-track diplomacy', peacebuilding, and contingency approaches and connected with liberal arguments about human security and the 'democratic peace' (Macmillan, 2003: 19). These contributions to second-generation thinking also imply that conflict requires social, political and economic engineering on the part of third-party interveners to remove the conditions that create violence.

The underlying ontology of conflict resolution is heavily predicated upon the understanding that individual agency should and can be exerted to assuage human needs and lead to social justice. From a global perspective, this 'cosmopolitan turn' in conflict resolution (Jones, 1999) empowered non-state actors and non-governmental organisations (NGOs) to assist in the development of peace based on the identification and allocation of human needs according to the voices of non-state and unofficial actors. Indeed, in providing a forum for the agency of individuals, and assuming that they will be in favour of a liberal form of peace, conflict resolution is also an inherently political approach that threatens elites who monopolise resources for their own alternative interests. Thus, conflict resolution while widely applied in conflict-affected societies from Cyprus to Northern Ireland, provides a radical perspective of a positive peace dependent upon the agency of the individual and civil society which is also both complementary and in tension with the acceptance of liberal norms. However, conflict resolution underestimates how entrenched structural violence or global injustice have become.

Conflict transformation

Conflict transformation can be regarded as the most emancipatory of the conflict management–conflict resolution–conflict transformation approaches to conflict. It pays more attention to the individual and the local, and believes that the structural bases of conflict can, and must, be addressed in order to truly deal with conflict causes and not merely conflict manifestations. Conflict transformation pays attention to issues of identity and believes that through self-examination, education and positive contact with the other, parties to a conflict can engage in reflective processes that consider conflict causation and maintenance factors. As such, conflict transformation places responsibility for addressing conflict on all participants – not just political or military actors. Unlike many other approaches to peace, it emphasises relationality and affect (Lederach, 1997). The whole-of-society approach makes conflict transformation potentially radical, costly and time-consuming. It is not merely about staunching conflict; it is about addressing the underlying factors. The radical potential of conflict transformation means that it is often regarded as an aspiration – a positive peace to be pursued once the negative peace of conflict management and conflict resolution have been reached. A full conflict transformation has not been attempted in any of the cases of crisis or conflict that are used as case studies in this chapter. Instead, parts of the conflict transformation agenda can be found in peacebuilding programmes and projects that form wider conflict response interventions. The conflict transformation agenda is particularly noticeable in people-to-people activities that seek to bridge intergroup divides.

Where it has been attempted, the conflict transformation has often been operationalised by international organisations and their proxies as part of complex multidimensional interventions. As a result, the good intentions of conflict transformation are often rendered into standardised and shallow formats that might use the language of rights and peace but are delivered in technocratic and limited ways. Conflict transformation, as operationalised as part of the contemporary liberal peace project, has a basis in a version of Kant's democratic peace argument and its focus on democratisation (Call and Cook, 2003: 233–246), and thus elides into development and marketisation, and on the rule of law and human rights. It introduced the global framework of a sustainable peace, which often rested upon an implicit agreement between international actors, the UN, international financial institutions (IFIs), and NGOs, on a 'peacebuilding consensus' aimed at the construction of the liberal peace as a response to post-Cold War conflicts (many of which revolved around collapsed or fragile states in the terminology of the day). This argument has been extended in practice by the recent UN documentation on 'sustaining peace' (UN, 2018).

The peacekeeping operations in Namibia, in Cambodia, Angola, Mozambique and El Salvador seemed to offer the hope that a conflict-transformation-inflected peace could go beyond merely monitoring ceasefires and would instead contribute to the democratisation of failing and failed states. But UN missions, even versions that showed aspirations to become more emancipatory and expansive, became subsumed in the wider liberal peace, meaning that interveners (peacekeepers, NGOs, donors, and officials) were now required to focus on democratisation, human rights, development, and economic reform. This became the blueprint in Cambodia, Bosnia, Kosovo, Sierra Leone, Liberia, DR Congo and East Timor. Peacekeeping, and the complexity of tasks associated with it, became part of global governance, which now became the new imaginary of peace in the minds of policy-makers. In this way, liberal peacebuilding represented a multilevel approach, attempting to incorporate the local, state and regional aspects of, and actors in, conflict – thus moving beyond the top-down, elite-led approaches developed in conflict management and conflict resolution. Lederach's vision of a people-centric conflict transformation became, instead, conflict transformation-lite or a hollowed-out version marked by compromise (Lederach, 1995). Certainly, international peace-support interventions sought to bring together a wider range of actors in peacemaking, including civil society, and sought to expand the range of concerns of peacemaking processes to include social, economic and development issues as well as security and politics (Lederach, 1997: 39). This approach to peacemaking had a trickle-down assumption, whereby it was thought that top-down mandates and the engineering of good governance processes and institutions would be gratefully received by populations and turn into a sustained peace.

Third-generation approaches gave rise to more comprehensive ambitions for peace, but also raised questions about the nature of the universal peace that they imply. The liberal peace requires multiple forms of intervention, which the theories of peacebuilding supply: UN peace operations, mediation and negotiation, development and humanitarian relief, and specialised reforms aimed to meeting international standards in areas from the security sector, the economy, the environment, border controls, human rights, and the rule of law. This effectively means that the liberal concept of peace revolves around the reform of governance, is highly interventionist, and has a rational and mechanical, problem-solving character. As Chopra argued (Chopra, 1996: 338), it engenders a mechanism whereby the UN, regional organisations, member states, and local actors, take control or monitor the instruments of governance (Chopra, 2000; UN, 2004; Carnegie, 1997: 2–3).

Yet, out of all UN attempts at democratisation since the end of the Cold War, around half had suffered some form of authoritarian regime within fifteen years. In addition, the role of IFIs has effectively driven economic structural adjustment and development projects through neoliberal strategies which have failed to provide the sorts of economic opportunities and welfare that would be expected within a liberal state (and indeed within the EU itself). In effect, liberal peacebuilding has been turned into a system of external governance rather than a process of contextual reconciliation. This indicates a failure to come to terms with the lived experiences of individuals and their needs in everyday life (Pouligny, 2006). There has emerged a gap between the expectations of peacebuilding and what it has actually delivered so far in practice, particularly from the perspective of local communities.

Critical approaches to peace

Critical approaches to peace represent a fourth generation of peacebuilding, which introduced new reflexivity and more relational dimensions into the discussion of a sustainable peace. In many ways they were faithful to the original aims of conflict transformation. It criticised peacebuilding, statebuilding and conflict resolution for being unable to overcome insidious practices of intervention upon host and recipient communities (Debrix and Weber, 2003: xv) and ignoring local claims and voices. It advanced a pluralist, critical and self-reflective approach (Patomaki, 2001: 732; Bourdieu, 1977) to peace, order and security, as well as a local turn (Mac Ginty and Richmond, 2013). Institutions, once moulded upon exported ideas of a state, had to be opened up to the cultural, customary dynamics of the local environment, and to have a beneficial impact on the everyday lives and needs of the post-conflict individual, as well as being cognitive of the external drivers of war. It pointed to issues of historical, distributive, social and environmental justice as integral to any sustainable form of peace.

This required a hybridised form of peacebuilding that allowed for mediation between the local and the international over peacebuilding praxis and social, political and economic practices that both deem plausible and acceptable (Boege *et al.*, 2008) from which a large scholarly and policy literature has subsequently emerged (Richmond *et al.*, 2011; Mac Ginty, 2011). A few significant hints of such an approach – for all its weaknesses – might be found in Northern Ireland, along with its EU Peace funding, which invested enormously in civil society, material improvement, and attempted to move away from the frameworks that fed nationalism and sectarianism (such as centralised power, territorialism, and hard borders). It is worth noting, of course, that this case was within the EU and this level of funding and attention would be difficult to replicate elsewhere.

A new crisis response framework

The categorisations outlined above (management–resolution–transformation–critical approaches to peace) have substantial levels of overlap and are best seen as a continuum, moving from the most conservative type of intervention (conflict management) to the most radical (critical approaches to peace). In complex peace operations, the first three types of intervention may be in operation simultaneously, or they operate sequentially. Transferring this conceptual progression to EU crisis management, the framework becomes: crisis management–crisis resolution–crisis transformation.

The elements of the tripartite framework resonate with the characterisation of EU interventions as realist, structuralist and liberal. We realise that any categorisation exercise will struggle when directed towards a complex and dynamic series of processes like EU crisis response. We see the categorisation exercise as a way of assisting conceptualisation, but not as a prescriptive straitjacket into which all aspects of EU crisis responses must fit. Instead, it is a way of sparking thinking about the normative ambitions of EU crisis response mechanisms and interventions, the interests that shape the translation of policy into practice, the rationalities and political economies that attend policy delivery, and the reception of policies once they hit the ground. This will help to examine the gap between institutionalist perspectives and critical peace and conflict perspectives. The latter encourages us to think about the reception of EU crisis responses on the ground and the extent to which they meet with agency, resistance and hybridisation.

Crisis management

Crisis management (CM) is the stabilisation or containment of a crisis, and is also often used as a generic term for all types of intervention in crises (Brecher and Wilkenfeld, 2000). It recognises that a crisis is on-going and aims to prevent further deterioration, contagion or spill-over into other forms of crises. The principal aim is limited: to prevent crises from spreading, destabilising regions or inflicting harmful repercussions on the EU. Crisis management works through short-term or limited-ambition interventions, but rejects long-term engagement with the underlying causes of the crisis, other than through balancing and stabilisation activities. Depending on the nature of the crisis, this can work at all levels, from elite diplomacy to on-the-ground activity involving a displaced population. There is much scope for humanitarian activity but less for complex political deals that may take time to negotiate. Hence, the crisis management toolkit of external crisis managers encompasses humanitarian assistance, budgetary support, mediation, donor conferences, border management missions, the establishment of no-fly zones and humanitarian corridors, while domestic crisis management may require ceasefire negotiations, security interventions, curfews and financial concessions. In prolonged crises, external crisis management can also stretch to sanctions, and short-term military interventions.

The worldview that informs crisis management is a realist perspective, which analyses crises through the prism of national interests and power relations. Crisis managers realise that security is a transnational concept in a globalised world, rendering national security vulnerable to contagion and spill-over effects of conflicts and crisis abroad. Yet, crisis management regards the state with its border regimes and defence mechanisms as a bulwark against negative effects of security interdependence.

The notion of 'management' suggests power relations in which the manager (in this case the EU) regards itself as in a position to manage (control) the crisis. In reality, the EU is likely to be acting in concert with other actors (or was essentially subservient to other actors as was the case with Libya), and a crisis, particularly in its emergent phase, is likely to be beyond the control of any actor or concert of actors. Many of the tools used in conflict management are thus aimed at containing the harmful repercussions of a crisis, and thus to prevent it from spreading or spilling over into other forms of crises. Crisis management can be seen as a first step that paves the way for more ambitious forms of intervention to follow. In some situations, however, crisis management is all that is possible over the longer term and crisis mode becomes a semi-permanent stance. In the case of Libya, movement along the CM–CR–CT–CCT trajectory seemed to be regressive, with policies based on engagement, institution-building, and limited forms of integration moving towards simple containment.

Our project found that EU engagement with external crises generated mainly crisis management responses. For instance, EU policies to mitigate the complex security crises in Libya (the lawlessness due to rebel infighting after the overthrow of Muammar al-Gaddafi) and Mali (the combined devastation of a secessionist uprising in the north, a military coup and a jihadist insurgency) demonstrated a narrow border management and security focus, which failed to respond to local security needs (Loschi *et al.*, 2018; Bøås *et al.*, 2018). In both contexts, crisis management was moulded on a Eurocentric rationale of threat containment. While the Libyan and Malian populations have been suffering from the infighting and general lawlessness of militia rule, economic instability and a lack of services, the EU was mainly concerned about weapons trafficking, jihadists crossing borders and migration to Europe. Prioritising its own interests, the EU authorised a Border Assistance Mission (EUBAM) in Libya in May 2013 and several border management programmes in Mali (Bøås *et al.*, 2018). This stands in stark contrast to a more conflict-sensitive approach to both countries, which needed to include the promotion of a national (or at least inter-regional) dialogue on power sharing, demobilisation of militias and joint statebuilding. In addition to the mismatch between EU's narrow interest in threat containment and local interests in a combined approach to the political, security and economic crises of their countries, the EU border management strategies failed to understand the complex border economies in both countries (Loschi *et al.*, 2018; Bøås *et al.*, 2018: 23). In Libya, the EUBAM blueprint for integrated border management was impossible to achieve in the Libyan context of disintegrated state authority (Raineri *et al.*, 2017). Equally poorly conceived remained the EU's mission EUNAVFOR MED. Its objective of boarding, seizing, searching and diverting human traffickers' vessels off the Libyan coastline was so mismatched with the political issues on the ground, that it could neither achieve a UN Security Council (UNSC) mandate nor an invitation from the Libyan authorities (Raineri *et al.*, 2017: 31).[3]

Another crisis management tool that the EU has deployed in several cases is the use of sanctions and conditionalities. In Libya, sanctions against specific individuals among the country's political elites, for instance, managed to remove some high-level resistance against the centralisation of political authority under the Libyan Political Agreement of 2015 (Raineri, 2017: 24). Individual EU sanctions were also applied to put pressure on Russia's annexation of Crimea – here, however, with less tangible outcomes (Raineri *et al.*, 2017: 53).

Crisis resolution

The increasing duration of crises as permanent situations have paved the way for more ambitious strategies of dealing with crises. In crisis resolution (CR), for instance, the ambitions are greater than in crisis management as human needs are the focus. This fits the ethos of EU engagement better than crisis management. Aside from stabilising the situation, the ambition is to 'resolve' the crisis, involving not only elites but also civil society. Often, this means reaching an agreement and as such it will often involve diplomatic, political and militant elites. Crisis resolution is focused on the needs of crisis-affected populations and considers economic marginalisation, conflicts and 'bad governance' as root causes of crises. An EU-sponsored programme on the restoration of local governance and reconciliation in crisis-affected areas of Ukraine provides an example for the latter (Raineri *et al.*, 2017: 47).

On-the-ground needs assessment – with a broader mandate but similarly localised as the 2012 needs assessment mission in Libya – can provide a good starting point. Accordingly, tools would focus on civil society-led debates in order to comprehend the complexity of local political economies, societal divisions and local power structures. Such complex understandings would feed into crisis resolution processes and elite-led diplomacy. Crises resolution may require burden-sharing agreements between the government at the epicentre of the crisis and neighbouring countries or international actors with an interest in regional and global stability, according to human needs provisions (now understood as human security).

However, the underlying approach to development remains constrained by neoliberal concepts of economic growth, which tend to centre on trade relations, governance reforms and investment climate, while its inclusion of civil society is limited to internationally operating actors and INGOs. Consequently, crisis resolution keeps crisis-afflicted economies locked into a precarious path towards development even if it highlights civil society processes.

The deal-making involved in crisis resolution raises questions of recognition and legitimacy. As formal agreements are being made, and as states and international organisations are often party to these agreements, issues of legitimacy are likely to arise. Crisis resolution suggests a longer term perspective on the crisis and its underlying causes.

Our research teams found little evidence for crisis resolution strategies among EU interventions. Civil society involvement may seem like a time-consuming endeavour to crisis responders. Yet, only the involvement of different societal perspectives on crises could help the EU to avoid designing responses that appear biased or self-interested, damaging its legitimacy on the ground. One of the few exceptions to this rule are the EU Capacity Building Mission (EUCAP) training programmes in proximity policing in Mali (Bøås *et al.*, 2018: 22). Here, police forces are trained to work with local communities on their security needs. In the context of the Malian security crisis, such an approach is particularly valuable as the ethnic biases of state security institutions have in the past undermined attempts at statebuilding (Bøås *et al.*, 2018).

Crisis transformation

Crisis transformation (CT) represents a more advanced form of crisis response, and one which closely resembles the goals of the EU on paper if not in practice. It recognises the pitfalls of short-term reactions and elite level deal-making and goes beyond the satisfaction of immediate needs in crisis-afflicted populations. It seeks to deal with the underlying causation and maintenance factors behind a crisis. Primarily, it seeks to lend rights to affected populations. In its attempts to develop an appropriate response strategy, crisis transformers involve a wide range of local perspectives on the crisis and its root causes. Much of the functionalist literature on EU integration, expansion, and engagement in the wider region is based upon this type of logic (Visoka and Doyle, 2015).

Rather than dealing with the fallout of a crisis as if its immediate effects could be easily and quickly reversed, crisis transformation considers the new contexts created by crises as permanent and seeks to accommodate those new realities. Mass exodus of refugee populations from conflict-affected regions, for instance, inflicts more than a short-term strain on host populations and government. Beyond housing and feeding those populations, a crisis transformation approach would offer host governments incentives to extend rights to refugees. An example of this approach can be seen in the EU's relaxation of its rules of origin in the EU-Jordan Association Agreement to benefit industrial production in Jordan that employs Syrian refugees.[4]

Crisis transformation includes non-elite actors in attempts to tackle the crisis. In practice, this means that crisis response networks have to be built from the ground up, starting with local actors at the epicentre of the crises, connected with regional and international organisations with the aim of sharing resources and coordinating crisis response strategies. Among the cases studied in this chapter, the Support Group for Ukraine (SGUA) constitutes the most serious attempt at crisis response coordination. SGUA was established to liaise between different EU aid efforts in Ukraine and those of its member states, while also facilitating the cooperation with other donors. Sadly, SGUA lacks credible links to its local counterparts, making it unproductive (Loschi *et al.*, 2018: 49) and disqualifying it as a genuinely transformative crisis response.

While offering assistance instantly in the heat of a crisis, crisis transformation considers the long-term effects of intervention: crisis response networks would incorporate local knowledge and offer capacity-building in return; its strategy aims to expand from the short-term to the medium and long-term based on the understanding that path dependency (either with the institutionalisation of intervention or with the power structures on the ground) could set in and spoil the outcome if based on a misguided understanding of the crisis. Hence, it builds regular review and monitoring milestones into its strategy in order to ward off negative long-term effects of short-term crisis response measures. It is a more long-term and costly response that operates at all levels of government and society.

Critical crisis transformation

The logical outcome of the thrust of EU policy, combined with the evolution of Peace and Conflict studies, along with the critical strands of EU studies indicates the possibility of more critical forms of crisis transformation (CCT) emerging in future, however. CCT would draw on the post-colonial, feminist, and more social democratic strand of thinking about the nature of peaceful order, fourth-generation thinking about conflict and peace, and an array of critical arguments about processes and aims of integration. It would combine the discursive and civil society approach of conflict/crisis resolution, with the more multidimensional and inclusive approach of conflict/crisis transformation, with a hybrid design of intervention-related institutions, crisis analysis and policies. An example for this would be a more inclusive version of the 'Political Framework for a Crisis Approach' (PFCA) as drafted by the EEAS in 2014 for the Libyan crisis. By bringing together all EU-internal expertise on Libya, critically assessing EU strategy in the country, identifying threats and outlining strategies for crises response, the Political Framework could have been the first step towards developing a hybrid crisis transformation framework. Yet, the lack of a systematic inclusion of Libyan partners and thus of EU-local consensus building in crises response disqualified the Political Framework as a transformatory approach. Strong hints of EU policy evolution may be found in documents such as *Shared Vision,*

Common Action: A Stronger Europe (European Union HR/VP, 2016), and in claims it has made about its goals in the Western Balkans and elsewhere, and the work that has gone into developing ECHO or multitrack forms of diplomacy (European Commission, 2009).

Associated practices would be based on dynamics of historical and distributive justice and the realisation of the relationality of global crises, avoiding core–periphery style discrimination as well as the limited goals of crisis management. It would recognise the materiality of needs as well as the importance of opening up to a multitude of local discourses in the attempt to understand and later resolve crises. Indeed, critical crisis transformation would try to distil its analysis of the causes of a crisis from a large variety of local and expert perspectives. Through such consultation processes, it might avoid premature narrowing of the crisis narrative, which is likely to set crisis response on the wrong path and facilitates the cascading of crisis through different spheres (Walby, 2015). It would also point to the need for broad institutional approaches, identifying institutions and instruments of crisis intervention in cooperation with local partners. Such a hybrid approach negotiates northern biases through localised claims and accepts that mobility is a legitimate mode of crisis response. It would recognise difference and would avoid inadvertently promoting centralised, state-centric, territorialised forms of government to the detriment of emancipatory and local forms of legitimacy. Moreover, it would require regular monitoring of the effectiveness of the crisis response. Most importantly, this would recognise that localised crises are often manifestations of wider structural and global justice oriented issues, which require the renegotiation of power relations (Gamble, 2014). This is where the EU might be most useful: to lend its weight to attempts to rectify these imbalances, which allow crises to resurface in different regions with devastating consequences for the affected societies.

It should be stressed that the elements of the CM–CR–CT–CCT framework might be seen as gradations along the same path. It could be that conditions do not allow anything more ambitious than minimal management and reaction. Over time, conditions may change and allow for more ambitious forms of intervention. Acute urgency and time limitations may constrain policy towards crisis management, but as situations become more protracted, it may tend to shift towards the longer term goals and processes implied by crisis resolution and transformation.

Applying the framework

We recommend the CM–CR–CT–CCT framework as it enables the examination of the actions and stances of the EU (and its partners, proxies and competitors) and the epistemologies and politics that lie behind them. It also points to the fact that, in line with more critical and interdisciplinary thinking, as well as with the more advanced claims of EU policy-making, a CCT framework may be plausible, drawing on the framework outlined above. The framework is proposed as a way of characterising EU stances in a systematic, comparative manner. It allows us to chart EU stances and policies in terms of the extent to which they may be characterised as realist and state/system-reinforcing (first- and second-generation peace interventions) or transformatory, welfarist and rights-based (third- and fourth-generation peace interventions). The framework pronounces on whether EU crisis response instruments and practices are orientated towards states and institutions or towards people and societies. Of course, the evidence so far points towards hybridised forms of crisis response that involve accepting (and possibly reinforcing) elements of crises. More important conceptually, crises are understood more from the perspective of the EU rather than from the perspective of the individual's or community's security and rights.

In terms of lessons learned, the decision-making and feedback processes that attend EU foreign and security policy-making, including crisis response (Peters, 2016: introduction) raise two main points. The first is that the policy-making process has limited scope for input from local actors (often the recipients or proposed 'beneficiaries' of crisis response). The nature of the EU, as a collection of states, means that many of its bureaucratic systems are designed to privilege elite forms of information that come from other states (or multilateral bodies). This has created a form of strategic paralysis with respect to peace, but it has been useful for engaging with migration and corruption issues. It means that EU crisis strategies are pushed back towards those associated with conflict management, leading at best to concurrence with the post-War on Terror 'stabilisation' framework as a form of contemporary counter-insurgency praxis.

A second point relates to the epistemologies and worldviews that lie behind conflict management, conflict resolution and conflict transformation and how they relate to the decision-making processes and assessment of 'success' and 'failure'. Crisis management as the most conservative of the perspectives is represented in Figure 7.1 (Chapter 7), where the setting of policy agendas and the requirement of consensus is limited to the EU, while external actors are expected to change their behaviour and comply. Conflict transformation, and particularly critical versions of that, would sit most uncomfortably with this way of defining 'success' or 'failure' and the structures of domination that it represents. The emphasis in conflict transformation on bottom-up and organic processes, inclusion of minorities, mutual learning as well as meaningful emancipation and empowerment would struggle with the linearity and controlled nature of institutionalised and formal processes. We are aware, of course, that Figure 7.1 represents a simplification and abstraction of very complex processes that involve multiple actors and processes, and events and exigencies are capable of throwing ordained and institutionalised processes off course. As explained in previous sections, a crisis management mind-set is likely to value path dependency and assess effectiveness and success as fulfilment of externally set goals. A crisis resolution mind-set, and more particularly that associated with crisis transformation, is more likely to be open to the analysis,

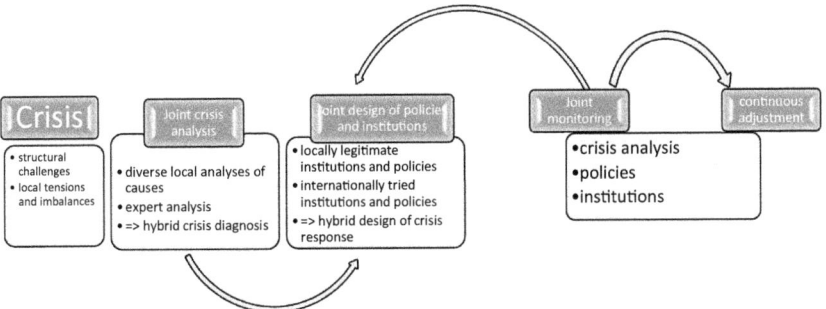

Figure 2.1 Critical crisis

agency and initiative of local actors. What appears to have arisen in EU engagements is a discursive framework that extends to and surpasses crisis resolution approaches, but in practice there exists a very traditional conflict and crisis management framework.

This represents a significant compromise on critical approaches to peace, which would require that crisis diagnosis and the design of policy instruments would be carried out jointly in cooperation with diverse actors from the crisis-affected context as depicted in Table 2.1, and engaging with a broader range of conflict dynamics as well as justice issues. This would open up the question of how crisis management would be framed through the eyes of the subalterns affected directly and indirectly by it, probably producing a hybrid version: still skewed towards the geopolitical and often Eurocentric interests of the EU, but at least more cognisant of the demands connected to the broader legitimacy of intervention, peacebuilding, and statebuilding.

Concluding discussion

The chapter has outlined three sets of taxonomies of crisis or conflict response:

- First–Second–Third–Fourth Generation peacebuilding
- Crisis management–Crisis resolution–Crisis transformation–Critical crisis transformation
- Realist–Structuralist–Liberal–Welfarist / Social Democratic responses

There are considerable overlaps between the three categorisations (thus pointing towards hybridisation). They can all be considered as constituting a continuum that moves from conservative to progressive and emancipatory stances.

A key observation from our studies has been the centrality of the EU in EU calculations rather than attempts to see crises in their own right or through the eyes of those in crisis locations. Crisis engagement represents EU security and political interests (in terrorism, migration, with weak common values), rather than those of disputant societies, or indeed of 'subaltern' actors. Indeed, looking back in the institutional history of EU crisis response shows a worrying

Table 2.1 Critical crisis transformation

	Operates in conjunction with other strategies	Is system compliant or system challenging?	Extends beyond top-down actors	Satisfies needs of conflict-affected societies	Extends rights to conflict-affected populations
Conflict/crisis management	(-)	compliant	(-)	(-)	(-)
Conflict/crisis resolution	(+)	compliant	(+)	short-term	(-)
Conflict/crisis transformation	(+)	challenging	(+)	medium-/long-term	(+)
(Critical crisis transformation)	(+)	(re-structuring)	(+)	short- to long-term	(+)

trend towards realist, securitised and self-interested interventions: the EU's Border Assistance Mission to Rafah, at the crossing point between Gaza and Egypt, with its main objective to foster confidence-building as a strategy to promote peace and strengthen the possibility of Palestinian statehood, shows that even border security missions can be normatively driven. Such priorities are a long way off from the EUBAM in Libya and other recent border assistance policies, whose purpose reflects mainly the EU's concern over issues of human trafficking and terrorism. Our case studies in this chapter, and indeed the case studies through this book, have shown that most EU crises responses are currently limited to crisis management with mostly unsuccessful or incomplete examples of further-reaching approaches.

If EU policies strive for a third and fourth generation of crisis transformation, EUNPACK research suggests that broader approaches are needed. It would have to engage with alternative forms of legitimate political authority outside of the modern state, it would be even less territorialised and more relational and networked across scales, and more focused on social assistance and consent. It would favour, in a somewhat contradictory manner, more external intervention if it were to be couched in such terms. In this way, the objectives inferred from ethnographic perspectives of crisis response, as compared with institutional and EU perspectives, transcend debates about shared or networked sovereignty, and humanitarian intervention, and are more in line with the normative but discursive frameworks of human rights and global justice to which the EU's policy was at least theoretically connected. However, fatigue with intervention, and a related retreat to concepts such as 'principled pragmatism'[5], subsidiarity and resilience, as a response to both material and normative overstretch, has undermined the EU's local peacebuilding authority and legitimacy in our cases.

We find no evidence for a graduated conflict response in our cases (although some variation was found in other cases in the EUNPACK project): strategies to contain risks in the EU's neighbourhood are the same as the approaches used further afield. We also find that crisis responses are not geared to the empirical, ethnographic dynamics of the conflicts, which have now been well documented and should be included in any responses. They are instead geared to the EU's centralised view of what constitutes a crisis for its core actors and policies: challenges to its model for integration, including its arguments for rights, democracy and capital; mass migration, influx of refugees and the weakening of states' ability to contain such movements; the risks for the destabilisation of the EU project's rationality of such factors, and the risks for the unity of specific member states. Attempts to resolve these contradictions have rarely been made. All of this points to the construction of crises often through political and discursive means.

The ontology of EU crisis management follows a realist rationale of prime interests for the broad rights of EU citizens, and the EU as a coherent state-like actor with hard borders, after which distance from a crisis enables a shift in the order to narrow security interests. This is despite an understanding – at a superficial level at any rate – of issues such as conflict sensitivity, gender, identity, mobility and the existence of alternative forms of political authority. Rather than engagement more with citizens' needs, the reverse patterns arises. In effect, this prioritises the interests of EU citizens and states over the rights of conflict-affected citizens but without resolving the contradictions between national interests and identity-based normative claims for security, EU interests and its liberal norms.

This chapter has sketched out what crisis resolution and crisis transformation could look like, and a way to measure existing stances. A needs and rights-focused approach to crises would help the EU to rescue its image of being a normative actor and position the EU as a progressive force in international politics. It offers the prospect of 'democratising' responses by working with and alongside local and non-elite actors, thus opening up opportunities for local ownership, partnership and – ultimately – sustainable forms of peace (a finding replicated in other chapters in this book). There are some signs of differentiated and modulated responses from the EU, and the range of actual and proposed responses covered in this chapter suggest room for a further hybridisation in crisis response – deftly changing the response in relation to an evolving crisis.

The major difference between crisis management and crisis transformation is that the latter works with the networks, agency and knowledge that already exist on the ground and connects its assistance to them. In other words, crisis transformation is able to move beyond states and formal political institutions. The grounding of crisis response in local politics helps to overcome two of the major downsides of crisis short-termism: the fragility of its resolution mechanisms as well the tendency to overreact in a way that spurs the forces that feed on social discontent (Runciman, 2016: 3–16). The continuous evolution of knowledge on any specific crisis requires a constant information flow between grassroots response and international decision-making. Crisis response mechanisms have to be regularly contrasted with local perceptions as might be observed with the EU crisis response strategies in Mali, Ukraine and Libya.

The timeline of any intervention and engagement is worthy of scrutiny. Crisis response thus needs to be considered on the basis of the path dependencies that it creates and are actors able to disengage with that path dependency: Who owns or identifies with the state that the EU tries to reinforce for the purpose of threat containment? Are EU interests in a crisis context aligned with the interests of crisis-affected societies? Does crisis intervention empower discredited or contested domestic elites? Would this erode the legitimacy of EU involvement in the eyes of crisis-affected populations? How can local agency and indigenous technical knowledge be incorporated into EU crisis response?

Creating and maintaining mutual trust and understanding between local and international crisis response requires more than bureaucratic models of regular reviews and formal consultation processes. Indeed, the abundance of such formalities has disheartened many crisis-affected communities (as becomes clear in many other chapters in this book). CCT is more closely attuned to the peace and security goals of the EU than crisis management, resolution, or transformation approaches applied so far. CCT offers the chance to create short- to long-term, multidimensional and yet locally modulated, sustainable and effective strategies to eradicate the root causes and longer-term consequences of both crises and conflicts, rather than merely their symptoms. Yet, as found in the EUNPACK project and as illustrated in many chapters in this book, EU foreign policy ambitions have been curbed and there is a trend towards stabilisation and securitisation. This accords more with conflict management than anything more progressive.

Notes

1 Indeed, solidarity in cases of terrorist attacks, man-made or natural disasters is contractually mandated in Art. 222 of the Treaty on the Functioning of the European Union (Treaty of Rome). Since the shape of this solidarity is not further defined though, this obligation cannot be enforced (see Bátora et al., 2016: 21).
2 In 2012, the Nobel Prize Committee honoured the EU for its advancements in the above fields with the Nobel Peace Prize.
3 The mission was eventually launched half a year later. However, it had to be re-dedicated from an anti-migration into an anti-terrorism policy.
4 European Commission (2020).
5 Multiple interviews and observations from our different case studies confirmed this argument.

References

Albrecht, P. and L. Wiuff Moe (2015) 'The simultaneity of authority in hybrid political orders', *Peacebuilding*, 3(1): 1–16.
Azar, E.A. (1990) *The Management of Protracted Social Conflict* (Aldershot, UK: Dartmouth Publishing).
Azar, E.A. and J.W. Burton (eds) (1986) *International Conflict Resolution: Theory and Practice* (Boulder, CO: Lynne Rienner Publishers).
Bátora, J., S. Blockmans, E. Ferhatovic, I. Peters, P. Rieker and E. Stambøl (2016) *Understanding the EU's Crisis Response Toolbox and Decision-Making Processes, EUNPACK Report (WP D4.1)* (Oslo: NUPI).
Bercovitch, J. (ed.) (1996) *Resolving International Conflicts: The Theory and Practice of Mediation* (London and Boulder, CO: Lynne Rienner Publishers).
Bercovitch, J. and J.Z. Rubin (eds) (1992) *Mediation in International Relations: Multiple Approaches to Conflict Management* (Basingstoke: Macmillan).
Berkowitz, L. (1993) *Aggression: Its Causes, Consequences and Control* (New York: McGraw-Hill).
Bøås, M., A.W. Cissé, A. Diallo, F. Kvamme and E. Stambøl (2018) 'The EU, Security Sector Reform and border management in Mali', *EUNPACK Working Paper 7.04* (Brussels: EUNPACK).
Boege, V., A. Brown, K. Clements and A. Nolan (2008) 'On hybrid political orders and emerging states: State formation in the context of "fragility"', in *Berghof Handbook Dialogue Series 8: Building Peace in the Absence of States: Challenging the Discourse of State Failure*

(Berlin: Berghof Research Center for Constructive Conflict Management), 15–35.
Bourdieu, P. (1977) *Outline of a Theory of Practice* (Cambridge: Cambridge University Press).
Brecher, M. and J. Wilkenfeld (2000) *A Study of Crisis* (Ann Arbor: University of Michigan Press).
Burton, J.W. and F. Dukes (eds) (1990) *Conflict: Readings in Management and Resolution* (London: Macmillan).
Calhoun, C. and G. Derlugian (eds) (2011) *The Deepening Crisis: Governance Challenges after Neoliberalism* (New York: New York University Press/SSRC).
Call, C.T. and S.E. Cook (2003) 'On democratization and peacebuilding', *Global Governance*, 9(2): 233–246.
Callinicos, A. (2010) *Bonfire of Illusions: The Twin Crisis of the Liberal World* (Cambridge: Polity).
Carnegie (1997) *Preventing Deadly Conflict: Final Report, Carnegie Commission on Preventing Deadly Conflict* (New York: Carnegie Corporation).
Chopra, J. (1996) 'The space of peace-maintenance', *Political Geography*, 15(3/4): 335–357.
Chopra, J. (2000) 'The UN's Kingdom of East Timor', *Survival*, 42(3): 27–40.
Comaroff, J. and J.L. Comaroff (2012) *Theory from the South: or, How Euro-America Is Evolving towards Africa* (London: Paradigm Publishers).
Debrix, F. and C. Weber (eds) (2003) *Rituals of Mediation* (Minneapolis: University of Minnesota Press).
Diehl, P.F. (2016) 'Exploring peace: Looking beyond war and negative peace', *International Studies Quarterly*, 60(1): 1–10.
Dollard, J., L.W. Doob, N.E. Miller, O.H. Mowrer and R.R. Sears (1939) *Frustration and Aggression* (New Haven, CT: Yale University Press).
Dunn, J.D. (2004) *From Power Politics to Conflict Resolution: The Work of John W. Burton* (Basingstoke: Palgrave Macmillan).
EEAS (2019) 'Crisis management and response' (Brussels: EEAS), https://eeas.europa.eu/headquarters/headquarters-homepage/412/crisis-management-and-response_en#Crisis+Response+System (accessed 1 June 2021).
European Commission (2009) *Communication from the Commission to the European Parliament, the Council, the European Economic and Social Committee and the Committee of the Regions – A Community Approach on the Prevention of Natural and Man Made Disasters. Document 52009DC0082* (Brussels: EC).
European Commission (2012) *State Aid, Crisis-Related Aid* (Brussels: EC).

European Commission (2020) 'Supporting Jordan in the context of the Syrian refugee crisis: A joint initiative on rules of origin' (Brussels: EC), http://ec.europa.eu/trade/policy/countries-and-regions/countries/jordan/index_en.htm (accessed 1 June 2021).
European Union HR/VP (2016) *Shared Vision, Common Action: A Stronger Europe. A Global Strategy for the European Union's Foreign and Security Policy* (Brussels: EU).
Ferguson, J. and A. Gupta (1992) 'Beyond "culture": Space, identity, and the politics of difference', *Cultural Anthropology*, 7(1): 6–23.
Galtung, J. (1969) 'Violence, peace, and peace research', *Journal of Peace Research*, 6(3): 167–191.
Galtung, J. (1998) *Peace by Peaceful Means: Peace and Conflict, Development and Civilization* (Oslo: PRIO / London: Sage).
Gamble, A. (2014) *Crisis Without End? The Unravelling of Western Prosperity* (New York: Palgrave Macmillan).
Giddens, A. (2014) *Turbulent and Mighty Continent: What Future for Europe?* (Cambridge: Polity).
Goldgeier, J.M. and M. McFaul (2001) 'The liberal core and the realist periphery in Europe', *Perspectives on European Politics and Society*, 2(1): 1–26.
Gurr, T. (1970) *Why Men Rebel* (Princeton, NJ: Princeton University Press).
Habermas, J. (2009) *Europe: The Faltering Project* (Cambridge: Polity).
Habermas, J. (2012) *The Crisis of the European Union: A Response* (Cambridge: Polity).
Hammarskjold, D. (1958) UN General Assembly, *Summary Study of the Experience Derived from the Establishment and Operation of the United Nations Emergency Force – Report of the Secretary-General*, UN doc. A/3943, 9 October.
Hay, H. (1996) 'Narrating crisis: The discursive construction of the "winter of discontent"', *Sociology*, 30(2): 253–277.
Isard, W. (1992) *Understanding Conflict and the Science of Peace* (Cambridge, MA and Oxford: Blackwell).
James, A. (1994) *Peacekeeping in International Politics* (Basingstoke: IISS/Macmillan).
Jones, D. (1999) *Cosmopolitan Mediation? Conflict Resolution and the Oslo Accords* (Manchester: Manchester University Press).
Kissinger, H. (1954) *A World Restored: Metternich, Castlereagh and the Problems of Peace 1812–1822* (Boston: Houghton Mifflin).
Kjaer, P.F. and N. Olsen (eds) (2016) *Critical Theories of Crisis in Europe: From Weimar to the Euro* (London and New York: Rowman & Littlefield).
Lederach, J.P. (1995) *Preparing for Peace: Conflict Transformation across Cultures* (Syracuse, NY: Syracuse University Press).

Lederach, J.P. (1997) *Building Peace: Sustainable Reconciliation in Divided Societies* (Washington DC: United States Institute of Peace).
Loschi, C., L. Raineri and F. Strazzari (2018) 'The implementation of EU Crisis Response in Libya: Bridging theory and practice', *EUNPACK Working Paper D.6.2.* (Oslo: EUNPACK).
Mac Ginty, R. and O.P. Richmond (2013) 'The local turn in peace building: A critical agenda for peace', *Third World Quarterly*, 34(5): 763–783.
Macmillan, J. (2003) 'Whose democracy, which peace? The "democratic peace" and liberal traditions on democracy and peace', paper prepared for the panel, 'The antinomies of the democratic peace', presented at the European Consortium for Political Research (ECPR) General Conference, Marburg, 18–21 September.
Manners, I. (2002) 'Normative power Europe: A contradiction in terms?' *JCMS: Journal of Common Market Studies*, 40(2): 235–258.
Offe, C. (2016) *Europe Entrapped* (Cambridge: Polity).
Patomaki, H. (2001) 'The challenge of critical theories: Peace research at the start of the new century', *Journal of Peace Research*, 38(6): 723–737.
Peters, I. (ed.) (2016) *The European Union's Foreign Policy Comparative Perspective: Beyond the 'Actorness and Power' Debate* (London and New York: Routledge).
Pietz, T. (2017) 'Flexibility and "stabilisation actions": EU crisis management one year after the Global Strategy', Policy Briefing (Berlin: Center for International Peace Operations (ZIF), September).
Pouligny, B. (2006) *Peace Operations Seen from Below: UN Missions and Local People* (London: Hurst).
Princen, T. (1992) *Intermediaries in International Conflict* (Princeton, NJ: Princeton University Press).
Raineri, L., A. Russo and A. Harrington (eds) (2017) 'How the EU is facing crises in its neighbourhood: Evidence from Libya and Ukraine', *EUNPACK Working Paper 6.1* (Oslo: EUNPACK).
Richmond, O.P., A. Björkdahl and S. Kappler (2011) 'The emerging EU peacebuilding framework: Confirming or transcending liberal peacebuilding?', *Cambridge Review of International Affairs*, 24(3): 449–469.
Roitman, J. (2016) 'The stakes of crisis', in P.F. Kjaer and N. Olsen (eds), *Critical Theories of Crisis in Europe: From Weimar to the Euro* (London: Rowman & Littlefield).
Runciman, D. (2016) 'What time frame makes sense for thinking about crises?', in P.F. Kjaer and N. Olsen (eds), *Critical Theories of Crisis in Europe: From Weimar to the Euro* (London: Rowman & Littlefield).
Runciman, W.G. (1972) *Relative Deprivation and Social Injustice: A Study of Attitudes to Social Inequality in Twentieth Century England* (London: Penguin Books).

UN (2004) *Report of the Secretary-General's High-Level Panel on Threats, Challenges, and Change, A More Secure World: Our Shared Responsibility* (New York: United Nations).

UN (2018) 'High-level Meeting on efforts undertaken and opportunities to strengthen the United Nations' work on peacebuilding and sustaining peace', 24–25 April: General Assembly Resolution, A/RES/70/262, 2016; Security Council Resolution S/RES/2282, 2016.

Visoka, G. and J. Doyle (2015) 'Neo-functional peace: The EU way of resolving conflicts', *JCMS: Journal of Common Market Studies*, 54(4): 862–877.

Walby, S. (2015) *Crisis* (Cambridge: Polity).

Whitman, R.G. (1998) *From Civilian Power to Superpower? The International Identity of the European Union* (Basingstoke: Palgrave Macmillan).

Zartman, I.W. (1982) *The Practical Negotiator* (New Haven, CT: Yale University Press).

Zartman I.W. (2003) 'The timing of peace initiatives: Hurting stalemates and ripe moments', in J. Darby and R. Mac Ginty (eds) *Contemporary Peacemaking* (London: Palgrave Macmillan), 19–29.

3

The potential and limits of EU crisis response

Pernille Rieker and Kristian L. Gjerde

Introduction

Research on the EU as a global actor has been largely dominated by normative or theoretical convictions or agendas. This has resulted in a sizeable literature focusing on how to understand the EU as an actor. The EU has been variously described as a civilian power (Duchêne, 1972), smart power (Nossel, 2004), normative power (Manners, 2002, 2006), cosmopolitan power (Sjursen, 2006), superpower (McCormick, 2007; Moravcsik, 2010) or a small power (Toje, 2011). This chapter takes a different starting point. Through an in-depth study of how EU foreign policy is implemented it aims to enhance our understanding of the functioning of the EU as an international actor. Rather than focusing on the EU's character, resources or how the systemic features of world politics condition its political behaviour, we concentrate on the Union's foreign policy repertoires and how these impacts the implementation of EU's external crisis response. Such a study will also allow us to conclude on whether the Union's approach can be understood as crisis management, crisis resolution or crisis transformation (see Chapter 2, this volume). The empirical focus is on several crises and conflicts of the past decade in what we may refer to as three concentric areas surrounding the EU: *the enlargement area* (Kosovo/Serbia), *the neighbourhood area* (Ukraine, Syria, Libya), *and the extended neighbourhood* (Afghanistan, Iraq, Mali). It is built on the assumption that while the logic of integration will affect the EU's approach in the two first cases, although in different ways, it will do so less or not at all in the extended neighbourhood.

The analysis draws on different types of sources. First, the discussion is based on a series of case studies undertaken within the framework of the EUNPACK project. Each case study was based on a series of standardised in-depth interviews and surveys undertaken in summer/autumn 2017 and will be referred to throughout this chapter.[1] Second, we wanted to gain insights into the official EU discourse about these countries/conflict areas. To this end, we 'scraped' more than seventy thousand press releases from the EC and the Council of the European Union.[2] We posit that this text collection is well suited for providing some quantitative contextualisation of the development of certain aspects of EU attention to various countries and issues. But first, we need to explain the concept of *foreign policy repertoire* and why it was chosen as a conceptual starting point for the purpose of this study.

The EU foreign policy repertoire in crisis response

Analyses of foreign policy behaviour have dominated IR theory and scholarship, but analytical tools for systematically exploring continuity and change are still lacking. This study explores these concerns from a new perspective by applying the concept of *repertoires of foreign policy*. Rather than focusing on actors' foreign policy character, resources and on how the systemic features of world politics condition certain types of political behaviour, we focus on the *repertoires* through which actors engage with one another. More precisely, we study the EU's foreign policy repertoire in one specific area – crisis response. Foreign policy repertoire is understood here as *the sum total of foreign policy instruments by a foreign policy actor* at any given point. This means that the analysis of an actor's use of instruments as well as the interaction of those instruments over time should reveal the logic of this actor's use of its repertoire. While such logics are analytical entities, we assume that they will correspond with an actor's *self-identity* and that all actors tend to develop relatively stable repertoires of power politics (Nexon and Goddard, 2018), composed of a set of instruments and logics that they deploy to enhance their relative influence, varying slightly according to the foreign policy field.

A close study of the EU's approach to crises indicates a *comprehensive approach to crisis* (European Commission and High Representative, 2013, 2015; High Representative, 2016) is seen as the Union's self-identity in this area. Such an approach addresses the whole crisis cycle from pre-crisis to post-conflict stabilisation, with a toolbox suitable for dealing with all these aspects, through 'soft' and 'hard' foreign policy tools. This means that conflict management is not in line with the EU's self-identity. Rather, it aims at having an approach more in line with conflict resolution and perhaps also with elements of conflict transformation.

But what we are interested in here is to investigate how well this EU self-identity and its policy objectives match with actual implementation of EU crisis response activities. In other words, is there an intention–implementation gap? Additionally, we examine a possible implementation–perception gap, which would be a mismatch between the EU's perceptions of its crisis response activities and local stakeholders' perceptions.

Self-identity, objectives, institutions and instruments

Since adopting a 'comprehensive approach' to crisis management in 2013 (European Commission and High Representative, 2013), the EU has spent considerable time and energy on streamlining its approach and improving internal coordination. New and protracted crises – the conflict in Ukraine, the rise of ISIS, the refugee situation in the South – have made improving external crisis response capacities a top priority (Blockmans, 2015). Thus, the EU has revised both the European Security Strategy (ESS) from 2003 and its ENP. The EU's 'Global Strategy', presented to the European Council in June 2016, offers a practical and principled route to conflict prevention, crisis response and peacebuilding, promoting human security through an 'integrated approach'. The meaning of the integrated or comprehensive approach has been expanded beyond the development–security nexus, and now encompasses a commitment to synergistic use of all tools available at all stages of the conflict cycle while paying attention to all levels of EU action – local, national, regional and global (Council of the European Union, 2016; High Representative, 2016).

Has all this improved the Union's actual capacity to act – or has it simply widened the 'capacity–expectations gap' identified by Christopher Hill (1993)? In the EU's external crisis response, this gap needs to be specified by two important and related elements. First, 'the intention–implementation gap', which relates not only to the capacity to make decisions based on predetermined objectives, responding with one voice and to deploying the necessary resources (central in Hill's contribution) – but also how these responses are implemented on the ground by EU institutions and member states, and how other actors – local and international – enhance or undermine the EU's activities. Second, there is the gap between the implementation of EU policies and approaches, and how these policies and approaches are received and perceived in target countries: 'the implementation–local reception/perceptions gap'. In order for the EU crisis response to be characterised as a type of conflict transformation, however, both gaps need to be plugged.

Rieker and Blockmans (2018) have surveyed the current state of EU crisis response capacity, presenting the EU's comprehensive approach to crisis and its capacities. Focusing mainly on the Union's resources and administrative capacities in this area, they find that the EU's capacity to act remains hampered by limited resources and a less-developed capacity to utilise available knowledge about the conflict at hand to ensure a conflict-sensitive approach.

Building on these insights, we take one step further to study the instruments and tools available to the EU for intervening throughout the crisis cycle, how they are implemented, and how they are perceived by local stakeholders. Such instruments may include diplomatic instruments (like dialogue and mediation) as well as economic instruments such as sanctions, and civil and military missions to enhance security and humanitarian/development aid.

So far, most research has studied EU capacity to handle crises from a top-down or European perspective, with less attention to the actual implementation phase and the implications of the implementation of EU crisis response, including local perceptions of these actions. Regarding its comprehensive or integrated approach, the EU also stresses the importance of 'local ownership' and 'conflict sensitivity'. But less is known about how or to what extent the EU has managed to achieve this. The aim of this article is to help fill this gap.

Combining qualitative approaches and text mining in the study of EU crisis response

The EU's objectives for crisis response are based on the Union's self-identity and inspired by the comprehensive approach. How have they been reflected in actual implementation in recent crisis response activities in the immediate, the near and the wider EU neighbourhood? While this issue has been addressed qualitatively through interviews and surveys in the various regions (these data are included in our analysis below), we will here complement it with a quantitative exploration of word usage in EU documents with the aim of highlighting the attention accorded by the EU to different parts of its comprehensive approach or power repertoires in this field. The main aim has been to trace development over time in the different regions. We have conceptualised the EU's comprehensive policy toolbox – the EU's repertoire for crisis response – as divided into three different agendas, which we postulate will be linked to different terminologies: a 'hard security' agenda linked with words such as 'sanctions' and 'border management', a 'soft security' agenda linked with words such as 'civil society' and 'good governance', and an 'integration' agenda linked with words such as 'integration' and 'association agreement' (see Table 3.1). While the first seems to be more in line with a traditional conflict management

Table 3.1 Selected 'category words'

Category	Selected 'category words'*
Hard security	border management, migration, refugees, security, stability, crime, trafficking, sanctions
Soft security	civil society, good governance, rule of law, dialogue, mediation, humanitarian aid, development aid
Integration	integration, enlargement, membership, conditionality, association agreement

* The following case-insensitive regular expressions were used to identify these categories in the texts: 'border management|migration|refugee|security (?! council)|stability|crime|trafficking|sanctions', 'civil society|good governance|rule of law|democra|dialog|mediation|humanitarian aid|development aid' and 'integration|enlargement|membership|conditionality|association agreement'

approach, both the soft security approach and the integration approach are more likely to include elements of conflict resolution and sometimes also conflict transformation.

To explore this, we first downloaded the entire press release archive of the EC (71,061 documents for the period 2000–16), which generally includes press releases and key decisions made by the European Council and the Council of the EU.[3] The goal was to see how our three categories of words appear together with mentions of the countries under study. As many documents are long and contain a number of different topics, we split these documents into their nearly four million component sentences[4] and examined how often the words in the three categories – 'category words' – appeared in the same sentences as the countries under study. Table 3.1 shows the words we have chosen to represent each category.

We should here underline that a different selection (and number) of words clearly could have changed the relative size of the categories. Therefore, what we want to explore is *the relative trend between the categories over time*, not one year or any overall sum taken in isolation. The aim is that Figures 3.1–3.6, which are based on this procedure and presented below, as a complement to the more qualitative case studies based on interviews and fieldwork, can illustrate developments of the EU's agenda in each case over time, as well as the differences in the EU's approach between these cases.

The power of conditionality, competing priorities and gap in expectations

In the enlargement area, the EU has the overarching ambition of creating stability through a process of integration based on the mechanisms of conditionality. This was long held to be a very efficient strategy, leading to a reunited and peaceful Europe after the end of the Cold War. Enlargement as such has been cited as the EU's most successful security-policy instrument. It could also be referred to as one of the strongest parts of the EU's foreign policy repertoires when dealing with this specific region.

However, although enlargement is seen as a foreign policy tool, enabling the EU to shape its environment according to its values and interests, this has not been a linear process. Since the 'big bang' enlargement of 2004, which led to ten new members, followed by Romania and Bulgaria in 2008, the process has slowed down. The combination of economic challenges and a more challenging geopolitical context has brought greater reluctance to further enlargement. However, there is still general agreement concerning the need to include the current Balkan candidate countries as soon as they fulfil the criteria. In 2013 Croatia joined the EU, while Serbia and Montenegro are official candidate countries and have started the negotiations process. According to an action plan issued by the EC in 2018, the ambition is for Serbia and Montenegro to be full members by 2025 (European Commission, 2018). First, however, both countries must improve in rule of law and governance; Serbia must also normalise its diplomatic relations with Kosovo.

How has the integration agenda, or the EU's *conditionality tool*, worked in the case of Serbia? To what extent has it considered the concerns of Kosovo? Instead of studying the process of enlargement as such, we focus on the actions taken by the EU and its member states to assist both Serbia and Kosovo in the process towards future membership. Here we examine aspects of the 'normalisation dialogue' between Belgrade and Pristina launched in 2013, as well as the implementation, practices, and perceptions on the ground of EULEX. We also enquire into the importance of this agenda with regard to agendas more dominated by either hard or soft security measures without necessarily being an integration agenda.

The key challenge here is that Serbia did not recognise Kosovo when it declared independence in 2008. A decade later, the official line of the Serbian government is that Kosovo remains an integral part of Serbia, despite the establishment of a parallel structure of government functions as well as the existence of various foreign and diplomatic missions with embassy status in Pristina and Belgrade (Bátora *et al.*, 2018). Here the EU has chosen to apply the practice, common in negotiations concerning international crises, of using ambiguous language as a way of achieving a buy-in by both the conflicting parties and gradual progress towards stabilisation of relations (Bátora *et al.*, 2018). In the EU governance literature, this is referred to as 'constructive ambiguity' – a term used in situations when member states or other parties to a negotiation cannot fully agree on an issue – and ambiguously worded agreements may then be interpreted differently in different international contexts. The underlying idea is that this might improve the lives of ordinary people and that it reflects the European method – seeking peace through practical cooperation rather than through grand rhetoric about the 'brotherhood of mankind' (Cooper, quoted in Bátora *et al.*, 2018: 13).

A typical example of such a method is the normalisation dialogue between Pristina and Belgrade: the language has remained sufficiently ambiguous to provide leeway for both sides to operate with varying interpretations (Bátora *et al.*, 2018: 12–13). While ambiguity may allow progress on difficult issues, it also has its costs. According to respondents from the embassies in both capitals, the whole concept of dialogue becomes artificial, superficial or too narrow to deliver (Bátora *et al.*, 2018: 13). In fact, conflicting interpretations also led to the derailing of the normalisation process in 2017.

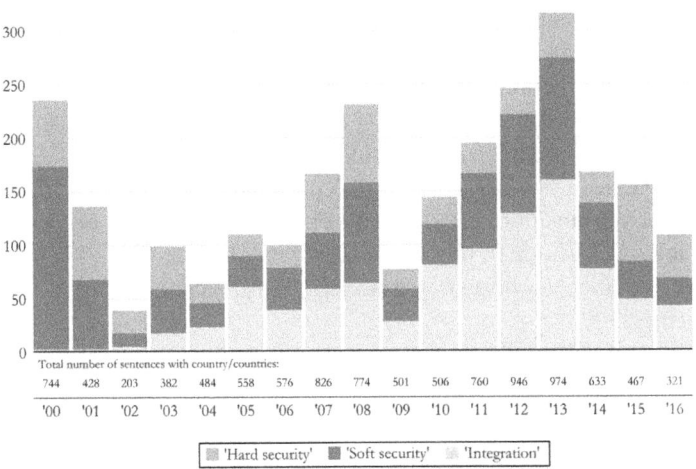

Figure 3.1 How terms reflecting different EU agendas appear in the same sentence as 'Serbia' or 'Kosovo' in our document collection (2000–16). Figures 3.1–3.6 are based on 3,870,946 sentences from 71,434 European Commission and Council of the European Union press releases. The figures show the number of sentences per year that include the country (or countries) and also include words from our 'agenda categories' for each category. All figures made using the ggplot2 in R package (Wickham, 2016)

The aim of the EULEX operation was threefold. First and foremost, to provide support to Kosovo's rule of law institutions. Second, to contribute to the Belgrade/Pristina Dialogue by assisting in the implementation of the dialogue agreement in the sphere of the rule of law. Third, to ensure that rule of law services are delivered until the progress of local authorities allows the complete transfer of executive functions to local authorities. Beyond this, the operation contributed to more over-arching objectives: increasing regional stability by preparing Kosovo for EU membership and minimising security threats to Europe emanating from Kosovo.

The EU has had these countries (and the conflict) on its agenda throughout the period. We see that the integration agenda has had a clear presence in our text material, but with a relative decline compared to the security (hard and soft) agendas since 2010.

While progress can be identified, and EULEX is perceived as an important watchdog against human rights abuses, the main challenge has been the conflicting sovereignty claims put forth by Kosovo-Albanians and Kosovo-Serbs. Both sides hold that there is a lack of conflict- or context-sensitivity on the part of the EU: 'while the local institutions are reporting to EULEX, communication only goes in one direction ... the EU is more interested in stabilization than in building democracy within the country' (Bátora *et al.*, 2018: 28). We have not pursued an in-depth analysis of EU attention to these questions in our collection of EU documents, but we do note that a quick search in this text material reveals scant use of concepts like 'conflict / context sensitivity', 'local ownership' or 'local partnership'.

Still, the EU's influence in this region is important, probably more so than that of other international actors. After all, this engagement is closely linked to the EU enlargement agenda. But there are also several obstructing factors. First, there is internal disagreement in the EU concerning the future status of Kosovo. Second, the instrumental use of ambiguity in the normalisation dialogue can promote cooperation – but it also leaves room for multiple interpretations that in turn may undermine trust among the parties. Third, the competing priorities of the EU in the region – stability versus democratisation – also hamper its effectiveness as an actor in the region. Further, poor conflict- and context-sensitivity limit the EU's capacity to deliver on democratisation *and* stabilisation, so priority goes to the latter. Finally, the discrepancy between the initial intentions of the EU and actual implementation of its policies on the ground has led to an expectations gap between the local population and the EU.

Crisis response in the neighbourhood

Also in its neighbourhood the EU has a special role due to its integration agenda. In parallel to the enlargement in 2004, the EU initiated the ENP to avoid new dividing lines in Europe. This led to aspirations in several post-Soviet states that they might – one day – become EU members; and in the South there was optimism concerning possibilities for closer cooperation and association that, in turn, would lead to greater prosperity in the region. While Russia was sceptical about the eastern part of this policy, it was, at the time, more concerned with NATO and its expansion plans. In the South, there were hopes that a relationship hitherto dominated by security concerns would lead to a mutually advantageous partnership. The ENP, further strengthened by the Eastern Partnership (EaP) in the East and the Union for the Mediterranean (UfM) in the South, was seen as an important instrument for (security) community building beyond EU borders, built on the same integration logic as in the enlargement area. While the conditionality mechanism was weaker (in the East) or non-existent (in the South), the objective was still that the EU would be able, by its soft security or *power of attraction*, to contribute to stability, security and prosperity in the neighbourhood.

The EU's soft power has been considerably weakened from 2011 onwards. After the short-lived 'Arab Spring', the Southern neighbourhood experienced a period of conflicts, wars and failed states. In the Eastern neighbourhood, the crisis in Ukraine and deteriorating relations with Russia have undermined the EU's influence over this region (Rieker, 2016). In fact, these experiences led to a revision of the ENP and the abandonment of the part of EU's self-identity based on the idea that regional integration would automatically lead to security. The revised ENP is less explicit as to possible future membership for the partner countries in the East, and more concerned with providing assistance to these countries in the work of building stronger institutions and good governance: downplaying the integration agenda, strengthening the general soft-security agenda.

Also in the South, there have been changes in the EU's approach. In response to the Arab Spring, there came a de-securitisation of the ENP in the South, with a brief period of greater focus on support for democratisation, and to civil society groups. However, maintaining this approach proved difficult as the Arab Spring faded out and was replaced by instability, wars and failed states. A combination of hard and soft security has gradually returned as the top priority for the EU in its relations with this part of the neighbourhood, a trend reconfirmed after the 2015 migration crisis and the series of terrorist attacks in Europe. That is not to say that other concerns have been completely abandoned. There is still the explicit ambition of tackling the root causes of migration and conflict in this region, but the integration agenda has been generally abandoned as a strategy for building security and prosperity. As the ENP has been the main framework for EU engagement in this region, the EU's main security policy tools – the Common Foreign and Security Policy (CFSP) and the CSDP – have played secondary roles. However, more recently, and linked to a changed regional security context, both Ukraine and Libya have experienced the deployment of CSDP missions. This shows that even though the overall trend seems to be greater degree of securitisation, the EU approach is complex and may include different elements.

How can the EU crisis response in one Eastern and one Southern conflict shed light on the EU crisis response repertoire in this area more generally – and how has it changed? Also here the analysis builds on the results of interviews and surveys (Ivashchenko-Stadnik *et al.*, 2018; Loschi *et al.*, 2018), complemented with a text-mining approach.

Crisis response in Ukraine: increasingly security-driven

The EU's reaction to the crisis in Ukraine, in the aftermath of the annexation of Crimea in March 2014, can be summarised as three groups of measures: first, *restrictive measures and sanctions against Russia;* second, *diplomatic measures* of supporting the dialogue within *the Normandy Format* between France, Germany, Ukraine

The potential and limits of EU crisis response   71

and Russia, combined with the financing of the Organization for Security and Co-operation in Europe (OSCE) Monitoring Mission in Ukraine aimed at monitoring implementation of the Minsk Agreement; and third, the *EU missions* in Ukraine. Since the crisis started in November 2013, the EU has had two permanent missions in Ukraine: the EU Advisory Mission (EUAM) for Civilian Security Sector Reform, which provides financial, technical and expert support for Ukrainian law enforcement and rule of law institutions and agencies; and SGUA, supporting the effective implementation and application of the EU–Ukraine Association Agreement by the Ukrainian government. The Support Group offers assistance in critical areas of reform and helps coordinate financial assistance to Ukraine on behalf of international financial institutions. In addition, the EU has continued to support the EUBAM in Moldova and Ukraine, operational since 2005.

The attention towards Ukraine (see Figure 3.2) is in line with expectations. Ukraine has been on the EU agenda since 2000 – increasingly so after 2004, when the ENP was launched and with the EaP a few years later (2009), and then peaking dramatically in 2014 and 2015 due to the crisis in Ukraine. The integration agenda featured increasingly in EU discourse from 2010, with a peak relative to the other categories in 2013. Since then, the figure seems

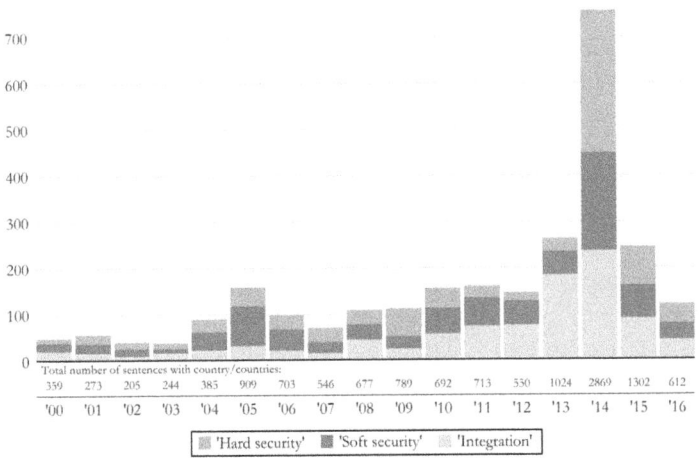

Figure 3.2 Ukraine 2000–16: terms reflecting different EU agendas

to tentatively support the claim that the EU's approach to Ukraine has become more characterised by a foreign policy agenda based on a combination of soft and hard security agendas, in addition to talk of integration.

The three groups of measures discussed above reflect the move towards support for reforms without mentioning the integration agenda. While this engagement is deemed important in Brussels, EU officials on the ground in Kiev mention three common problems. First, the workflow is too slow, and involves too many bureaucratic procedures. Second, there is a gap between the goals and ambitions of local partners and the EU. Finally, doubts among the local population as to the EU agenda lead to some degree of mistrust (Ivashchenko-Stadnik *et al.*, 2018).

The EUBAM is an exception here, as it is seen largely as a success – probably because it is a more specific mission that provides technical assistance in a clearly defined sector. Local interlocutors indicate that the EU engagement is perceived positively at the general level, but that it is insufficient and has difficulties in adapting rapidly to changing needs. There are fears that the EU's need to balance its relations with Russia will overshadow its engagement in Ukraine in the long run (Ivashchenko-Stadnik *et al.*, 2018).

Crisis response in Libya: limited and security-driven

While Libya is also part of the ENP on paper, this has never been fully activated. Unsurprisingly, relations between Libya and the EU have remained dominated by a security agenda. The post-Gaddafi period has proven particularly challenging for the EU, as there is no functioning government in Libya to cooperate with. The unstable situation also represents a direct security threat to the EU, as the 2015 migration crisis clearly showed. The EU has responded by giving priority to immediate security threats instead of focusing on more long-term solutions like capacity-building and SSR. The EU has undertaken two CSDP missions in Libya: the naval operation EUNAVFOR MED (Operation Sophia) and EUBAM Libya. Both are directed towards handling the migration challenge. Beyond these operations, the EU has launched a Trust Fund for Africa and Libya, and ECHO is engaged with humanitarian aid (Loschi *et al.*, 2018).

The initial aim of the EUNAVFOR MED operation was to disrupt the business model of human smuggling and trafficking networks by capturing and destroying the vessels used. While the intentions were good, the result was that the smugglers simply replaced their vessels with cheaper, dangerous rubber boats, leading to increased profits for the smugglers as well as more deaths at sea. There is also the difficulty of stopping the main traffickers and getting them prosecuted. Networks are robust and adapt rapidly. However, there is also reason to believe that there has been insufficient understanding of these networks and how they work, and of the malfunctioning of the Libyan judicial system.

The EUNAVFOR MED mandate has now been adapted and changed, and the overall operation has been more successful – also in the eyes of Libyans. EU vessels have been patrolling the waters outside Libyan cities known to harbour jihadist organisations; since 2017, the EU has expanded its activities to include the fight against oil smuggling, which fed territorial militias, fuelling the war economy and preventing the internationally recognised government from establishing its authority. It has been argued that the inclusion of these tasks has improved the overall coherence and led to greater acceptance of the EU crisis response in Libya (Loschi *et al.*, 2018). But not all EUNAVFOR MED activities have been so successful. Because of the lack of authorisation to operate inside Libyan waters, the training part of the operation was not implemented systematically; this also revealed the lack of knowledge about the competence and the needs of the local agency (Loschi *et al.*, 2018). When it became known that Libyan coastguard officers, trained by the EU, had been responsible for misconduct and abuses of human rights, it was recognised that this part of the operation had failed.

The civilian CSDP mission EUBAM Libya was launched in May 2013, mandated to help the Libyan authorities to develop a concept for integrated border management in Libya. As border management is challenging in a country that lacks a consolidated state apparatus able to control its territory, the EUBAM was seen as an appropriate tool for fostering border management across the country, at least if it could manage to improve coordination with EU member states, like Italy, also engaged in Libya. But EUBAM Libya was also tasked with conducting the preliminary planning of a possible future CSDP mission for more comprehensive SSR, aimed at countering irregular migration and the smuggling of migrants. With the mission's mandate changing and broadening, the specificities of Libya's security sector and its lack of governance represented major challenges (Loschi et al., 2018). The EU failed to take these aspects into account – showing how lack of in-depth knowledge about the situation on the ground, and thus the lack of a genuine bottom-up perspective, can hamper operations and prevent success (Loschi et al., 2018: 12–15).

Beyond the CSDP operations, the EU Trust Fund for Africa and Libya was established to provide rapid, flexible, effective response to the migration-related emergency situation. The Fund was directed towards programmes that would manage mixed-migration flows in Libya by expanding space and supporting local socio-economic development. While the intention was precisely to ensure local ownership of rapid-impact stabilisation projects by creating job opportunities, re-structuring local services, and reinforcing education services, this initiative has also been criticised for being too top-down in orientation and for marginalising the role of local stakeholders. In response, the Commission will now ensure that all projects undergo a 'conflict sensitivity assessment' (Loschi et al., 2018: 17).

Despite these recent changes, the EU's approach to the Libya crisis has remained basically unchanged since the 2014 recognition of the security crisis in the country. Moreover, short-term objectives seem to have taken precedence over more strategic long-term objectives. As migration became securitised and framed as an emergency, the EU and its member states have focused increasingly on protecting European interests and not those of the local population. The EU crisis response in Libya has been characterised by a huge gap between intentions and actual implementation, and thus also a gap in expectations.

Attention to Libya has varied over time. Not surprisingly, there was a peak in 2011 (see Figure 3.3). Hard security has been dominant, but is not the only agenda present in the EU discourse: the EU has also been concerned with softer measures. The 'integration' category is also present in our material in certain periods, with a relative peak when the ENP was launched in 2004. Since then, the security agenda in general and hard security in particular has

The potential and limits of EU crisis response 75

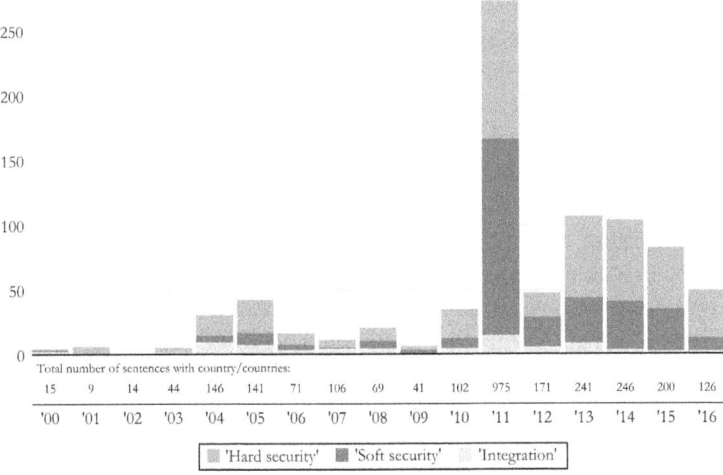

Figure 3.3 Libya 2000–16: terms reflecting different EU agendas

dominated, but the continued focus also on softer measures show also here that a securitisation is not the whole story.

The wider neighbourhood: Afghanistan, Iraq and Mali

Beyond Europe and its neighbourhood, the EU's approach changes character, and is no longer defined or steered by the logic of integration. Thus, in many ways, EU policy towards more distant countries comes closer to regular foreign policy. But exactly what is it that characterises EU policy in the wider neighbourhood? Is it dominated by a hard or a soft security agenda? To what extent are the concerns of conflict sensitivity and local ownership taken into account? Here we briefly examine the EU's engagement in three countries – Afghanistan, Iraq and Mali – and how it is perceived by local stakeholders (Suroush, 2018; Mohammed, 2018; Bøås *et al.*, 2018).

Crisis response in Afghanistan

With Afghanistan, the main EU engagement is the EU Police Mission (EUPOL). At the G8 conference in Geneva in April 2002, the donor community for Afghanistan decided on a division of labour for establishing and training Afghan security forces. Among the EU member states, the UK was assigned to combatting drugs, Italy to revision of the justice sector and Germany as the lead on police reform. On 23 April 2007, the EU Council decided to establish EUPOL in Afghanistan, intended as a non-executive mission, focused on monitoring, mentoring, advising and training (Suroush, 2018). In terms of staff and budget, EUPOL was a minor player in Afghan police reform – at least compared to NATO and the United States – but it provided a 'civilian surge' complementing the US/NATO military deployment. It also had a small but important role in the construction of the new Police Staff College in Kabul, where it was particularly committed to the promotion of policewomen and the inclusion of human rights in Afghan police training. According to local stakeholders, EUPOL had a real but limited impact on the civilian aspects of Afghan police reform.

EUNPACK project surveys in Kabul show that 69 per cent of the respondents had heard about EUPOL and 75 per cent of the staff at ministries and in the police were trained by EUPOL. The gender and the human rights programme emerged as the best-known programme in addition to the establishment of the Police Staff College according to a survey undertaken in Kabul (Suroush, 2018). However, EUPOL has been criticised for failing to apply the SSR model due to security concerns, weak domestic institutions, institutional discord within and between Euro-Atlantic institutions, and lack of commitment to the EUPOL mission (Suroush, 2018: 18). At the local level, Afghan police have expressed discontent with EUPOL's long and complicated decision-making procedures.

Beyond its limited but generally positive impact on the ground, EUPOL was also seen as important by the EU itself: as an opportunity to expand its role as a global actor and also because it would promote the comprehensive approach to post-conflict reconstruction and peacebuilding. While Afghanistan was most frequently discussed in 2001 and 2002, it was accorded considerable attention throughout the period under study (see Figure 3.4). Not surprisingly, security-related words dominate, but, judging by the choice of words used in our data material, the EU seems to have maintained a balance between discussing 'hard' and 'soft' security.

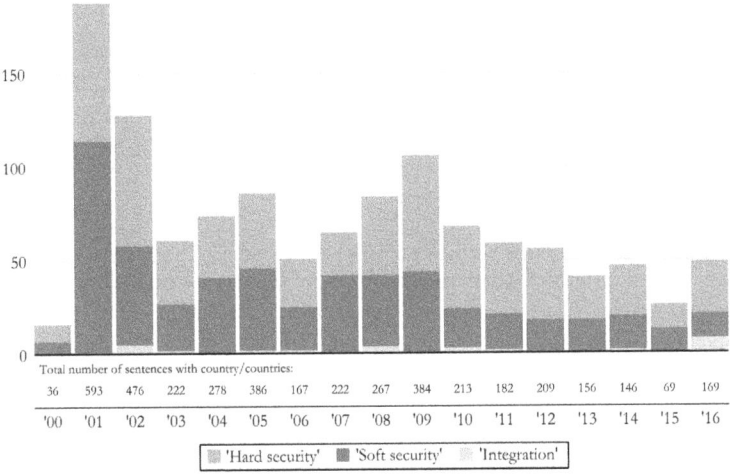

Figure 3.4 Afghanistan 2000–16: terms reflecting different EU agendas

Crisis response in Iraq

Since the toppling of the regime of Saddam Hussein in March 2003, the EU has come to play an active and supportive role in Iraq. The EU's financial and political footprint remained relatively light in the early years following the invasion in Iraq but increased later in preparation for the two elections, held in January and December 2005, with a training programme for election observers and the dispatch of electoral observers to Baghdad. Later, the EU maximised its engagement when it realised that a failed Iraq would weaken the existing regional order, negatively impacting the interests of many EU member states (Mohammed, 2018). The EU engagement has involved financial support to the post-war reconstruction phase; 2005 saw the launch of the EU Integrated Rule of Law Mission for Iraq. EU–Iraq relations were underpinned by two agreements: a Memo of Understanding on energy cooperation, and a Partnership and Cooperation Agreement. Once the EU established permanent presence in Iraq, it became engaged in providing support for strengthening the state's governance structure in many different areas.

Mention should be made of the EUJUST LEX-Iraq mission, as well as the EU's work on reconstruction, development, and humanitarian aid. The former sought to promote closer collaboration among actors throughout the criminal justice system, strengthen the management capacity of officials for the police, judiciary and penitentiary, and improve skills and procedures in criminal investigation with full respect for the rule of law and human rights (Mohammed, 2018).

Our text collection shows that the general attention accorded to Iraq was at its highest in the first half of the period, starting from 2003, which is not surprising. The 'soft security' vocabulary seems to have been relatively more dominant in EU attention towards Iraq in this early period, with 'hard security' being more dominant later (see Figure 3.5). Results from surveys and interviews show that the EU lacks visibility in Iraq and that many people are unaware of its engagement. In particular, they have difficulty distinguishing between the EU's engagement as such and that of individual member states. Humanitarian assistance was best known; less familiar were the EU's efforts in development aid and rule of law.

While Iraqis in general held rather good impressions of the EU, those able to distinguish between the member states as well as local stakeholders who had been working with the EU on the ground claimed that the EU's engagement lacked sustainability and

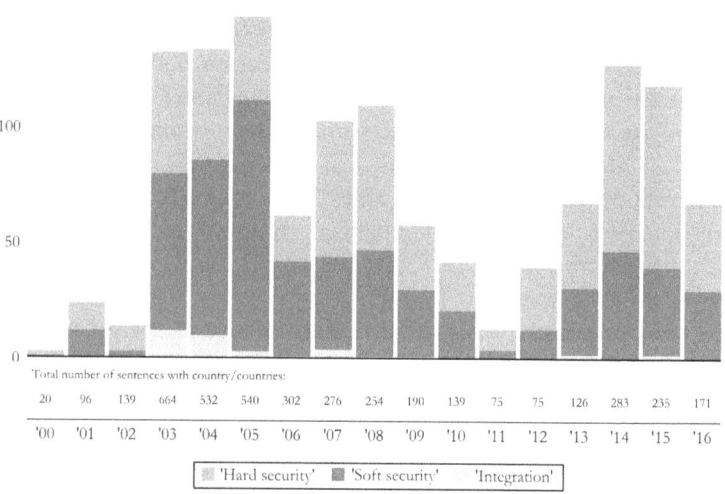

Figure 3.5 Iraq 2000–16: terms reflecting different EU agendas

continuity; they also expressed doubts about the impact of EU activities. The main reasons highlighted were limited resources and insufficient understanding of the situation on the ground.

Crisis response in Mali

The EU's concern with fragile states in Sahel is nothing new. This became evident through the EU Strategy for Security and Development in the Sahel (EEAS, 2011). The conflict that erupted in Mali in 2012 pushed the issue higher up the agenda, and the migration crisis in 2014/15 made the Sahel a high-politics concern for Europe. Various actors are involved in Mali: the UN with MINUSMA, France with its Operations Serval and Berkhane, and the deployment of two EU police and military training missions – EUCAP Sahel Mali (2015–) and the European Training Mission (EUTM) to Mali (2013). The EU is also involved in border management through the EU Trust Fund.

However, security in Mali is deteriorating, and the conflict has spread to the centre of the country (Bøås *et al.*, 2018). Both MINUSMA and the French operations have lost much of their initial popularity. So far, the EU has been less affected. However, as many local Malians have problems in understanding what the EU interventions are, and in distinguishing between EU and French actions, their anger and frustration with France may also affect the EU. The French approach is criticised for defining the crisis as caused by foreign terrorist insurgencies, which some see as a convenient excuse for not dealing with the underlying internal causes of conflict and the drivers of violence (Bøås *et al.*, 2018).

Further, it is argued that even though EUTM Mali and EUCAP Sahel Mali were well-intentioned, they ended up producing mixed results on the ground. The main challenge with the EU training mission is that it remains a non-executive mission: it does not participate in combat, nor accompany the Malian armed forces in operational zones. With EUCAP it is the change of mandate that is seen as the key problem. It was established in 2015 with a mandate to support the restoration of state authority in Mali (EUCAP, 2018), but it soon came to concentrate mainly on Mali's counter-terrorism services and support to Malian authorities regarding irregular migration, including trafficking and border control (Bøås *et al.*,

2018). As the EU sees the 'problem of porous borders' as a key challenge in Mali and in the Sahel more broadly, it is also involved in several other projects with border mandates, as with the new funding tool, EU Emergency Trust Fund (EUTF), which has the mainstreaming of migration management in all EU external action as its core objective. EUTF is not a separate mission, but a fund that operates through other programmes and missions. One of these is the G5 Sahel, where the EU has deployed a designated border expert to support the G5 Permanent Secretariat elaborating a regional border strategy for Mali/Mauritania, for Mali/Niger/Burkina Faso, and for the border between Niger and Chad.

The EU crisis response in Mali is characterised by a clear gap between intentions and implementation. As the stated goal is to contribute to the restoration of state authority in Mali, and this will take time, the EU perspective has gradually become more short-term and security-driven – in turn, offering limited potential to build legitimate, operational and sustainable police and armed forces.

For Mali, data from our web-scraping exercise show that attention from the EU has increased from virtually zero since 2000, with a peak in 2012–13 (Figure 3.6). Further, the 'hard security' agenda

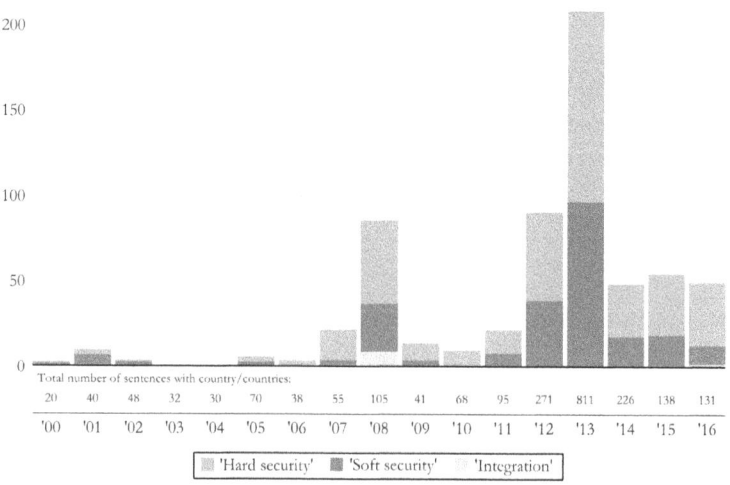

Figure 3.6 Mali 2000–16: terms reflecting different EU agendas

appears to predominate over the 'soft security' agenda, in line with the EU being seemingly more focused on handling issues like trafficking, terrorism and crime, than on contributing to good governance and democracy-building.

The intention is to leave a 'light footprint' through building ownership with local partners, but in reality, programme design has generally come from policy-makers in Brussels who are worried about terrorism, trafficking and refugees. This lack of conflict sensitivity is clear from Council documents, where the distinctions between the different groups in Mali are blurred. Although the training of the Malian army is appreciated, it is argued that there has been too much focus on short-term technical training. Also, the fact that EUTM personnel train an army at war without being able to monitor trained soldiers in action considerably limits the mission's ability to provide valuable follow-up, and see whether the training actually works. There is a need to improve border control, but it is challenging to stop illegal trafficking while facilitating trade in general. Moreover, the various training programmes proposed are often not relevant for the local context. This lack of context sensitivity may be linked to the huge turnover in EU staff, as personnel never get time to familiarise themselves with the local context (Bøås *et al.*, 2018).

Concluding remarks

What has this comparative study of the Union's approach to these different crises revealed about the EU's foreign policy repertoire as regards crisis response? How has this repertoire been applied in relation to crises in three concentric areas surrounding the EU: the enlargement area (Kosovo/Serbia), the neighbourhood area (Ukraine, Syria, Libya), and the extended neighbourhood (Afghanistan, Iraq, Mali)? Finally, how have EU missions and activities been perceived locally – is there a match or a mismatch between EU intentions and implementation, and the perceptions of local stakeholders?

The most apparent trend is the shift towards a greater focus on security rather than integration, in the enlargement area and in the neighbourhood area; and an increase in the harder security agenda in the region referred to here as the 'extended neighbourhood' – especially in the Mali crisis, which is closest to the EU; but also to some extent in Afghanistan and to a lesser extent in Iraq. Another key finding is the general lack of understanding of the local situation, and poor conflict sensitivity, both of which are likely to limit the impact of EU crisis response. This indicates that the EU has not yet implemented a crisis response approach that can be characterised by Crisis Transformation.

The first trend indicates a certain match between EU intentions and the implementation in the field of crisis response. Here the EU engagement is in line with the main orientation of the 2016 Global Strategy, *Shared Vision, Common Action: A Stronger Europe* (European Union HR/VP, 2016), which emphasises the need to safeguard the security of European citizens and the EU as such – to be pursued through an approach referred to as 'principled pragmatism'. This represents a deviation from the more normative approach outlined in the 2003 ESS, *A Secure Europe in a Better World*, where the emphasis was on creating security through processes of Europeanisation and the promotion of European values. Ironically, the EU has now managed to plug the intention–implementation gap – but by adjusting its intentions rather than actual implementation.

Also taking into account the limitations with this line of inquiry that we pointed out above, the analysis of the presence of 'category words' for the countries/conflicts under study also seem to suggest a general trend whereby security – hard or soft – is given more attention relative to an 'integration' vocabulary.

Concerning the match or mismatch between on-the-ground implementation on the one hand and local perceptions of this engagement on the other, interviews and surveys in the various countries show that in all crises where the EU has been engaged, it has been criticised by local populations for not taking into consideration the specificities of the conflict, and thereby also largely failing to provide local ownership or show conflict sensitivity. A quick search in our database of EU documents also showed that concepts like conflict- or context-sensitivity or local partnership and local ownership were never mentioned, or very rarely.

In conclusion, while the intention–implementation gap has been closed by adjusting intentions, the gap between implementation and local perceptions is still far from being closed. While the emphasis on security may be understandable, given the current geopolitical context, it marks a move away from the EU's self-identity of having a comprehensive repertoire in the area of crisis response. That being said, the continuing lack of conflict sensitivity is probably the most obvious limit of the EU repertoire in crisis response and shows the continued persistence of a top-down, Brussels-centred approach and an approach that is limited to the management and potentially resolution of crisis rather than crisis transformation.

Notes

1 For more information, take a look at www.eunpack.eu
2 For details, see below.
3 The Commission press release database (http://europa.eu/rapid/) does not appear to include the documents summarising the meetings of the various configurations of the Council of the European Union after the first half of 2013. For the period 2013–16, we manually added 313 such documents, to increase the consistency of the data over time.
4 Using the spaCy (Honnibal and Johnson, 2015, see https://spacy.io/) Python library. The premise is not that the recognition of sentence boundaries in the texts is flawless, but that it is good enough for our purposes.

References

Bátora, J., K.M. Osland, F.M. Kvamme and S. Stojanovic (2017) 'Public perceptions of the EU's role in crisis management in North Mitrovica', Policy Brief D.5.3, EUNPACK project.

Bátora, J., M. Navrátil, K.M. Osland and M. Peter (2018) 'The EU and international actors in Kosovo: Competing institutional logics, constructive ambiguity and competing priorities', EUNPACK Working Paper D.5.2, EUNPACK project.

Blockmans, S. (2015) 'The 2015 ENP Review: A policy in suspended animation', CEPS Commentary, 1 December, www.ceps.eu/system/files/SB%20ENP%20Review%20CEPS%20Commentary.pdf (accessed 2 October 2020).

Bøås, M., A.W. Cissé, A. Diallo, F. Kvamme and E. Stambøl (2018) 'The EU, security sector reform and border management in Mali', EUNPACK Working Paper D.7.4, EUNPACK project.

Council of the European Union (2016) 'Taking forward the EU's Comprehensive Approach to external conflict and crises', *Action Plan 2016–17*, Joint Staff Working Document SWD(2016) 254 final (19 July) (Brussels: European Commission).

Duchêne, F. (1972) 'Europe's role in world peace', in R. Mayne (ed.), *Europe Tomorrow* (London: Fontana), 32–47.

EEAS (2011) 'Strategy for security and development in the Sahel' (Brussels: EEAS), http://eeas.europa.eu/archives/docs/africa/docs/sahel_strategy_en.pdf (accessed 3 September 2020).

EUCAP (2018) 'EUCAP Sahel Mali mandate', https://eucap-sahel-mali.eu/about_en.html (accessed 1 June 2021).

European Commission (2018) 'A credible enlargement perspective for and enhanced EU engagement with the Western Balkans', Communication from the Commission to the European Parliament, the Council, the European Economic and Social Committee and the Committee of the Regions, COM(2018) 65 final (Strasbourg: European Commission).

European Commission and High Representative (2013) 'The EU's Comprehensive Approach to external conflicts and crises', Joint Communication to the European Parliament and the Council, JOIN (2013) 30 final (Brussels: European Commission and High Representative of the Union for Foreign Affairs and Security Policy).

European Commission and High Representative (2015) 'Taking forward the EU's Comprehensive Approach to external conflict and crises, Action Plan 2015', Joint Staff Working Document SWD(2015) 85 final (Brussels: European Commission).

European Union HR/VP (2016) *Shared Vision, Common Action: A Stronger Europe. A Global Strategy for the European Union's Foreign and Security Policy* (Brussels: EU).

Hill, C. (1993) 'The capability–expectations gap, or conceptualizing Europe's international role', *Journal of Common Market Studies*, 31(3): 305–328.

Honnibal, M. and M. Johnson (2015) 'An improved non-monotonic transition system for dependency parsing', *Proceedings of the 2015 Conference on Empirical Methods in Natural Language Processing* (Lisbon: Association for Computational Linguistics), 1373–1378.

Ivashchenko-Stadnik, K., R. Petrov, P. Rieker and A. Russo (2018) 'Implementation of the EU's crisis response in Ukraine', EUNPACK Working Paper D.6.3, EUNPACK project.

Loschi, C., L. Raineri and F. Strazzari (2018) 'The implementation of EU crisis response in Libya: Bridging theory and practice', EUNPACK Working Paper D.6.2, EUNPACK project.

Manners, I. (2002) 'Normative power Europe: A contradiction in terms?', *JCMS: Journal of Common Market Studies*, 40(2): 235–258.

Manners, I. (2006) 'Normative power Europe reconsidered: Beyond the crossroads', *Journal of European Public Policy*, 13(2): 182–199.

McCormick, J. (2007) *The European Superpower* (New York: Palgrave Macmillan).

Mohammed, K. (2018) 'The EU crisis response in Iraq: Awareness, local perception and reception', EUNPACK Working Paper D.7.2, EUNPACK project.

Moravcsik, A. (2010) 'Europe, the second super power', *Current History* (March): 91–98.

Nexon, D.H. and S.E. Goddard (2018) 'Repertoires of power politics', Conference Paper, International Studies Association Annual Convention, San Francisco, 4–7 February.

Nossel, S. (2004) 'Smart power: Reclaiming liberal internationalism', *Foreign Affairs* (March/April).

Rieker, P. (ed.) (2016) *External Governance as Security Community Building: The Limits and Potential of the European Neighbourhood Policy* (London: Palgrave Macmillan).

Rieker, P. and S. Blockmans (2018) 'Towards a conflict sensitive EU crisis response?', paper prepared for the panel, 'The EU, crisis response, and the intentions–implementation gap', International Studies Association Annual Convention, San Francisco, 4–7 February.

Sjursen, H. (2006) 'What kind of power?', *Journal of European Public Policy*, 13(2): 169–181.

Suroush, Q. (2018) 'Assessing EUPOL impact on Afghan police reform (2007–2016)', EUNPACK Working Paper D.7.3, EUNPACK project.

Toje, A. (2011) 'The European Union as a small power', *JCMS: Journal of Common Market Studies*, 49(1): 43–60.

Wickham, H. (2016) *ggplot2: Elegant Graphics for Data Analysis*, 2nd edn (Cham: Springer).

4

The EU's integrated approach to crisis response: learning from the UN, NATO and OSCE

Loes Debuysere and Steven Blockmans

Introduction

In a follow-up to the 2013 Joint Communication on the 'EU's Comprehensive Approach to external conflict and crises', the 2016 EU Global Strategy on Foreign and Security Policy (EUGS) set out to implement an 'integrated approach to conflict and crises'. The notions of comprehensiveness and integration are widely present in multilateral approaches to crisis management, with the UN having introduced the 'integrated mission' concept already in the late 1990s. Other actors have followed, including the United States and individual EU member states, NATO and the EU. A comprehensive approach refers to the strategic objective of coordination and integration among different civilian and military actors involved in the conflict cycle, in order to enhance the effectiveness of tackling manifestations of instability and conflict (Faleg, 2018; Kammel and Zyla, 2018). Accordingly, a comprehensive approach involves action using a full range of tools – political, economic, civilian and military – to solve a single conflict or crisis complex (Smith, 2012). Yet different actors configure comprehensiveness differently in their policies, which leads to divergences in the practical implementation of comprehensiveness.

In theory, a comprehensive and integrated approach should be able to span a wide repertoire of policy responses to crises and emergent crises. This could span crisis management, crisis resolution and crisis transformation, and even suggests the possibility of flexible or calibrated crisis responses whereby a 'mix and match' approach was deployed. Depending on circumstances, an integrated and comprehensive approach could allow for the modulation of crisis response over time (perhaps shifting from crisis management to a more participatory crisis transformation mode) or having different approaches operating simultaneously in the same territory. As this chapter demonstrates, a theoretical flexibility is not easily translated into real world stances and actions.

This chapter identifies four potential difficulties that may arise when integrating levels, tools and phases of conflict. First, coordination between various actors may prove difficult due to complex or conflicting processes and interests. Hence, 'effective multilateralism' – a doctrine included in the 2003 ESS – serves as a prerequisite for an 'integrated' approach in what are often crowded theatres. Second, a process of integration may undermine local ownership. While integration seeks to improve the coherence and coordination of any international intervention, it could in fact weaken or overlook the indispensable input of local actors (Tardy, 2017). Third, the process of integrating responses to conflict ought to happen in a conflict-sensitive way. Efficient and comprehensive responses need to consider the complexity and multilayered nature of a given conflict, in order to anticipate how interventions will impact and interact with dynamics on the ground. Finally, in setting up an integrated approach to conflict, different priorities, values and interests that underpin an organisation's agenda, may clash. While the EU may claim that 'interests and values go hand in hand' (European Union HR/VP, 2016), evidence from practice – especially in those conflict contexts that pose migration challenges to the EU – shows that this does not necessarily hold true.

We seek to address these four challenges facing the EU's integrated crisis response, while comparing the approach of other key players in conflict settings. In order to do so we first provide a broader overview of how the EU's integrated approach compares to the policy approaches of the UN, OSCE and NATO, that is, the three international organisations on whose side the EU most often serves to prevent, manage and/or sustainably resolve conflicts and crises. Next, based on empirical findings collected from the EU Horizon 2020-funded EUNPACK research project, which aimed at analysing how the EU and its member states respond to crises on the ground throughout the conflict cycle,[1] the four challenges that risk hampering successful implementation of an 'integrated' approach are discussed, with a principal focus on the EU's approach to conflicts and crises. This links with EUNPACK's two major threads that are also running through this book: an overall EU trend towards securitisation, and an assessment of the extent to which an established framework of interpreting responses to conflicts (to categorise as conflict management, conflict resolution or conflict transformation) could be mapped onto crisis management, crisis resolution and crisis transformation. This part of the chapter starts from concrete experiences in the conflict settings, thus addressing potential intention–implementation gaps, and consists of two sections. The discussion first revolves around how challenges of multilateralism, local ownership and conflict sensitivity have panned out in the EU's (and, to a lesser extent, other actors') responses in the conflict zones of Afghanistan, Iraq, Kosovo, Libya, Mali and Ukraine. The chapter then takes up the example of crises involving migration in order to discuss the fourth challenge: how the EU is balancing its interests and values in Libya, Mali and Ukraine, compared to other actors. We conclude by synthesising specific lessons drawn from highlighted examples that can assist in addressing the intention–implementation gap that characterises the so-called 'integrated' approaches of the EU in particular when compared with other actors.

The inside looking out: HQ approaches to external crisis response

The EU's integrated approach

Since 2003, the EU has aspired to contribute to conflict prevention, crisis management and post-conflict peacebuilding through civilian and/or military means (see Dijkstra *et al.*, 2016; Dijkstra *et al.*, 2017). The 'nexus between security and development' (Anderson *et al.*, 2003; Chandler, 2007) took centre stage in the 2003 ESS, according to which security is a precondition for development. Building on the spirit of structural integration espoused by the Treaty of Lisbon, the EC and the High Representative in 2013 issued a joint communication introducing the EU's 'comprehensive approach' to external conflict and crises. This approach combined the use of EU instruments and resources and required the shared responsibility of EU-level actors and member states. Identifying local ownership as one of the main tenets of EU crisis response, the joint communication represented a shift from a top-down to a bottom-up policy approach (Richmond et al., 2011). But already in 2016 the comprehensive approach was superseded by the EU Global Strategy's 'integrated approach' to external conflicts and crises.

According to the EUGS (European Union HR/VP, 2016: 9–10, 28–29), the integrated approach is:

- *Multi-phased*, allowing the EU to act 'at all stages of the conflict cycle, acting promptly on prevention, responding responsibly and decisively to crises, investing in stabilization, and avoiding premature disengagement when a new crisis erupts';
- *Multi-dimensional*, drawing on 'all available policies and instruments aimed at conflict prevention, management and resolution', bringing together diplomatic engagement, CSDP missions and operations, development cooperation and humanitarian assistance;
- *Multi-level*, acting to address the complexity of conflicts 'at the local, national, regional and global levels';
- *Multi-lateral*, engaging all players 'present in a conflict and necessary for its resolution … [partnering] more systematically on the ground with regional and international organizations, bilateral donors and civil society', to build sustainable peace 'through comprehensive agreements rooted in broad, deep and durable regional and international partnerships'.

The scope and actions of the EU's integrated approach to external conflicts and crises have been defined in a working document of the EEAS and the EC (EEAS, 2017: 8). The EU's tools for integrated responses are said to encompass different policy phases, such as planning and implementation; address all stages of the conflict cycle, from prevention to recovery; and advance essential cross-cutting issues, such as the evolution from early warning to preventive action. A new directorate in the EEAS devoted to the 'Integrated Approach for Security and Peace' (Directorate ISP) has become the main coordination hub for EU conflict cycle responses. Created in March 2019 and nestled under the Managing Directorate for CSDP and Crisis Response, Directorate ISP encompasses the old unit for Prevention of conflicts, Rule of law/SSR, Integrated approach, Stabilisation and Mediation (PRISM), which was regrouped with other CSDP parts of the house. The new directorate packs divisions responsible for, inter alia, concepts, knowledge management and training; conflict prevention and mediation; and international strategic planning for CSDP and stabilisation. It is flanked by the Directorate Security and Defence Policy (SECDEFPOL) and cooperates closely together with the Commission's Foreign Policy Instruments (FPI) service and the Directorate-General for International Cooperation and Development (DG DEVCO) Resilience and Fragility Unit.

By expanding the 'comprehensive approach', EU policy-makers sought to reframe the EU's response to fragility and external conflicts and crises. In conceptual terms, the integrated approach increases the level of ambition of EU interventions. The EU seeks to address instability more strategically, that is, by going beyond operational crisis response and integrating a better sequencing of the political, security and economic dimensions of crisis response to deal with the root causes of conflict. This new level of ambition is reflected in the strong linkages between the 'integrated approach' and other follow-up actions to the EUGS, particularly the 'strategic approach to resilience in the EU's external action', a joint communication which highlights the relevance of investing in upstream conflict prevention, crisis response and conflict resolution (High Representative, 2017). This document recognises that 'the traditional linear division of labour between humanitarian aid and development cooperation has been changing' in the face of a fluid landscape of protracted crises, global challenges and risks. Pressures on states, societies, communities and individuals 'range from demographic, climate change, environmental or migratory challenges beyond the power of individual states to confront, to economic shocks, the erosion of societal cohesion due to weak institutions and poor governance, conflict, violent extremism, and acts of external powers to destabilize perceived adversaries' (High Representative, 2017: 3).

Whereas the comprehensive approach synchronised a wide range of instruments in a horizontal way, the integrated approach places various components of EU response under a single authority (Tardy,

2017: 3) – that is, Directorate ISP. In operational terms, the implementation of the integrated approach could enhance EU conflict sensitivity by strengthening capacities in the fields of early warning, conflict analysis and prevention; to reframe the EU's stabilisation approach, integrating various political, security and development components to make sure that transition between crisis management and stabilisation is more coherent and inclusive, integrating (rather than coordinating) different levels of EU action; and to more effectively link all levels of EU responses with those of other multilateral actors and regional organisations (UN, OSCE, NATO, AU), ensuring consistency in international community interventions.

The UN's integrated approach

In conceptual terms, the 1992 *Agenda for Peace* (UN, 1992) was the first serious attempt to generate a greater sense of unity in conflict cycle management, placing the UN front and centre of the international community's efforts to prevent, manage and durably resolve armed conflict in line with the basic principles laid down in both the UN's Charter and human rights covenants. In response to the need felt in Africa, the Balkans and elsewhere to run increasingly large and multidimensional peace support operations (Gelot, 2016), the UN Secretariat of the Department of Peacekeeping Operations (DPKO) and the Department of Political Affairs (DPA) were created. This first stab at 'structural' integration was followed by an attempt at 'strategic' integration. Based in part on the lessons learned from peacekeeping failures in the late 1990s and early 2000s (de Coning, 2008), the 'strategic' integration drive, encapsulated in the Brahimi Report, promoted the idea that all UN entities, agencies, funds and programmes should cooperate under a single UN flag, to maximise the impact of their collective resources (Koops *et al.*, 2015). An analysis of the weaknesses and obstacles to integration led the Panel on the United Nations Peace Operations to recommend the formation of an 'integrated mission task force' – that is, an integrated HQ-level response to be developed at the earliest stages of the crisis response planning process, bringing together different departments of the UN Secretariat (DPKO, DPA, OCHA), agencies, funds and programmes (e.g., UNDP, UNICEF, UNHCR) for mission-specific support.

An 'integrated mission concept' was pioneered for Kosovo in 1999 in order to ensure an effective division of labour between the different actors on the ground (Eide *et al.*, 2005: 12; Weir *et al.*, 2006). In operational terms, the main innovation of the integrated mission concept was that the functions of the Resident Coordinator (RC) and the Humanitarian Coordinator (HC) were morphed into the mandate of a Deputy Special Representative of the Secretary-General (DSRSG). This double-hatting allowed the DSRSG to better represent the humanitarian and development dimensions in planning, coordinating, managing, and evaluating the mission. UN entities on the ground, including mission components, UN Country Team and specialised agencies were technically distinct but brought under the same leadership. Guidelines for an 'Integrated Mission Planning Process' (IMPP) became operational as of 2008 when the broader and more strategic 'integrated approach' was adopted under the leadership of UN Secretary-General Ban Ki-moon (UN, 2008). This approach recognised that integration requires a system-wide process whereby all different dimensions and relevant UN agents should act in a synchronised, sequenced and coherent fashion, also with the Bretton Woods institutions (International Monetary Fund and World Bank Group), all operating as one integrated UN system at the country level, and in a coordinated fashion with extra-UN actors. In other words: 'effective multilateralism' within and outside of the UN family.

A new push for the UN's integrated approach has been catalysed by the adoption of the 2030 Agenda for Sustainable Development in 2015 (UNGA, 2015) and the report of the UN High-Level Independent Panel on Peace Operations (HIPPO) (UN, 2015). The HIPPO report recommended ways of achieving the full potential of UN operations. These included strengthened early warning, analysis, strategy and planning mechanisms, thereby bolstering conflict sensitivity in order to design missions better and be able to respond flexibly to changing needs on the ground; and a renewed emphasis on investing in capacities and local ownership to play a more preventive and inclusive role in addressing emerging crises.

The institutional reform process of the UN peace and security pillar launched by Secretary-General António Guterres in 2017 is beginning to bear fruit after implementation started in the first half of 2019. DPA was reconstituted as the Department for Political and

Peacebuilding Affairs (DPPA) and DPKO as the Department of Peace Operations (DPO). Three Assistant Secretary-Generals (ASGs) are responsible for regions and the Standing Principals Group is tasked with increasing the coherence and coordination between DPPA-DPO and regional ASGs. The Department of Field Support (DFS) has also been restructured, to reduce fragmentation, expand capacities/activities and ensure faster deliveries, and is now the Department of Operational Support (DOS). The new structures should address the main problems identified by the HIPPO report, namely reducing competition and duplication within the Secretariat and ensuring a spectrum of operations that are customised to address country contexts better (Cliffe, 2017: 3–4). If properly implemented, then the ongoing reform may well turn the UN into the world's most sophisticated integrated system for conflict prevention, crisis management and peacebuilding.

The OSCE's comprehensive and cooperative security approach

The OSCE's comprehensive approach to 'in area' conflicts and crises is rooted in its core mandate as a forum for political and security dialogue among members and has been fully embodied in the organisation's joint actions since its creation. The comprehensive approach emanates from the three 'baskets' of the 1975 Helsinki Final Act: the politico-military, the economic-environmental, and the human dimension. The approach presumes a direct relationship between peace, stability and wealth, on the one hand, and the values of democratic institutions, the rule of law, respect for human rights and the development of a market economy on the other. The principle of 'indivisibility' of the comprehensive approach implies that an increase in security for some participating states should not be detrimental to the security of other states. The notion of 'cooperative security', a variant to the principle of 'effective multilateralism', is also central to the OSCE's operational rationale and aims at the prevention of security threats and zero-sum games, rather than efforts to counter them. The OSCE builds on the acceptance of binding commitments that limit military capabilities and actions, through confidence-building and reassurance measures. These values and strategic principles were reiterated and reinforced over time, through a series of documents, including the 1990 Charter of Paris for a New Europe, the 1999 Charter for European Security, and the 2003 OSCE Strategy to Address Threats to Security and Stability in the Twenty-First Century.

This shows that the integrated approach of the EU does not just have to be about institutions working together, but that should also include a more comprehensive view of conflict, in particular the nexus with (under)development. Reinforcing comprehensive action along the strands of conflict prevention, crisis management and post-conflict rehabilitation, the OSCE addresses challenges that pose a threat across borders, such as climate change, terrorism, radicalisation and violent extremism, organised crime, cyber-crime and trafficking of all kinds. In its cross-dimensional activities, the OSCE starts from virtually the same value-base as the UN and the EU to work towards gender equality, engage with local youth across the peace and security agenda, and promote comprehensive approaches to managing migration and refugee flows:

> The EU, like the OSCE, addresses security in a comprehensive manner… from conflict prevention, mediation and cross-border cooperation, to respect for human rights and fundamental freedoms; from the promotion of the rule of law and democracy, to strengthening States' resilience to trans-national threats. (EEAS, 2018)

Its institutions include the Office for Democratic Institutions and Human Rights, the High Commissioner on National Minorities and the Representative on Freedom of the Media.

Despite a value-based and comprehensive approach to cooperative security being engrained in the DNA of the OSCE, the organisation suffers from significant operational limitations (i.e., ineffective multilateralism). This is mainly due to the different priorities and perspectives on European security of the participating states; negative attitudes to the organisation from a number of participating states; the consensus-building nature of the organisation, which is difficult and time-consuming; the absence of effective mechanisms to sanction violations of the body's core principles; limited resources; the lack of clear implementation criteria for the wide range of activities; and the disparate ways and means for (self-)assessment and implementing lessons learned. In an effort to enhance a conflict-sensitive approach to crises, the 2011 Vilnius

Ministerial Council (OSCE, 2011) called for enhanced coordination to strengthen the OSCE's analysis, assessment and engagement capacities in all phases of the conflict cycle. It led to the consolidation of the organisation's early warning capacity and resources; the creation of a systematic mediation-support capacity within the Conflict Prevention Centre; the adoption of guidance materials on dialogue facilitation, taking on the UN principles of active mediation; and the creation of a rapid deployment roster. Capacity-building for the comprehensive approach was accelerated by the deployment of an OSCE Special Monitoring Mission to Ukraine in 2014. Yet many of these capacities remain in suspended animation. Since the eve of the 40th anniversary of the Helsinki Final Act, Russia has violated Ukraine's borders, territorial integrity and freedom from non-interference in domestic affairs – thus shaking the very foundations of European security on which the OSCE rests and ignoring the monitoring mission's observations.

NATO's comprehensive approach

The 2006 Riga Summit Declaration was the first official NATO document to refer to the Alliance's so-called comprehensive approach to 'out of area' conflicts and crises. Drawing on the experiences in Afghanistan and Kosovo, NATO's comprehensive approach was conceived as a way to respond better to crises by involving a wide spectrum of civil and military instruments while fully respecting the mandates and decision-making autonomy of all involved. As the need for proper mechanisms of cooperation with other international actors and civilian agencies was considered particularly acute at the early planning stage of an operation, NATO adapted its operational planning to improve support for civilian reconstruction and development (Gheciu, 2012). Developing closer ties with the EU, the UN and other international organisations constituted a critical part of this approach: a better division of mandates would help NATO to perform better in theatre.

NATO's Strategic Concept of 2010 affirmed that the Alliance would engage, 'when possible and necessary, to prevent crises, manage crises, stabilize post-conflict situations and support reconstruction', and that a 'comprehensive political, civilian and military approach is necessary for effective crisis management' (NATO,

2010: 19). The strategic concept called for NATO to enhance intelligence-sharing within the organisation, intensify political consultations among allies, form a civilian crisis management capability to liaise more effectively with civilian partners, enhance integrated civilian-military planning, and develop the capability to train local forces in crisis zones (NATO, 2010: 21–22). A plan was developed to stimulate the transformation of NATO's military mind-set into a comprehensive modus operandi with a clear emphasis on effective multilateralism both within and outside of the organisation and combined with local ownership.

Against the backdrop of a rapidly evolving security environment, the 2016 Warsaw Summit called for a review of the strategic concept and an action plan with new elements for conflict prevention, countering hybrid threats, cyber-security and operational cooperation at sea and on migration. Based on a joint declaration of 10 July 2016, forty-two concrete actions for implementation in the aforementioned areas were developed to boost NATO-EU cooperation. In December 2017, an additional set of thirty-four actions was endorsed, including on three new topics: counter-terrorism; military mobility; women, peace and security. These efforts at generating more complementarity and effective multilateralism have contributed to improving NATO's own conflict sensitivity, internal organisation and crisis management instruments. That said, the military culture remains overwhelmingly predominant in the Alliance. In theatre, NATO remains the *primus inter pares* in supporting or undertaking military engagement in crisis situations.

Conceptual convergence but different institutional logics

The analysis in this section reveals a gradual conceptual convergence of headquarters' approaches in dealing with conflicts and crises. In their constituent charters and relevant policy documents, the UN, OSCE, NATO and EU spell out in more or less explicit detail four key virtues in the implementation of their comprehensive/integrated approach to conflicts and crises: being conflict-sensitive; pursuing effective multilateral coordination (within the organisation and with international actors); upholding the organisation's values; and ensuring local ownership. Divergences between the organisations' approaches arise from variances in their mandates to deal with conflicts and crises 'in area' (UN, OSCE, NATO) and/or 'out of area' (NATO, EU) by employing predominantly civilian (OSCE) or military (NATO) means or a combination thereof (UN, EU). Differences in the autonomy of the organisations' bodies to prepare for and decide on action determine the speed, scope and duration of implementation.

In what follows, empirical data gathered by EUNPACK partners from a range of conflict areas (Afghanistan, Iraq, Kosovo, Libya, Mali and Ukraine) are used to illustrate the extent to which crisis responders are led by the four above-mentioned virtues in implementing their so-called integrated approach. The principal focus will be on the EU's external action.

The outside looking in: field experience

Effective multilateralism

In a follow-up to the doctrine of 'effective multilateralism', as outlined by the 2003 ESS, the 2016 EUGS has listed 'effective global governance' among its five priority objectives. The EU thus continues its commitment to preserving, strengthening and coordinating multilateral processes, albeit in a more pragmatic and flexible fashion. Since interventions in Mali, Libya, Ukraine, Kosovo, Afghanistan and Iraq have attracted a multiplicity of actors, it makes sense to see how multilateral processes play out in external crisis response and what challenges they raise. In general, the EU has worked in various coalitions and strategic partnerships with the UN (the EU's most consistent partner), NATO (in Afghanistan, Iraq, Libya, Kosovo) and the OSCE (in Ukraine, Kosovo). The involvement of all actors has undergone major changes and shifts over time, never really finding a winning formula (Peters *et al.*, 2018: 6).

Kosovo, which was fully entrusted to the administration of a UN peacekeeping operation, UNMIK (United Nations Interim Administration Mission in Kosovo), was initially governed by a four-pillar structure under the leadership of the Special Representative of the Secretary-General (SRSG), with the UN in charge of civil administration, the United Nations High Commissioner for

Refugees (UNHCR) in control of the humanitarian aid programme, the OSCE responsible for democratisation and institution-building and the EU focused on economic reconstruction (Bátora *et al.*, 2017: 13–14). In both Afghanistan and Iraq, the United States assumed the role of agenda-setter, leaving little room for other actors to determine the course of peace- and statebuilding. While the United States focused heavily on fighting the insurgency and fostering security ('security first'), the civilian aspects of the EU's reconstruction efforts took place under the leadership of the UN (Peters *et al.*, 2018: 1). In Mali, it was France who was the agenda-setter and driving force behind Western and EU engagement. The UN (MINUSMA mission), together with the Economic Community of West African States (ECOWAS) and the African G5 Sahel Joint Force, were the most important actors outside the military-security realm (Peters *et al.*, 2018: 6). The EU plugged into the ongoing multilateral effort by training the military and offering civilian support in modernising the police, gendarmerie and national guard. In Libya, after a NATO-led intervention, the UN (UNSMIL) has played a crucial role in the country's political mediation and reconciliation process. However, in the wake of the difficulties that the UN's initiative is facing, many international players have joined the multilateral process, yet also started to compete with one another to gain in Libya (Mezran and Varvelli, 2017: 18). The EUBAM had to relocate to Tunis as a result of the worsened security situation. And EUNAVFOR MED – Operation Sophia (see next section), the only CSDP operation for which the EU has been criticised for over-reacting and launching a military operation without a UN Security Council mandate covering all phases of the mission, was terminated by certain member states annoyed by the 'pull factor' it had on migrants. In Ukraine, some experts have rated the EU as the second most active international actor dealing with the country's conflict, together with the United States. Its role went much further than the SSR mission and presented a nearly full-spectrum approach to the crisis complex. The OSCE has had a supportive function, but did not shape conflict developments (Ivashchenko-Stadnik *et al.*, 2018: 11–12). This short overview shows that, generally speaking, the EU tends to arrive late in 'theatre', resulting in a reactive rather than pro-active role in shaping multilateral relations on the ground. This framed and mostly securitised the EU's crisis response. So far it is really only in the case of Ukraine that the EU is trying to move the needle towards conflict transformation.

Based on EUNPACK findings, three concrete and interrelated pitfalls or challenges with regard to multilateralism were identified for the EU. First, a lack of coherence among the response of key international actors has hampered effective conflict management. While the presence of many actors can improve international engagement – funds, facilities and efforts are successfully coordinated – our collective research findings illustrate that when coordination is lacking, the sheer multiplicity of parallel or competing decisions and programmes will almost inevitably have negative implications (Peters *et al.*, 2018: 3). For example, in Kosovo, the overlapping focus by multiple actors, including the EULEX mission, led an OSCE official to argue that the area of rule-of-law assistance is so crowded that the local judiciary suffers from 'training fatigue' (Bátora *et al.*, 2018: 18, n31). Conflicting ambitions and difficult cooperation have been especially present in EU-NATO relations. In response to the crisis in Libya, for example, EU members disagreed about whether an EU military mission (as advocated for by France) or a broader alliance under the NATO flag (as advocated by Italy) was the appropriate answer. Eventually, the EU decided to set up the military operation EUFOR on 1 April 2011, tasked with assisting the efforts of the UN humanitarian agency in Libya. However, humanitarian actors never requested the intervention of EUFOR, at least in part because a NATO-led military operation was already operating with a UN mandate. The short-lived EUFOR Libya mission illustrates the initial lack of coordination and the problem of unilateral action on the EU side (Ivashchenko-Stadnik *et al.*, 2017: 13). In Afghanistan, EUPOL also suffered from difficult coordination with NATO. Despite the 2002 Berlin Plus arrangements, which allow the EU to use NATO intelligence and assets for CSDP missions, EUPOL was limited in its access to NATO's provincial bases due to the veto by Turkey (a NATO ally) over a dispute with EU member Cyprus (Suroush, 2018: 13). Similarly, in Mali, the EUTM has lacked budget for military and defence, which resulted in the EU being unable to provide equipment for its mission. EEAS officials complained that while the EU supports NATO, it has not received the same support from NATO for its missions. The lack of equipment and the financial constraints for security have dealt a blow to the credibility of the EU in Mali (Heinemann, 2017: 55).

Second, the responses by the EU and the member states have also lacked internal cohesion, which has hampered the effectiveness of the EU response. The decision of five member states not to recognise Kosovo as an independent and sovereign state, for example, has prevented the EU from pursuing a clear institutional logic in assisting the country's political order. This, in turn, has left space for competing claims of sovereignty and authority by the governments in Pristina, Belgrade and local actors in the Kosovo Serbian municipalities in Northern Kosovo (Bátora *et al.*, 2018: 30). In Afghanistan, the lack of coordination between various EU policy tools and funding instruments and those of the member states has obstructed the implementation of the 'comprehensive approach' (Peters *et al.*, 2018: 21). Concretely, coordination has been difficult between the EU Special Representative (EUSR), the delegation of the EC, EUPOL and the bilateral missions by member states, as member states have, for example, felt that joining EUPOL translated in losing national influence and visibility on the ground. As a consequence, France, Italy, the Netherlands, Portugal and Spain committed forces to the NATO training mission rather than to EUPOL (Tripathi and Ferhatovic, 2017: 43). In Ukraine, the EU has faced difficulties in effectively coordinating both old (pre-conflict) and new (post-conflict) EU initiatives in the country. Coordination has been weak, for example, between the Commission-led SGUA and the delegation in Kiev, or between the EUBAM and EUAM missions (Ivashchenko-Stadnik *et al.*, 2017: 61).

Third, unilateralist tendencies by actors have constrained the impact of other key actors, including the EU. Notable cases are Afghanistan and Iraq, where Washington was the gatekeeper for the role of other actors. In Afghanistan, the strong push of the United States after 9/11 for an international intervention, marginalised other actors, including the UN, to shape the peace- and statebuilding agenda in Afghanistan (Peters *et al.*, 2018: 3). By launching a contested military intervention in Iraq, the United States also stirred major rifts both within NATO and among EU members, pitting the United States and its allies against those EU member states which opposed the war. This division undermined both organisations and 'resulted in a lack of harmonisation between European institutions, individual states and NATO in relation to capacity building and democratisation in Iraq' (Burke, quoted in Peters, 2017: 44). In Mali, France rapidly launched a unilateral military operation in Mali (Opération Serval), after the 2012 rebellion and coup d'état. France's role has had an impact on the EU, as Malians have considerable difficulties separating the EU's activities from what France has undertaken bilaterally. Given France's former colonial role and the issues this may raise in terms of local (rather than neo-colonial) ownership, some (Cissé et al., 2017: 8) have argued that it is in the EU's interest to set its activities apart from those of France.

Conflict sensitivity

Conflict sensitivity – that is, the awareness of how interventions interact with the conflict situation on the ground and the ability to minimise negative impacts of these interventions ('do no harm') – turns out to be another challenge rather than a virtue that arises when trying to implement a comprehensive crisis response. In the context of the Libyan conflict, some have argued (Loschi et al., 2018: 23) that EU conflict sensitivity needs to be strengthened, especially when compared with other international actors' crisis response. While a 'Conflict Sensitivity Leadership Group' and 'Assistance Forum' have been set up to ensure greater attention to the topic, most EU officers (re)located in Tunis only have a vague understanding of these tools. NGO officers and conflict sensitivity specialists have expressed fears that the EU approach to conflict sensitivity has been superficial, lacking genuine commitment and adequate knowledge.

Concretely, a lack of conflict sensitivity on the part of the EU has been most notable in the EU's outsourcing of migration management to Libyan authorities and the setting up of detention centres, which fuelled a criminal economy of exploitation and trafficking. As such, the EU may have been unintentionally empowering non-state armed actors and militias, given the links that exist between security officers and trafficking networks on the ground (Loschi et al., 2018). In an earlier phase of the conflict, NATO also misjudged the local context by underestimating the resistance a military campaign would face. While NATO planners expected that the air campaign would contribute to overthrowing Gaddafi in a matter of weeks, loyalists to the Gaddafi regime proved able to count on support from African mercenaries, including labour migrants and marginalised communities from Southern Libya (Ivashchenko-Stadnik *et al.*, 2017: 13).

In the case of Mali, the EU's conflict sensitivity has also been limited. Background talks with EEAS officials in Brussels revealed a lack of awareness and knowledge about the concept of 'conflict sensitivity', with the concept at one point being dismissed as a 'luxury concept' (Peters *et al.*, 2018: 19). It does not come as a surprise, then, that both EUTM and EUCAP produced very mixed results on the ground, as a result of the EU crisis response being imported, rather than set up via a bottom-up approach (Bøås *et al.*, 2018: 24). Indeed, policy documents are developed in Brussels, with limited consultation with local partners in Mali (Bøås *et al.*, 2018:15). The EU's conflict sensitivity has also been questioned in the context of the EU's close cooperation with the Malian government, despite clear links between the state and local militias, according to non-partisan experts (Heinemann, 2017: 55). As these are hot conflicts, we'll have to see whether the EU's approach will change.

In Iraq, one concern raised by academics and civil society activists was that the EU approaches the whole of Iraq as a single unit, while on the ground no such entity exists. Implementing the same projects in all governorates, as the EU tends to do, does not necessarily make sense, as each area has its own needs and is bound by unique dynamics (Mohammed, 2018: 16). In Afghanistan, external actors were also lacking a proper understanding and sensitivity towards the needs of locals, which explains why the intervention in Afghanistan was not successful. A fundamental problem was that Western actors lacked the knowledge, power or legitimacy to transform Afghanistan, being isolated from Afghan reality (Stewart, 2013; Tripathi and Ferhatovic, 2017: 51). Also, the UN failed the test of conflict sensitivity in Afghanistan, when it allowed funding for reconstruction to be processed through corrupt state-structures (Peters *et al.*, 2018: 5).

Local ownership

A third virtue for the successful implementation of the integrated approach to conflicts and crises is 'local ownership'. This principle ensures that local concerns and needs are at the heart of conflict management and peacebuilding. In Libya, the prompt and top-down actions that the EU took to tackle Libya's 'migration crisis', seemed not to reflect principles of participatory planning and local ownership. Local stakeholders felt marginalised, feeling that they had to sign-off pre-conceived projects with limited consultation about their inputs, priorities and needs (Loschi *et al.*, 2018: 15). Whereas the EU did seek to ensure 'local ownership' – for example, by supporting local authorities and communities in dealing with the migration crisis within the framework of the EU Trust Fund (EUTF) – this proved to be a double-edged sword in the midst of a civil war fuelled by multipolar competition. Indeed, cooperation with local municipalities stirred competition and opportunism among local actors and negatively impacted the local economy. Other international actors pursued a different strategy in this regard. The UNDP, for instance, promotes the involvement of municipal governments in stabilisation programmes, always in combination with central government representatives, such as the Ministry of Infrastructure. This helps to respect intergovernmental relations between national and sub-national levels and, simultaneously, to enhance the legitimacy of the Government of National Accord (Loschi *et al.*, 2018: 17).

In Mali, in order to ensure local ownership, the EU not only works together with the Malian government, but also with other actors including the African Union (AU), the Economic Community of West African States (ECOWAS), the West African Economic and Monetary Union (WAEMU), the G5 Sahel and the Lake Chad Basin Commission (LCBC). While the EU has actively sought to cooperate with regional organisations – more than was the case in Afghanistan or Iraq, for example (Peters *et al.*, 2018: 4) – there is little mention in its documents of the importance of working with local bodies and communities (Heinemann, 2017: 43; Vogelaar, 2018). In practice this has resulted in an information deficit with local Malian stakeholders reporting problems understanding the EU's approach and how to interpret concepts like SSR and 'border management'. Simultaneously, to what extent do EU priorities of border management align with the priorities of local stakeholders and communities (Bøås *et al.*, 2018: 7)? For example, EU reinforcement of border control as a means to manage migration flows might undermine border economies, which are a lifeline for marginalised communities, and might be at odds with regional law which states that citizens of ECOWAS countries are free to move across borders within the ECOWAS space (Bøås et al., 2018: 24). Similarly, the free health care that ECHO provides for the population as part of humanitarian relief actually goes against Malian law, which forbids free care provision. As a consequence, even when training is provided to local staff to take over the work, the provision of health care will be stopped (Heinemann, 2017: 47).

In Afghanistan, similar problems emerged in relation to local ownership. While the EU welcomed coordinated efforts to support the Afghan government in promoting an Afghan-led and Afghan-owned peace process, it quickly found that pursuing local ownership does not necessarily translate into, for instance, more successful SSRs. In a context where there is no monopoly of force and no stable political system, relying on local actors does not necessarily foster a more depersonalised, formalised and rationalised exercise of power through the state. The UN faced the same problem with its 'light footprint' approach that welcomed local ownership yet underestimated the extent to which professional leadership and institutional capacity of national/local actors had been eroded during years of conflict (Tripathi and Ferhatovic, 2017:11). While ostensibly a good idea, local ownership can in practice mean ineffective policy (Peters et al., 2018), especially when not implemented in a conflict-sensitive way.

The EU's 'principled pragmatism' and the case of migration

We will be guided by clear principles. These stem as much from a realistic assessment of the current strategic environment as from an idealistic aspiration to advance a better world.... Principled pragmatism will guide our external action in the years ahead. (European Union HR/VP, 2016: 16)

We need as Europeans, as the European Union, to be extremely clear, united and firm with our own compass in mind: the set of values, principles and interests that guide our action on the global scene. (Mogherini, 2018)

Upholding institutional principles and values in responding to conflict situations constitutes a final virtue and challenge underpinning the EU's integrated approach to external conflict. Indeed, the EU prioritises European values and principles in its rhetoric and speeches about external action (cf. quotes above), with '*principled pragmatism*' (italics added) figuring as an overarching leitmotif in the EU's Global Strategy. In practice, however, the EU has struggled to make good on idealism. The EU approach to migration in its wider neighbourhoods (Libya, Ukraine, Mali) shows how the EU tries to straddle the line between interests and values and how its approach is received by other actors, both local and international, in conflict zones.

Libya provides the clearest illustration of an EU struggling to uphold its principles in the face of pragmatic Member State interests. While the EU has been present on the ground since 2011, the Council in March 2015 hinted at a new CSDP mission in Libya that would focus specifically on migration and security, as irregular migration was increasingly seen as a threat to the interests of EU member states (Ivashchenko-Stadnik *et al.*, 2017: 26). A major shipwreck involving a migrant boat in April 2015 eventually led to the launch of CSDP mission EUNAVFOR MED – Operation Sophia with the aim of breaking the business model of refugee smugglers along routes in the central Mediterranean. What followed was a shift in the EU's crisis response, henceforth perceiving the interlacing conflicts and crisis in Libya as a 'mere' migration issue, thus bringing into question the comprehensiveness of the EU's crisis response. Rather than investing in longer term strategic DDR and SSR processes, which would address some of the root causes of the Libyan crisis, the EU presented short-term solutions, such as coastguard capacity-building to intercept migrants bound for Europe (Loschi *et al.*, 2018: 23).

EUNVAFOR MED began training the Libyan coastguard in late October 2016. This included, according to official documents, a substantial emphasis on human rights law (Loschi *et al.*, 2018), however, they show little evidence of a genuine commitment to core EU values by the trainers. Moreover, the EU faced difficulties when selecting candidates for the training seminars, with some individuals involved in human trafficking appearing among the beneficiaries of the EU support (El Kamouni-Janssen and de Bruijne, 2007;

Amnesty International, 2017). Seen through this prism, it is hardly surprising that Libyan coastguard officers have been accused of abusive behaviour towards both migrants and NGOs engaged in Search and Rescue (SAR) operations. By outsourcing border control to Libya and its coastguards, the EU has resorted to unsafe detention schemes within Libya. Various NGOs have documented the dreadful conditions in Libya's detention centres, which at worst can be seen as a direct result of the EU's restriction of migrants' safe passage to Europe (Loschi *et al.*, 2018: 15).

The examples of coastguard trainings and detention centres bring into question both the conflict sensitivity and value-based approach that the EU claims to uphold as part of its 'integrated approach'. They are but two illustrations of a decoupling of normative rhetoric and practice in Libya, which is undermining the reputation of the EU and its crisis response (Loschi *et al.*, 2018: 23). Indeed, despite persistent rhetoric on the part of the EU to uphold 'UN-EU priorities to human rights and, International Humanitarian Law, including the protection of children and other persons in vulnerable situations in conflict and post-conflict areas' (Council of the European Union, 2018: Conclusion 8), the UN has strongly condemned the EU securitisation of migration in Libya. It contends that the Union's strategy of containment has been 'catastrophic' and 'inhuman', and calls for the decriminalisation of irregular migration (Loschi *et al.*, 2018: 24). UN High Commissioner for Human Rights Michelle Bachelet issued a statement in September 2018 saying that

> [i]n the context of the EU's ongoing discussions to establish so-called 'regional disembarkation platforms', the prospect of the EU outsourcing its responsibility to govern migration to States with weak protection systems is disturbing. Without prejudice to the ongoing discussions, the authorities should recall that respect for the rights of all migrants must be assured, including those in the most vulnerable situations, and processes must be established to ensure that relevant actors be held to account if they fail to meet basic international standards. (OHCHR, 2018, np)

Several NGOs have deliberately declined to apply for EU funding in order to distance themselves from the EU's controversial migration policies in Libya (Loschi *et al.*, 2018: 16). In short, the

EU's natural allies in terms of norms and values have not endorsed the Union's 'pragmatic turn' in Libya.

In Ukraine, while migration flows from here have not been framed as a security threat to the EU, in contrast to the Libyan example, the EU's crisis response has also comprised efforts in the realm of border security and border management (Ivashchenko-Stadnik *et al.*, 2017: 63). Since the referendum in Crimea in March 2014, the ongoing conflict in the eastern provinces has created a problem of internally displaced people and refugee flows, with over 1.5 million Ukrainians seeking asylum or other forms of legal stay in neighbouring countries in 2017 (Ivashchenko-Stadnik *et al.*, 2018: 17). As a consequence, the EU has sought to foster further investment in cross-border cooperation with neighbouring countries and its CSDP mission EUBAM was mandated to strengthen border security. However, EUBAM's mandate of consolidating pillars of statehood and stability has reportedly clashed with the informal and extra-legal economies in situ, which risks further conflict (Ivashchenko-Stadnik *et al.*, 2017: 63).

Apart from conflict-insensitive designs, the EU has also been blamed for double standards in its asylum policies with regard to potential asylum-seekers who migrate to Europe through Ukraine. Human rights defenders have reported a gap between the EU's human rights rhetoric and its operational recommendations to Ukrainian authorities: 'in fact, the EU is interested in not allowing potential asylum-seekers and refugees into Ukraine' (Ivashchenko-Stadnik *et al.*, 2018: 19, n78). The EU's enforcement of discriminatory practices on the border has led to violations of conventional commitments and contrasts with the human rights perspective adopted by the International Organization for Migration, a UN migration agency based in Ukraine.

In Mali, the EU's external action has also been perceived as serving its own interests rather than being 'a force for good' (one of the aims of the 2003 European Security Strategy). After the spike in migration in 2014–15, Mali rose to the top of the EU's political agenda, resulting in the deployment of a police and a military training mission (EUCAP and EUTM). The EU perceived the 'problem of porous borders' as the key challenge and threat in Mali, which led to migration management being mainstreamed in all EU external action in Mali (Bøås *et al.*, 2018: 12). This disproportionate focus on security and border management, combined with a lack of subsequent monitoring, has indirectly led to human rights abuses, as the EU cooperated with disputed actors like the Malian Armed Forces (FAMa) in restoring state authority (Ba and Bøås, 2017: 20). The EU's focus on border controls has also conflicted with the freedom of movement and trade, guaranteed by an ECOWAS convention for citizens of ECOWAS member states (Bøås *et al.*, 2018: 21).

There is concern in Mali that, unlike the UN's neutral approach to conflicts and crises, the EU's 'principled pragmatism' focuses too much on protecting its own interest in containing migration flows to Europe. To counter this sentiment, the EU Delegation in Bamako has since late 2017 been developing a second component to PARSEC – a programme aimed at enhancing the security in the Mopti and Gao regions – to help the state respond to the basic needs of the local populations (Bøås *et al.*, 2018: 12). This attempt to build trust between state and local communities moves beyond mere security provision. This may be the only bottom-up, comprehensive and potentially conflict-sensitive project in an otherwise Brussels-driven 'integrated approach' (Bøås *et al.*, 2018: 23).

Conclusion

The comparative analysis of headquarters' approaches to 'comprehensiveness' shows that the EU and the UN exhibit the most ambitious efforts to reform their structures and procedures to achieve an integrated approach to conflicts and crises. They have done so by incorporating lessons learned across the whole spectrum of action, taking a broader systemic and strategic stance, through the guidance provided respectively by the EUGS and by the HIPPO report. Integration efforts by NATO and the OSCE have been more focused: enhancing the OSCE's conflict sensitivity through early warning, analysis, strategy and planning and transforming NATO's capacities to tackle hybrid threats.

Policy documents illustrate how the EU has shown a steady evolution from a narrow concept of civilian-military coordination – that is, a blueprint followed by NATO albeit from the opposite perspective – to a broad notion of systemic coherence similar to that employed by the UN. However, experiences in Afghanistan,

Iraq, Kosovo, Libya, Mali and Ukraine point towards at least four challenges the EU is facing when attempting to effectively implement its integrated approach in conflict settings.

First, the multidimensional nature of conflicts and security threats requires proper coordination among international partners, to produce inter-agency synergies and to avoid overlaps, waste of resources and unintended consequences. Infamous for its slow crisis responses, the EU has faced challenges in fostering multilateral coherence, both among its own ranks and with other international actors – particularly NATO. Indeed, an important issue to bear in mind when thinking of the crisis management, crisis resolution, and crisis transformation options is that of pace: to what extent can particular responses be mobilised and sustained over time. Crisis transformation in particular requires a long-term vision (and the planning and budgeting to match) that is often in conflict with many of the more prosaic national and institution-wide political concerns that were highlighted in this chapter.

Second, aside from declaratory claims in official documents on EU crisis response, empirical evidence from Libya, Afghanistan, Mali and Iraq shows that 'conflict sensitivity' is only sullenly accepted, if not a completely neglected concept in practice (Peters *et al.*, 2018: 20). Especially in Libya, the EU has been blamed for a lack of conflict sensitivity compared with other international actors operating on the ground. While crisis management may not require particular sensitivity, it seems important that crisis resolution, and especially crisis transformation are dependent on participation, a knowledge of constituencies, and an ability to take on board cultural and social expectations as well as localised political economies. Well-working crisis sensitivity requires knowledgeable personnel and institutional systems that allow the observations from this personnel to feed into the system.

Third, both the EU and other multilateral actors' crisis response have recurrently failed to ensure and prioritise the participation and needs of domestic actors in their crisis response (Peters *et al.*, 2018). Even when local ownership was on the agenda, a lack of conflict sensitivity sometimes resulted in local, yet corrupt or ineffective actors, aggravating a crisis or conflict and undermining peacebuilding efforts. As above, meaningful participation in crisis response requires system in place that can recognise the importance of local interlocutors and different ways of interpreting and narrating crises.

Finally, the examples of Libya, Ukraine and Mali illustrate the kind of challenges which are likely to dog the EU for years to come (ESPAS, 2015: 9), and show an increasingly self-interested focus on migration in the EU's crisis responses. This narrow focus is thwarting the Union's self-proclaimed commitment to a 'integrated' approach to conflicts and crises. EUNPACK research shows that in none of the above-mentioned cases there seems to be a strategy that combines conflict prevention, conflict management and peacebuilding. In spite of persistent rhetoric about human rights and democratic values, normative concerns have progressively faded in policy documents (Ivashchenko-Stadnik *et al.*, 2017: 63). More pragmatic security and stabilisation imperatives are now centre stage, effectively subordinating the EU's role as a transformative power and affecting its credibility compared to less interest-driven and more value-based actors like the UN. Ukraine is perhaps the exception that proves the rule. Indeed, according to the findings presented in this chapter, the EU does not easily fit into a narrative of straightforward securitisation or a shift from conflict management to conflict transformation.

Note

1 The Horizon 2020 EUNPACK data consist of standardised in-depth interviews and surveys undertaken in summer/autumn 2017.

References

Amnesty International (2017) *Libya's Dark Web of Collusion: Abuses against Europe-bound Refugees and Migrants* (London: Amnesty International, December).

Anderson, M.B., L. Olson and K. Doughty (2003) *Confronting War: Critical Lessons for Peace Practitioners* (Cambridge, MA: CDA).

Ba, B. and M. Bøås (2017) *Mali: A Political Economy Analysis*. Report commissioned by the Norwegian Ministry of Foreign Affairs (Oslo: NUPI).

Bátora, J., K. Osland and M. Peter (2017) 'The EU's crisis management in the Kosovo-Serbia Crises', EUNPACK Working Paper, D. 5.1, EUNPACK project.

Bátora, J., M. Navrátil, K.M. Osland and M. Peter (2018) 'The EU and international actors in Kosovo: Competing institutional logics, constructive ambiguity and competing priorities', EUNPACK Working Paper D.5.2, EUNPACK project.

Bøås, M., A.W. Cissé, A. Diallo, B. Drange, F. Kvamme and E. Stambøl (2018) 'The EU, security sector reform and border management in Mali', Working paper on the implementation of EU crisis response in Mali, EUNPACK Working Paper, D.7.4, EUNPACK project.

Chandler, D. (2007) 'The security–development nexus and the rise of "anti-foreign policy"', *Journal of International Development*, 10(4): 362–386.

Cissé, A.W., A. Dakouo, M. Bøås and F. Kvamme (2017) 'Perceptions about the EU crisis response in Mali – a summary of perception studies', EUNPACK Policy Brief, D.7.7, EUNPACK project.

Cliffe, S. (2017) 'UN Peace and Security Reform: Cautious steps in the right direction' (New York: NYU Center on International Cooperation, September).

Council of the European Union (2018) Council Conclusions on Reinforcing the UN-EU Strategic Partnership on Peace Operations and Crisis Management: Priorities 2019–2021, 18 September, Brussels: Council Secretariat (12264/18).

de Coning, C. (2008) *The United Nations and the Comprehensive Approach* (Copenhagen: Danish Institute for International Studies).

Dijkstra, H., P. Petrov and E. Mahr (2016) 'Reacting to conflict: Civilian capabilities in the EU, UN and OSCE', EU-CIVCAP Report DL 4.1.

Dijkstra, H., E. Mahr, P. Petrov, K. Đokić and P. Horne Zartsdahl (2017) 'Partners in conflict prevention and peacebuilding: How the EU, UN and OSCE exchange civilian capabilities in Kosovo, Mali and Armenia', EU-CIVCAP Report DL 4.2.

EEAS/European Commission (2017) Issues paper for the Political and Security Committee (PSC). 'EEAS/Commission services' issues paper suggesting parameters for a concept on Stabilisation as part of EU Integrated Approach to external conflicts and crises' (Brussels: EEAS/COM).

EEAS (2018) 'The EU enhances its operational cooperation with the OSCE', Press release, 22 June (Brussels: EEAS).

Eide, E.B., A.T. Kaspersen, R. Kent and K. von Hippel (2005) 'Report on Integrated Missions: Practical perspectives and recommendations', Independent Study for the Expanded UN ECHA Core Group, May.

El Kamouni-Janssen, F. and K. de Bruijne (2007) *Entering the Lion's Den: Local Militias and Governance in Libya*, Clingendael Crisis Alert Report (Clingendael: CCA).

European Strategy and Policy Analysis System (ESPAS) (2015) *Global Trends to 2030: Can the EU meet the Challenges Ahead?* (Brussels: ESPAS).

European Union HR/VP (2016) *Shared Vision, Common Action: A Stronger Europe. A Global Strategy for the European Union's Foreign and Security Policy* (Brussels: EU).

Faleg, G. (2018) 'The EU: From comprehensive to integrated approach', *Global Affairs*, 4(2–3): 171–183.

Gelot, L. (2016) 'The legitimacy of peace operations in volatile environments: Between state-centred and people-centred standards', *Journal of Regional Security*, 11(2): 123–142.

Gheciu, A. (2012) 'Communities of security practices in the age of uncertainty', *Journal of Regional Security*, 7(2): 151–162.

Heinemann, R. (2017) 'The European Union's crisis response in the extended neighbourhood: The EU's output effectiveness in the case of Mali', EUNPACK Working Paper D.7.1, EUNPACK project.

High Representative (2017) Joint Communication of the European Commission and the High Representative to the European Parliament and the Council, 'A Strategic Approach to Resilience in the EU's External Action', JOIN (2017) 21 final (Brussels: EU).

Ivashchenko-Stadnik, K., R. Petrov, L. Raineri, P. Rieker, A. Russo and F. Strazzari (2017) 'How the EU is facing crises in its neighbourhood: Evidence from Libya and Ukraine', EUNPACK Working Paper D.6.1, EUNPACK project.

Ivashchenko-Stadnik, K., R. Petrov, P. Rieker and A. Russo (2018) 'Implementation of the EU's crisis response in Ukraine', EUNPACK Working Paper D.6.3, EUNPACK project.

Kammel, A.H. and B. Zyla (2018) 'The comprehensive approach to EU crisis management: Contexts, lessons identified, and policy implications', *Journal of Regional Security*, 13(1): 39–63.

Koops, J., N. MacQueen, T. Tardy and P.D. Williams (2015) *The Oxford Handbook of United Nations Peacekeeping Operations* (Oxford: Oxford University Press).

Loschi, C., L. Raineri and F. Strazzari (2018) 'The implementation of EU crisis response in Libya: Bridging theory and practice', EUNPACK Working Paper D.6.2, EUNPACK project.

Mezran, K. and A. Varvelli (eds) (2017) *Foreign Actors in Libya's Crisis* (Milan: Atlantic Council & ISPI).

Mogherini, F. (2018) Opening speech by HR/VP Federica Mogherini at the annual EU Ambassadors Conference, Brussels, 3–7 September.

Mohammed, K. (2018) 'The EU Crisis Response in Iraq: Awareness, local perception and reception', EUNPACK Working Paper D.7.2, EUNPACK project.

NATO (2010) 'Active engagement, modern defence: Strategic concept for the defence and security of the members of the North Atlantic Treaty Organization', adopted by Heads of State and Government at the NATO Summit in Lisbon, 19–20 November.

OCSE (2011) Vilnius Ministerial Council Decision No. 3/11 (2011) 'Elements of the conflicts cycle, related to enhancing the OSCE's capabilities in early warning, early action, dialogue facilitation and mediation support, and post-conflict rehabilitation', MC.DEC/3/11, 7 December.

OHCHR (2018) 39th Session of the Human Rights Council, Opening statement by UN High Commissioner for Human Rights Michelle Bachelet, Geneva, 10 September 2018.

Peters, I. (2017) 'The European Union's crisis response in the extended neighbourhood: The EU's output effectiveness in the case of Iraq', EUNPACK Working Paper D.7.1, EUNPACK project.

Peters, I., E. Ferhatovic, R. Heinemann, S. Berger and S.M. Sturm (2018) 'European Union's crisis response in the extended neighbourhood: Comparing the EU's output effectiveness in the cases of Afghanistan, Iraq and Mali', EUNPACK Working Paper D.7.1 (part 4), EUNPACK project.

Richmond, O.P., A. Björkdahl and S. Kappler (2011) 'The emerging EU peacebuilding framework: Confirming or transcending liberal peacebuilding?', *Cambridge Review of International Affairs*, 24(3): 449–469.

Smith, M.E. (2012) 'Developing a "comprehensive approach" to international security: Institutional learning and the CSDP', in J. Richardson (ed.), *Constructing a Policy-making State? Policy Dynamics in the EU* (Oxford: Oxford University Press), 253–269.

Stewart, R. (2013) 'What went wrong in Afghanistan? Trying to do the impossible', *Foreign Policy* (4 March).

Suroush, Q. (2018) 'Assessing EUPOL impact on Afghan police reform (2007–2016)', EUNPACK Working Paper D.7.3, EUNPACK project.

Tardy, T. (2017) 'The EU: From comprehensive vision to integrated action' (Brussels: EU Institute for Security Studies, February).

Tripathi, S. and E. Ferhatovic (2017) 'The European Union's crisis response in the Extended Neighbourhood: The EU's output effectiveness in the case of Afghanistan', EUNPACK Working Paper, D.7.01 (Oslo: EUNPACK project).

UN (1992) *An Agenda for Peace: Preventive diplomacy, peacemaking and peace-keeping*. Report of the Secretary-General pursuant to the statement adopted by the Summit Meeting of the Security Council on 31 January 1992. A/47/277S – S/24111, 17 June.

UN (2008) Decision Number 2008/24 – Integration, Decisions of the UN Secretary-General, 25 June, Policy Committee (New York: United Nations).

UN (2015) Report of the High-Level Independent Panel on United Nations Peace Operations (HIPPO) on uniting our strengths for peace: politics, partnership and people (A/70/95/–S/2015/446), 17 June.

UNGA (2015) 'Transforming our world: The 2030 Agenda for Sustainable Development' (New York: UNGA, 25 September).

Vogelaar, G. (2018) 'Local ownership, inclusivity and civil-military synergy in EU external action: The case of EU support to security sector reforms in Mali', *Journal of Regional Security*, 13(2): 105–130.

Weir, E.A. (2006) 'Conflict and compromise: UN integrated missions and the humanitarian imperative' (Accra: Kofi Annan International Peacekeeping Training Centre).

5

Securitisation of the EU approach to the Western Balkans: from conflict transformation to crisis management

Kari M. Osland and Mateja Peter

Introduction

While much of the EU peacebuilding capacities and mechanisms are relatively new, the EU has acted as a crisis response actor in the Western Balkans since the mid-1990s.[1] This region, now part of the enlargement area, has long been an incubator and a test ground for the EU peacebuilding toolkit. The Western Balkans is the region where the EU has not only financially invested the most, but where the Union enjoys the greatest clout. Unlike in other regions addressed in this book, the Union is one of the most, if not the most, influential external actors in the Western Balkans. The proximity of the region also means that the Western Balkans problems have spill-over effects on the Union. For normative and/or self-interested reasons, the EU has heavily supported programmes and mechanisms with conflict transformation ambitions. These structural reforms with longer timelines have been particularly targeted at the rule of law sector in the region.

In this chapter, we look at the implementation and perception of the EU's largest investment into the rule of law sector in the Western Balkans: EULEX.[2] Established in 2008, this CSDP mission took over justice functions from UNMIK. While its operation has been extended multiple times, the mission has entered a drawdown stage, focusing on mentoring and advising local institutions. But for the first ten years of its existence, EULEX was the only EU mission with an executive mandate. EU judges, prosecutors, investigators and customs officials were embedded into Kosovo's rule of law institutions, directly dispensing justice in the most sensitive criminal proceedings. While consultations with local counterparts were increasing over time as part of local ownership policies (Ejdus, 2017), for much of its existence, EULEX had full authority to transfer any case to its own docket, thus at least in theory not just supervising but also governing the local rule of law system.

We argue that while the design of EULEX suffers from problems typically associated with liberal peacebuilding operations – lack of local ownership, technocratic approaches, and lack of accountability – the mission mandate embodied ambitions for conflict transformation. However, as the EU increased its presence and commitment to Kosovo and the region in the late 2000s, it became increasingly difficult to reconcile its own conflicting priorities for the region, a problem we have previously described as the first proximity paradox in peacebuilding (Osland and Peter, 2019). EULEX implementation therefore got compromised and the mission became the casualty of the Union's increasingly securitised crisis management approach to the Western Balkans (cf. Ioannides and Collantes-Celador, 2011; Kmezić and Bieber, 2017). In this, the EU is mirroring broader trends in contemporary international operations, which have all but abandoned any conflict transformation ambitions and are now primarily deployed to manage and contain conflicts to their regions (Peter, 2019: 40). We see this as particularly problematic for an actor whose self-image as a 'normative power' (Manners, 2002), is underpinned by an assumption that its influence in the world in gained through 'the power of ideas' (Galtung, 1973: 33).

We build our argument by drawing on experiences of those most directly responsible for the execution of the EULEX mandate and those directly affected by its outcomes. Our data was collected as part of the EU Horizon 2020-funded EUNPACK project and comes from twenty-five in-depth interviews with practitioners familiar with the day-to-day work of the mission and its reception on the ground. These interviews were conducted in Mitrovica and Pristina in October 2017. In selecting interviewees, we paid special attention to implementers of the executive mandate, such as EULEX judges and prosecutors, and others intimately familiar with the relationship between the executive and the capacity-building work in the rule of law sector in Kosovo. These selections were done to avoid building our understanding of EU practices solely on the basis of meetings with EU gatekeepers in the field (Ejdus and

Juncos, 2018). To gauge how the mission is perceived by local actors, we spoke with local judges and civil society actors, representing NGOs, research institutes and media, all with deep familiarity with the rule of law in Kosovo and the EU assistance to the sector. These were selected according to a snowball selection procedure, where we wanted to find people with a representative view from different ethnic parts of society, based on a context- and gender-sensitive understanding of the local dynamics in Kosovo. Local perceptions were gathered from Kosovo-Albanian (majority) and Kosovo-Serb (minority) representatives. In all our interviews, we were interested in challenges as identified by our interlocutors, seeking to understand how practitioners are assessing the situation and what meaning they are ascribing to their actions and to the actions of the EU.

The chapter is organised into five sections. After this introduction, the second section provides the framework for the argument, focusing on the different modes of conflict response highlighting a recent shift from conflict transformation to conflict management in international interventions. The third section draws on critical peacebuilding literature outlining how the mandate and the design of the mission were undermining its conflict transformation objectives. In the fourth section, we show how these transformation ambitions of the mission were fundamentally eroded in practice through de-prioritisation of the rule of law in EU policy towards the region. While designed as a conflict transformation mission, in practice, EULEX became a conflict management one, with the EU responding to crises of immediate concern at the expense of longer term priorities. We conclude with some broader observations on EU-specific challenges in mounting what was an executive statebuilding mission in its immediate neighbourhood.

From conflict management to conflict transformation – and back

International responses to conflicts have changed dramatically since the beginning of the 1990s, with both conflict theory and best practice developing in parallel. As the nature of conflict dynamics changes, international responses needed to adapt. In the typology elaborated in Chapter 2, a distinction is made between different types or generations of conflict response, stretched on a continuum from the more conservative to the more progressive responses: conflict management–conflict resolution–conflict transformation–critical conflict transformation. While there are considerable overlaps between these categories, each ideal type is commonly associated not just with a certain type of international presence but also with a specific era of international responses.

Conflict management has the most contained ambitions and is commonly equated with political realism. This approach relies to a large degree on the intervening third parties and is characterised by a limited state-centric discourse with local elites. Such an approach is most commonly associated with the Cold War era international responses to conflicts and is epitomised in the development of UN peacekeeping principles: consent, limited use of force, and non-interference in internal affairs (UN, 2008). International responses are not supposed to resolve the underlying conflict, but are instead designed to prevent them from escalating into a broader conflict, thus containing them to the region of origin. *Conflict resolution* is framed as a second generation of responses partly arising as a critique of conflict management. This approach is more structural in that it focuses on understanding the root causes of conflict, including underdevelopment. It highlights the need for full representation of all voices and issues in conflicts, in contrast to the state-centric approach adopted in conflict management. Stress is put on individual agency; human needs are seen as universal and there is an embedded view that contact with the 'other' leads to deconstruction rather than a reification of conflict. The primary local in such an approach is not the state or its elites, but civil actors and 'normal' people.

Conflict transformation is a type of response developed in the post-Cold War era and sought to merge the top-down approach of conflict management with the bottom-up approach of conflict resolution. Bolstered by the broader consensus in the international community, the idea was to not just manage and contain conflicts, but to transform societies emerging from conflicts. The liberal peacebuilding project became central to such conflict responses, with international agencies assisting in building states. Such an approach was underpinned by a broad understanding among key international actors who saw the continued stability of a (post) war state closely linked to adequate standards in other areas, including the rule of law, policing, and developmental and social issues. Peacebuilding became intertwined with statebuilding (Paris and Sisk, 2009: 1–2).

This shift corresponds with a trend in UN peacekeeping where UN interventions changed from keeping peace to helping societies recovering from conflict in creating new government institutions and strengthening existing ones (Paris, 2004). By building functional and legitimate institutions, peace would follow. Engagement of civil society is emphasised in these programmes with the idea that non-state actors would hold state institutions accountable. However, given the strong emphasis on reforms of the state and its institutions, the bottom-up dimension was deprioritised in practice, becoming an add-on to peacebuilding operations. Even more, external donors and actors continued to be in the driver's seat of the reforms, obstructing any real chance of local ownership of these processes. Similar blueprints were applied from one country to another, with international peacebuilding efforts implemented through bureaucratic, technical solutions, where thematic expertise is prioritised over local/country knowledge (Autesserre, 2014: 68–69). To complicate the impact of these responses further, such efforts have largely been perceived as unaccountable, with their staff acting with impunity (Caplan, 2005; Visoka, 2012).

While this third type of conflict response has been ambitious in its aims and scope, such interventions have created a range of unexpected consequences and a large expectation gap on the side of the people living in the affected countries. As noted by Richmond (2010: 30–31), 'the very ontology and related epistemology of the liberal peace are being disputed by local communities, not necessarily on an ideological basis, but quite often because of its failures to provide sufficient resources to support the everyday lives of such communities'. Critical scholars have therefore argued for a fourth generation of conflict response – *critical conflict transformation* (Richmond et al., 2016). The key here is a hybridised form of peacebuilding that connects the local and the international, focusing on a beneficial impact on the everyday lives of the people in question.

But while scholars have pointed to the need to properly engage the bottom-up aspects of conflict transformation, in practice, international responses to recent conflicts have gone in the opposite direction. This return from conflict transformation to conflict management has been most extensively explored in UN peace operations (Peter, 2015; Gelot, 2017; Hunt, 2017; Tull, 2018; de Coning and Peter, 2019; Laurence, 2019), but the EU responses to conflicts have also increasingly come under scrutiny. Youngs (2004: 415) contends that 'instrumentalist security-oriented dynamics persist within the parameters set by norms defining the EU's identity', something that is carried over into its conflict responses. Raineri and Strazzari (2019: 544) show on the examples of Mali and Libya that 'EU investments in sector-specific capacity building are geared to the enhancement of sovereign prerogatives in neighbouring states', thus returning EU policies back to a conflict management/containment era. This problem has been noted also in the literature on the Western Balkans, with Ioannides and Collantes-Celador (2011) maintaining that CSDP missions in the region are increasingly guided by the 'internal–external security nexus'. Similar argument has been made in the literature on 'stabilitocracy' (Kmezić and Bieber, 2017), which concludes that the EU has become content in supporting autocratically minded leaders, who guarantee stability of the region. In this chapter, we explore how this shift to conflict management has impacted a mission designed to transform the conflict.

EULEX as a liberal peacebuilding mission: a problematic conflict transformation project

EULEX, while in many ways an idiosyncratic peacebuilding endeavour for the EU, is in other ways an archetypical example of a statebuilding mission associated with the liberal peacebuilding era of international interventions. As a first step, the mission therefore needs to be understood and critiqued as a liberal peacebuilding project. In this section, we show that EULEX objectives embody conflict transformation ambitions, but that its design suffers from structural flaws endemic to a liberal peacebuilding project. Critiques raised by rule of law experts we interviewed concerned a missing bottom-up dimension, a technocratic approach to a political problem, and unaccountability of the mission.

A major component of liberal peacebuilding is 'directed at constructing or reconstructing institutions of governance' (Chesterman, 2004: 5), with rule of law being one of the most prominent aspects (Osland, 2019). Since the early 1990s, international actors have assisted local police and judiciary in building up their independence, while simultaneously attempting to democratise these institutions by instilling accountability and human rights standards in their work. Rule of law institutions are supposed to chiefly embody equality before the law, which in societies emerging from ethnic conflicts translates into supporting a multi-ethnic police and judicial system. The assumption is that a functioning legal system would provide alternative conflict resolution mechanisms and that its multi-ethnic nature would ensure that these mechanisms are unbiased in their treatment of previously fighting groups.

Such an approach is reflected in the core objective of EULEX, which is supposed to

> [a]ssist Kosovo, judicial authorities and law enforcement agencies in their progress towards sustainability and accountability and in further developing and strengthening an independent multi-ethnic justice system and multi-ethnic police and custom service, ensuring that these institutions are free from political interference and adhering to internationally recognised standards and European best practices. (European External Action Service (EEAS), 2018)

Both EULEX and its predecessor mission UNMIK were underpinned by the idea that building accountable institutions would aid in post-conflict reconciliation. Independence and adherence to international standards were and remain major problems in the Kosovo judiciary with the mission's core objective responding to the problem identified not just by international actors, but also local ones. Public perception studies consistently raise rule of law as a major concern. One such study, conducted by a network of civil society organisations in 2016, showed that 62 per cent of respondents expressed no trust in Kosovo judiciary, with 60 per cent claiming they did not trust prosecutors. Asking about the level of corruption, prosecutors topped the list (jointly with the parliament), with 63 per cent of respondents deeming that corruption was widespread among them. The Kosovo judiciary was close third with 61 per cent seeing it as widely corrupt (Emini, 2016). This lack of independence of local judiciary was continuously brought up in our interviews as well, with one Kosovo-Albanian interlocutor saying that the main challenge to the rule of law in Kosovo is that judges and prosecutors are politically appointed, sending a message to the citizens that the justice system is not independent.[3] When EULEX was launched, locals had high expectations that the EU would tackle this endemic problem. One Kosovo-Albanian we interviewed, intimated, 'we had high expectations and it proved to be a big disappointment'.[4]

Although independence of the local rule of law institutions was and remains a major concern, the perceived bias against minority groups in the Kosovo judicial system is what influenced the design of EULEX and its predecessor mission even more. Unlike most international missions, which focus on capacity-building through training and advice, EULEX and UNMIK were missions with executive mandates, meaning that they directly exercised judicial and police functions. The UN Security Council resolution 1244, which established a UN transitional administration over Kosovo, allowed for a possibility of an executive mandate in all aspects of civilian administration (UN, 1999). While international police officers were deployed immediately after the ceasefire, the UN initially relied on local judges and prosecutors to dispense justice across Kosovo. A Joint Advisory Council, composed of international and Kosovo representatives, selected these and as no Kosovo-Serb jurist applied, the composition of the Kosovo judicial system became entirely ethnically Albanian (Skendaj, 2014: 89). Such a system was widely seen as biased against Kosovo minorities (O'Neill, 2001) and it was this bias that led to a change in the international policy and the eventual deployment of international judges and prosecutors. Bias against minorities represents a concern to this day and as our interviews with EULEX officials on the ground highlighted, integration of Kosovo-Serb judges from the so-called parallel institutions is seen by them to be a chief priority for the EU. Supporting the normalisation process between Pristina and Belgrade, entailing also the integration of Kosovo-Serb judiciary, is one of four areas EULEX is supposed to focus on.[5]

However, by trying to address the problem of bias in the local judiciary and thus creating UNMIK/EULEX as executive statebuilding missions, the international community/EU created other problems for its conflict transformation ambitions. Critiques raised in our interviews correspond well with what authors writing in the critical peacebuilding tradition have uncovered elsewhere. EULEX had an almost non-existent bottom-up dimension, it adopted a highly technocratic approach, and experienced problems with accountability. All these problems were magnified due to the executive nature of the operation.

One of the main critiques in the critical peacebuilding literature is that liberal peacebuilding exercises lack a strong bottom-up component, which undermines their conflict transformation potential. To respond to these critiques, international actors promote the idea of local ownership (von Billerbeck, 2015; Ejdus, 2017). While such policies are designed to create stronger consultation mechanisms with beneficiaries of international efforts (including non-state actors), in practice, they fail to deliver. Scholars point to a gap between the discourse and practice, as international actors often perceive the devolution of agency to local actors as endangering the achievement of their overall goals (von Billerbeck, 2015; Lemay-Hébert and Kappler, 2016). The lack of a bottom-up component is amplified in missions with executive mandates, such as EULEX, as these missions are put in place to temporarily substitute problematic local institutions. An executive rule-of-law mission therefore by definition needs to insulate its activities from local actors if it wants to maintain that it is acting as an independent judiciary. Nonetheless, these missions still design programmes purporting to pursue local ownership.

Our interviews confirmed these findings. Both EULEX and local experts agreed that local ownership is an in-built problem for executive missions, concluding that even with the best intentions, the design of the mission was never going to allow for implementation of what was written on paper. Several civil society interlocutors maintained that proper discussion happened only with elites, which was ironic as that was the layer the EU and EULEX were supposed to hold accountable. One Kosovo-Albanian concluded, 'there is a structured platform for dialogue with civil society ... but there is no room for criticising the EU'.[6] This lack of consultation was a particularly serious concern for minority representatives, who saw the mission and the EU focusing on high-level conflict management at the expense of peacebuilding on the ground, something we return to in the next section. According to one Kosovo-Serb: 'The local institutions are reporting to EULEX but communication only goes in one direction. The local community and institutions do not have anything to say for designing the mission and this is very problematic as for local ownership.... They don't understand the need of the local community – they don't ask them – and in some cases, they know what is going on but they are not interested.'[7]

Others were more sympathetic arguing that things could have been worse. One Kosovo-Albanian civil society representative contended: 'We see the EU here on the ground as very active.... We are asked to give general views on different themes and topics and are invited to those where we have expertise.'[8] Local judges similarly intimated having a good working relationship with their EULEX counterparts, seeing variation more as a matter of personalities: 'some really listen to local interpretations, others are more dismissive'.[9] Another argued that what helped was that most EU judges came from legal systems that had similarities with Kosovo's.[10] EULEX judges and prosecutors broadly shared these opinions, simultaneously arguing for a need to be insulated from interference in their own work and stronger consultation mechanisms with the civil society at the policy level.[11] Several criticised the mission for starkly separating its executive and capacity-building work in its 2012 review, which meant that the EU staff, who were directly exposed to local judges and prosecutors, could neither mentor them nor receive their feedback on the work of the mission.[12] One EULEX prosecutor concluded that given the little interaction between the strengthening and the executive side of EULEX, even informal feedback from local counterparts, does not reach people who oversee local ownership policies.[13]

Another critique found in much of the peacebuilding literature is that such missions are overly technocratic thus prioritising thematic knowledge over local expertise (Autesserre, 2014: 68–69). Peacebuilding is implemented as a one-size-fits-all approach, 'peace from IKEA' (Mac Ginty, 2008: 145). The conclusion in these studies point to a limited conflict transformation potential of statebuilding missions by arguing that '[a]lthough peacebuilding is committed to positive peace, its discourses and practices tend to depoliticise peace' (Goetschel and Hagmann, 2009: 66). Both local and EULEX experts were highly critical of the technocratic policies the EU and the management of the mission adopted, with nuanced reading of differences in their accounts revealing how EULEX staff internalised a technocratic approach themselves.

Furthermore, both local and EULEX experts agreed that in planning of the mission, the EU was focused on what worked best for the EU, not what was most needed or appropriate for Kosovo. As a result, the mission had a major problem due to the high turnover of its staff. Staffing for EULEX follows a similar logic to staffing for other CSDP missions: officials are either seconded by member states or contracted by the mission itself. This system was widely seen as inappropriate for the type of mission EULEX was, with one interlocutor arguing that when you take over executive functions, you take over state functions, meaning that the turnover rate is incompatible with the tasks you are asked to take on: 'in legal proceedings, you cannot change an investigator every year'.[14] This turnover particularly impacted seconded staff, where the decision on the length and the possible extension of their mandate rests with the sending state. At the time of interviews, roughly three quarters of staff working in the Executive Division were seconded.[15] On the other hand, contracted staff are hired on short, but renewable, contracts and were therefore seen to be under a bigger pressure to perform to the wishes of the management. A local judge argued that this system influenced the quality of EULEX judges wanting to come to Kosovo and also the perception of their rulings. These were not deemed to be of the highest standard.[16] Another interlocutor maintained that since the mission preferred seconded staff (as these are paid by the sending states), it repeatedly appointed to managerial posts people that lacked the required legal training and experience.[17] Overall, the impression was that the specificities of staffing an executive mission were not thought through in advance nor have been properly understood by Brussels since.

But there was also a clear sense among our local interlocutors that EULEX staff themselves internalised the bureaucratic nature of their job, not seeing their work as political. Speaking to EULEX executive staff on their expectations and what they would consider a successful mission, they spoke of 'working on difficult cases',[18] 'providing independent justice',[19] and 'leading by example'.[20] They were not naïve, but EULEX staff clearly prioritised processes and standards.[21] They were there to implement a technical mandate and did not have high expectations of their contributions to fighting corruption. In contrast, a local judge grumbled about the length of time it took EULEX judges to resolve a case, saying an EU judge handles less than two cases, while he needs to finish six or so in a year.[22] This slow handling of justice was particularly palpable during the handover period and one EULEX official shared that the core of his work represented handing over more than five thousand cases they had been working on to local authorities. Around twelve hundred cases were inherited from UNMIK and many were still on EULEX's docket ten years later.[23] This broad sense of EULEX's technocratic approach was shared also by civil society representatives. One Kosovo-Albanian explained that they expected EULEX to go after the big fish and that this expectation had not been met. He argued that the challenge for EULEX was that they were asked for results early on to show that the EU was effective and therefore the more 'low hanging fruits' were picked, such as the drug cases, which would not be hard to go after for the locals either.[24] A minority representative confirmed this narrative, arguing that 'when you see the cost of the EULEX mission, you would expect more results'.[25]

A further problem plaguing peacebuilding missions is their perceived unaccountability. Both media reports and academic studies are rife with examples of international staff breaking or skirting legal and ethical rules. In the UN context, reports of sexual abuse have haunted several major peace operations, as have stories of embezzlement and corruption (Simic, 2009; Grady, 2010; Kanetake, 2010; Jennings and Bøås, 2015). While international organisations have put policies in place to address these (e.g., UN, 2003; UN, 2017), such policies are most often poorly implemented. What further complicates the relationship with locals is that most accountability processes happen through international channels, far removed from where the violation took place. For rule of law missions, and especially executive rule of law missions, the perception that they might be corrupt is even worse than other violations, given that they are supposed to support and serve as an example of an independent judiciary or a police force. And this was a major problem for EULEX.

While every single interviewee with direct experience with EULEX, including internationals not employed by the mission and local judges and staff, categorically rejected any knowledge of endemic corruption within the mission, our civil society interviewees were of a different opinion, perceiving EULEX as corrupt and thus enabling corrupt local elites. Perception studies mentioned above reflect this sense. According to one Kosovo-Albanian, the general perception is that EULEX is not doing anything about the main problem in Kosovo: 'there is a lot of political interference and no MPs in prison'. She linked this lack of action on local corruption with corruption within EULEX: '78 per cent think that rule of law institutions – locals and EULEX – are influenced by politicians according to a recent poll. We are losing faith in the EU.'[26] Another majority representative was even more explicit, stating 'they [EULEX] cannot fight corruption because they are so involved in corruption themselves.'[27] Several interviewees pointed to the blame game happening between employees in Kosovo justice institutions and EULEX, with neither willing to clean up its own ranks.[28] As one Kosovo-Albanian phrased it: 'The reason why they [local institutions and EULEX] don't fight corruption is that they have interest there themselves.'[29] Others saw corruption within EULEX being just one aspect of the problem, arguing that the mere presence of EULEX allowed for political interference in local judiciary to persist. One interviewee argued that EULEX, even if not directly corrupt itself, merely represents an additional layer of governance, resulting in more ways for their own politicians to avoid being held accountable.[30] As the blame game continued, the local judiciary could hide behind the mistakes of the international mission.

While a preliminary investigation by the EULEX mission itself found no evidence of corruption among EULEX staff and the independent Jacqué Report (EU, 2015) echoed this, rumours and allegations of corruption had been flourishing for a long time before EU took any action (cf. Capussela, 2015). People's negative perceptions are difficult to change, but it seems that the EU also did little to address Kosovar's concerns. Jean-Paul Jacqué criticised the EU for not opening an investigation into the allegations immediately as '[t]his would have prevented the issues that later arose in connection with the use of secret and special procedures, which fuelled suspicions of a cover-up' (EU, 2015: 8). And while EULEX staff similarly rejected the idea of broad corruption, they agreed that action was needed. If EU findings and EULEX narratives were correct and this truly was a misperception, responding to suspicions of political interference and corruption would have been crucial for any international mission, even more so for one with an executive mandate to fight corruption itself.

The above section highlighted ways that EULEX design was undermining conflict transformation ambitions the EU had set for its operation. In the next section, we further show that not only was the design and the bureaucratic top-down nature of the mission a problem, but that the EU fundamentally undermined its status also in practice, by de-prioritising the core objective of the mission: the rule of law.

EULEX as a casualty of EU's competing priorities: from conflict transformation to conflict management

Over the last decade, as the EU has been increasing its role in Kosovo, the contradictions in its approach have become more apparent. In this section, we show how EULEX became the casualty of the EU's competing priorities for the region. We outline the increasing EU presence in and engagement on Kosovo before laying out four overarching political objectives of the EU. We then show how EULEX's core objective – the rule of law – was sacrificed as part of an increasingly securitised approach to the region. While EULEX was pursuing longer term conflict transformation objectives, the EU began focusing on immediate crisis management.

By the mid 2000s, the EU wanted to increase the stakes by highlighting its own special relationship with the region, one that other states – especially Russia and the United States – and other international organisations did not share. In 2005, the EC published a Communication highlighting its contribution to making Kosovo's European perspective a reality, thus linking Kosovo's future to its own (European Commission, 2005). In its 2008 Enlargement Strategy, the Commission announced its intention to present a feasibility study on Kosovo (European Commission, 2008). One of the main priorities in ensuring this European perspective is the rule of law. Almost simultaneously as Kosovo proclaimed its independence, in February 2008, the Council of the European Union in one Joint Action established both the EUSR and EULEX Kosovo (Council of the European Union, 2008a). These two missions are still the main EU bodies on the ground, with EUSR now also double-hatted as the Head of the EU Office (not Delegation, due to Kosovo's contested status).

In addition to its substantial ground presence, the EU is involved in broader diplomatic, humanitarian, development and economic relations with Kosovo and the region. The EU's engagement has increased in this area as well. The most notable of these is the EU-facilitated dialogue for the normalisation of relations between Belgrade and Pristina, which started in 2011 and is from 2014 facilitated by the High Representative for Foreign Affairs and Security Policy/Vice-President of the Commission (Bátora et al., 2017).[31]

With such a heavy footprint of EU institutions and the concurrent presence of EU member states on the ground, it is unsurprising that the EU has multiple objectives for what it wants to achieve with its presence on the ground. While objectives specific to individual actors – such as economic interests of a member state – contribute to shaping EU policies and priorities, we identify four overarching political objectives that the EU is pursuing in Kosovo:

1. *Conflict management:* normalisation of relations between Kosovo and Serbia, and Kosovo-Serbs and Kosovo-Albanians;
2. *Conflict transformation:* supporting an independent judiciary free from political interference; strengthening democracy and rule of law;
3. *European security:* minimising security threats to Europe emanating from Kosovo, due to high levels of organised crime and its links to European criminal networks;
4. *EU as an international actor:* through its presence in Kosovo the EU is building its own nascent foreign policy capacities and maintaining the status as a global player.

These objectives can be identified in multiple EU documents (European Commission, 2005, 2008; Council of the European Union, 2008a, 2008b; European Union HR/VP, 2016; EU, 2019) and were mentioned also in our interviews. The EU stresses that they are pursued simultaneously and in parallel to each other. However, there are underlying tensions between them and in implementing the mandate of the mission, it matters which of these objectives is prioritised. The last two objectives in many ways have more to do with the EU than Kosovo. More importantly for our discussion, to achieve these objectives, the EU needs to work with different local constituencies. Objectives (1) and (3) require an elite buy-in; they are top-down approaches. Elite consent is needed for the normalisation of relations between Serbia and Kosovo and for continued cooperation of local authorities on transnational organised crime and terrorism. Objective (2), on the other hand, at its heart, requires insulating justice institutions from these same local elites. It hinges on bottom-up engagement and support, as elite accountability cannot be achieved from the outside. A manifest tension between EULEX priorities is reflected already in the mandate, where the mission is supposed to both '[be] fighting political interference ... and [act in] support [of] the EU-facilitated dialogue between Belgrade and Pristina ... in the sphere of rule of law'.[32]

While the EU was seen by our interlocutors as uniquely positioned to address Kosovo's rule of law problems, its *sui generis* character and competing objectives in and for the region presented EU-specific challenges resulting in de-prioritisation of the mission's main objective: the rule of law. The proximity of the region to the Union means that EU's objectives for Kosovo are broader and more intertwined with EU's internal concerns, impacting how the executive rule of law mission was implemented (Osland and Peter, 2019). Other objectives – conflict management, internal security and EU actorness – were deemed to be more important to the EU and the EU was seen as often abandoning its longer term rule of law reforms for immediate crisis management. As more immediate concerns required an elite buy-in, accountability of these same elites was seen to be lost along the way. One EULEX official commented that Brussels spends an immense amount of energy on the normalisation process, often at the expense of 'the real problems' with the Kosovo judiciary.[33]

Throughout our interviews, several used the phrase 'stabilocracy' or 'stabilitocracy', referring to a weak democracy with autocratically minded leaders, who enjoy external legitimacy by claiming to provide pro-Western stability in the region (Kmezić and Bieber, 2017). In its essence, it is an exchange of stability for lenience on matters of democracy and rule of law. A majority representative encapsulated this thinking: 'The EU came to strengthen the rule of law here but did the opposite. The purpose was to make the local judges competent enough for EULEX to leave – but today it is worse than it was in 2008. [The] EU is more interested in stability with Serbia than with what is going on within the country.'[34] Another saw the main challenge to the sector being in 'a political class which has been installed for the sake of stability.... But these political leaders have embedded the structures of corruption and organised crime – the underground is becoming part of the mainstream politics'.[35] The EU was seen to be needing these leaders for greater purposes with no interest in holding them accountable.

This sentiment resonated with what EULEX staff told us about how they sensed that the EU maintained a balance between various strong groups needed for broader political agendas. Many listed subtle forms of pressure: EU prosecutors were let known informally that a certain person should or should not be indicted; EULEX Head of Judges reassigned a sensitive case from a certain judge; interim court measures were not implemented by EULEX police; the content of press statements was changed somewhere above; issues raised about the handling of a case never received a reply, etc.[36] These examples illustrate the atmosphere among staff and one EULEX employee argued that she constantly feels like there are other things at work. She continued that when things are a bit out of the ordinary, staff are never told why they happen the way they do and that this is not how an independent judiciary is supposed to function. She spoke of a constant consideration of other EU objectives by the management, resulting in the mandate of the mission not being implemented properly.

Other examples related to cases EULEX was seen as prioritising. While the European Court of Auditors (2012: 10) concluded that given the international nature of organised crime, EU security objectives had not been adequately integrated into the mission, our interlocutors offered different opinions. One of them argued that the biggest impact coming out of EULEX deployment was the international police cooperation. He continued that through the EU presence on the ground, EULEX investigators were helping build cases in their home countries and that more had been done on this than on the organised crime in Kosovo itself.[37]

Broader political considerations not related to the primary objective of the mission were a source of constant frustration to EULEX staff and some openly stated that despite its heavy footprint, the EU was not serious about the rule of law in Kosovo. This lack of normative commitment was recognised as the core problem for the mission also by our local interlocutors. According to our experts, the EU's broader political objectives and its prioritisation of the dialogue process between Pristina and Belgrade may have come at the expense of contributing to building transparency and democracy. The conflict of interest became obvious as some of the individuals, who were deemed by the general public as prime candidates for EULEX investigations, were the very same individuals that the EU relies on as partners for the dialogue process. Locals and internationals alike agreed that the stability argument (conflict management) not only trumped the good governance argument (conflict transformation) but actively undermined its implementation. The bottom-up dimension, an essential component of conflict transformation, was seen as absent from the EU's approach.

Conclusions

This chapter analysed the EU's crisis response in the Western Balkans through the lens of EULEX. By exploring how those immediately responsible for mandate execution and those directly affected by its outcomes perceive EULEX, we discover gaps that highlight the pitfalls of direct and ingrained political interference in the mission's work. While EULEX has been seen as an important watchdog for preventing further human rights abuses, the EU's approach to Kosovo and the region continues to be characterised by competing priorities: the EU's broader political objectives impact the mission's legal work and hamper the EU in achieving a coherent and impactful rule of law policy. In turn, this decreases the local populations' trust and approval of EULEX and ultimately undermines the EU's overall goals of promoting good governance and a European perspective for Kosovo. This tension highlights the incompatibility of the EU's short-term focus on crisis management and the more long-term focus on crisis transformation.

While we know that conflicts do not develop in a linear fashion, we still tend to think of conflict *responses* as broadly linear processes where learning accumulates and transmutes to a more ambitious endeavour. In Kosovo, the international community first

Securitisation of the EU approach to the Western Balkans 133

engaged in conflict management trying to stabilise the crisis with military and police presence, but soon expanded its ambitions to conflict transformation. UN and EU assistance to the rule of law sector, including the two executive missions, have been the best examples of the international community's conflict transformation plans. As a priority, these missions focused on accountability and good governance. However, our findings suggest that due to the emphasis put on the normalisation process between Belgrade and Pristina, which to a large degree is an elite-driven process, the bottom-up accountability and good governance ended up compromised. It is pertinent to ask, whether this is due to the conflict response adapting to the changing terrain or whether the EU abandoned its normative commitments to the region. Our interviews suggest the answer is the latter.

Notes

1 This chapter has received funding from the EU's Horizon 2020 research and innovation programme under grant agreement number: 693337. The authors would like to thank Beti Hohler, Tringa Naka and Florian Qehaja for their help in conducting fieldwork. They would also like to thank the editors for their feedback on earlier drafts.
2 Parts of this book chapter draw on material published as Osland and Peter (2019).
3 Interview Osland with local actor 5, 24 October 2017.
4 Interview Osland with local actor 6, 28 October 2017.
5 Interviews Peter with EULEX staff 1, 3 and 6, 23 and 24 October 2017.
6 Interview Osland with local actor 1, 23 October 2017.
7 Interview Osland and Peter with local actor 11, 26 October 2017.
8 Interview Osland with local actor 5, 24 October 2017.
9 Interview Peter with local judge 1, 25 October 2017.
10 Interview Peter with local judge 2, 25 October 2017.
11 Interviews Peter with EULEX staff 4 and 8, 24 and 27 October 2017.
12 Interview Peter with EULEX staff 7, 27 October 2017.
13 Interview Peter with EULEX staff 6, 24 October 2017.
14 Interview Peter with EULEX staff 10, 27 October 2017.
15 Interview Peter with EULEX staff 1, 23 October 2017.
16 Interview Peter with local judge 2, 25 October 2017.
17 Interview Peter with EULEX staff 6, 24 October 2017.
18 Interview Peter with EULEX staff 4, 24 October 2017.

19 Interview Peter with EULEX staff 9, 27 October 2017.
20 Interview Peter with EULEX staff 6, 24 October 2017.
21 Interview Peter with EULEX staff 4 and 6, 24 October 2017.
22 Interview Peter with local judge 2, 25 October 2017.
23 Interview Peter with EULEX staff 1, 23 October 2017.
24 Interview Osland with local actor 7, 25 October 2017.
25 Interview Osland and Peter with local actor 9, 26 October 2017.
26 Interview Osland with local actor 5, 24 October 2017.
27 Interview Osland with local actor 6, 28 October 2017.
28 Interview Osland with local actor 5, 24 October 2017 and with local actor 6, 28 October 2017.
29 Interview Osland with local actor 7, 25 October 2017.
30 Interview Osland with local actor 1, 23 October 2017.
31 For an overview of links on the EU's relations with the Western Balkans, see https://eeas.europa.eu/regions/western-balkans/7859/western-balkans_en (accessed 13 January 2018).
32 EULEX Kosovo, mandate of the Strengthening Division, see www.eulex-kosovo.eu/?page=2,3 (accessed 13 January 2018).
33 Interview Peter with EULEX staff 6, 24 October 2017.
34 Interview Osland with local actor 8, 25 October 2017.
35 Interview Osland with local actor 1, 23 October 2017
36 To completely protect the anonymity of interviewees on this sensitive issue, no reference to specific interviews is made in this paragraph. This is something that was promised to the interlocutors (Peter).
37 Interview Peter with EULEX staff 2, 23 October 2017.

References

Autesserre, S. (2014) *Peaceland: Conflict Resolution and the Everyday Politics of International Intervention* (Cambridge: Cambridge University Press).

Bátora, J. K. Osland and M. Peter (2017) 'The EU's crisis management in the Kosovo-Serbia crises', EUNPACK Working Paper, D.5.1, EUNPACK project.

Caplan, R. (2005) 'Who guards the guardians? International accountability in Bosnia', *International Peacekeeping*, 12(3): 463–476, doi: 10.1080/13533310500074549.

Capussela, A.L. (2015) *State-Building in Kosovo: Democracy, Corruption and the EU in the Balkans* (London: I.B. Tauris).

Chesterman, S. (2004) *You, The People: The United Nations, Transitional Administration, and State-Building* (Oxford: Oxford University Press).

Council of the European Union (2008a) Council Joint Action 2008/124/CFSP of 4 February 2008 on the European Union Rule of Law Mission in Kosovo, EULEX Kosovo. Official Journal of the European Union, L 42/92.

Council of the European Union (2008b) 'Javier Solana, EU High Representative for CFSP, announces the start of EULEX Kosovo' (S400/08) (2008b), www.consilium.europa.eu/uedocs/cms_Data/docs/pressdata/en/declarations104524.pdf (accessed 12 January 2018).

de Coning, C. and M. Peter (eds) (2019) *United Nations Peace Operations in a Changing Global Order* (Cham: Palgrave Macmillan).

Ejdus, F. (2017) '"Here is your mission, now own it!" The rhetoric and practice of local ownership in EU interventions', *European Security*, 26(4): 461–484, doi: 10.1080/09662839.2017.1333495.

Ejdus, F. and A.E. Juncos (2018) 'Reclaiming the local in EU peacebuilding: Effectiveness, ownership, and resistance', *Contemporary Security Policy*, 39(1): 4–27.

Emini, D. (2016) *The Citizens' Opinion of the Police Force: The Results of a Public Opinion Survey Conducted in Kosovo*, Pointpulse (Prishtina: Kosovar Centre for Security Policy), https://pointpulse.net/wp-content/uploads/2016/09/POINTPULSE-2016-KOS-ENG.pdf (accessed 13 January 2018).

European Commission (2005) 'A European Future for Kosovo' COM (2005) 156 (Brussels: Communication from the Commission, 20 April), http://europa.eu/rapid/press-release_IP-05–450_en.htm (accessed 13 January 2018).

European Commission (2008) 'Enlargement Strategy and Main Challenges 2008–2009' (Brussels: Communication from the Commission to the Council and the European Parliament, 5 November).

European External Action Service (EEAS) (2018) *European Union Rule of Law Mission in Kosovo (EULEX)* (online), www.eulex-kosovo.eu/?page=2,16 (accessed 7 January 2018).

European Court of Auditors (2012) *European Union Assistance to Kosovo Related to the Rule of Law*, Special Report No. 18, www.eca.europa.eu/Lists/ECADocuments/SR12_18/SR12_18_EN.PDF (accessed 13 January 2018).

EU (2015) *Review of the EULEX Kosovo Mission's Implementation of the Mandate with a Particular Focus on the Handling of the Recent Allegations*. Report to the attention of the High Representative/Vice President of the European Commission, Ms Federica Mogherini. Brussels (31 March), www.eulex-kosovo.eu/?page=2,11,201 (accessed 13 January 2018).

EU (2019) 'The European Union's Global Strategy: Three years on, looking forward' (Brussels: EU), https://eeas.europa.eu/sites/eeas/files/eu_global_strategy_2019.pdf (accessed 13 January 2018).

European Union HR/VP (2016) *Shared Vision, Common Action: A Stronger Europe. A Global Strategy for the European Union's Foreign and Security Policy* (Brussels: EU), https://eeas.europa.eu/sites/eeas/files/eugs_review_web_0.pdf (accessed 13 January 2018).
Galtung, J. (1973) *The European Community: A Superpower in the Making* (London: Allen & Unwin).
Gelot, L. (2017) 'Civilian protection in Africa: How the protection of civilians is being militarized by African policymakers and diplomats', *Contemporary Security Policy*, 38(1): 161–173, doi: 10.1080/13523260.2017.1291564.
Goetschel, L. and T. Hagmann (2009) 'Civilian peacebuilding: Peace by bureaucratic means? Analysis', *Conflict, Security & Development*, 9(1): 55–73, doi: 10.1080/14678800802704911.
Grady, K. (2010) 'Sexual exploitation and abuse by UN Peacekeepers: A threat to impartiality', *International Peacekeeping*, 17(2): 215–228.
Hunt, C.T. (2017) 'All necessary means to what ends? The unintended consequences of the 'robust turn' in UN peace operations', *International Peacekeeping*, 24(1): 108–131, doi: 10.1080/13533312.2016.1214074.
Ioannides, I. and G. Collantes-Celador (2011) 'The internal–external security nexus and EU police/rule of law missions in the Western Balkans', *Conflict, Security & Development*, 11(4): 415–445, doi: 10.1080/14678802.2011.614127.
Jennings, K.M. and M. Bøås (2015) 'Transactions and interactions: Everyday life in the peacekeeping economy', *Journal of Intervention and Statebuilding*, 9(3): 281–295.
Kanetake, M. (2010) 'Whose zero tolerance counts? Reassessing a zero tolerance policy against sexual exploitation and abuse by UN Peacekeepers', *International Peacekeeping*, 17(2): 200–214.
Kmezić, M. and F. Bieber (eds) (2017) *The Crisis of Democracy in the Western Balkans. An Anatomy of Stabilitocracy and the Limits of EU Democracy Promotion*, Policy Study (Belgrade/Graz: BiEPAG, March).
Laurence, M. (2019) 'An "impartial" force? Normative ambiguity and practice change in UN Peace Operations', *International Peacekeeping*, 26(3): 256–280, doi: 10.1080/13533312.2018.1517027.
Lemay-Hébert, N. and S. Kappler (2016) 'What attachment to peace? Exploring the normative and material dimensions of local ownership in peacebuilding', *Review of International Studies*, 42(5): 895–914, doi: 10.1017/S0260210516000061.
Mac Ginty, R. (2008) 'Indigenous peace-making versus the liberal peace', *Cooperation and Conflict*, 43(2): 139–163, doi: 10.1177/0010836708089080.

Manners, I. (2002) 'Normative power Europe: a contradiction in terms?' *JCMS: Journal of Common Market Studies*, 40(2): 235–258.
O'Neill, W.G. (2001) *Kosovo: An Unfinished Peace* (Boulder, CO: Lynne Rienner Publishers).
Osland, K.M. (2019) 'UN policing – the security-trust challenge', in C. de Coning and M. Peter (eds), *United Nations Peace Operations in a Changing Global Order* (Cham: Palgrave Macmillan), 191–209.
Osland, K.M. and M. Peter (2019) 'The double proximity paradox in peacebuilding: Implementation and perception of the EU rule of law mission in Kosovo', *European Security*, 28(4): 493–512, doi: 10.1080/09662839.2019.1649658.
Paris, R. (2004) *At War's End: Building Peace After Civil Conflict* (Cambridge: Cambridge University Press).
Paris, R. and T.D. Sisk (eds) (2009) *The Dilemmas of Statebuilding: Confronting the Contradictions of Postwar Peace Operations* (Abingdon: Routledge).
Peter, M. (2015) 'Between doctrine and practice: The United Nations peacekeeping dilemma', *Global Governance*, 21(3): 351–370.
Peter, M. (2019) 'Peacekeeping: Resilience of an idea', in C. de Coning and M. Peter (eds), *United Nations Peace Operations in a Changing Global Order* (London: Palgrave Macmillan), 25–44.
Raineri, L. and F. Strazzari (2019) '(B)ordering hybrid security? EU stabilisation practices in the Sahara-Sahel Region', *Ethnopolitics*, 18(5): 544–559, doi: 10.1080/17449057.2019.1640509.
Richmond, O.P. (ed.) (2010) *Palgrave Advances in Peacebuilding: Critical Developments and Approaches* (London: Palgrave Macmillan).
Richmond, O.P., S. Pogodda and R. Mac Ginty (2016) 'Towards critical crisis transformation', EUNPACK Working Paper D.3.2, EUNPACK project.
Simic, O. (2009) 'Rethinking "sexual exploitation" in UN peacekeeping operations', *Women's Studies International Forum*, 32(4): 288–295.
Skendaj, E. (2014) *Creating Kosovo: International Oversight and the Making of Ethical Institutions* (Ithaca, NY: Cornell University Press).
Tull, D.M. (2018) 'The limits and unintended consequences of UN peace enforcement: The Force Intervention Brigade in the DR Congo', *International Peacekeeping*, 25(2): 167–190, doi: 10.1080/13533312.2017.1360139.
UN (1999) UNSC Resolution 1244 S/RES/1244(1999) (10 June).
UN (2003) *Secretary-General's Bulletin: Special Measures for Protection from Sexual Exploitation and Sexual Abuse* ST/SGB/2003/13 (9 October).
UN (2008) *United Nations Peacekeeping Operations: Principles and Guidelines* (New York: UN DPKO/DFS).

UN (2017) *Report of the Secretary-General on Special Measures for Protection from Sexual Exploitation and Abuse: A New Approach*, A/71/818 (28 February).

Visoka, G. (2012) 'The "Kafkaesque accountability" of international governance in Kosovo', *Journal of Intervention and Statebuilding*, 6(2): 189–212, doi: 10.1080/17502977.2012.655603.

von Billerbeck, S.B.K. (2015) 'Local ownership and UN peacebuilding: Discourse versus operationalization', *Global Governance*, 21(2): 299–315, doi: 10.1163/19426720–02102007.

Youngs, R. (2004) 'Normative dynamics and strategic interests in the EU's external identity', *JCMS: Journal of Common Market Studies*, 42(2): 415–435.

6

The paradoxes of EU crisis response in Afghanistan, Iraq and Mali

Morten Bøås, Bård Drange, Dlawer Ala'Aldeen, Abdoul Wahab Cissé and Qayoom Suroush

Introduction

This chapter is based on extensive field research carried out within the framework of the EU Horizon 2020-funded project EUNPACK by four of the partner institutes: the Norwegian Institute of International Affairs (NUPI), the Middle East Research Institute (MERI) in Erbil, the Alliance for Rebuilding Governance in Africa (ARGA) and the Afghanistan Research and Evaluation Unit (AREU). In close cooperation, researchers from these institutes engaged with EU interventions in Afghanistan, Iraq and Mali over a period of three years. This engagement including a mixed-methods approach of qualitative interviews and surveys of target populations of supposed beneficiaries of EU programming. In total, more than a hundred qualitative in-depth interviews were carried out in Afghanistan, Iraq and Mali with members of the EU delegations, European training personnel, local and national government representatives, civil society organisations, academics and other stakeholders. Surveys targeting supposed beneficiaries of EU programming were also implemented in each country with a sample of together five hundred respondents (see Bøås *et al.*, forthcoming).

In this chapter we use the substance of all these data to conceptualise the obstacles that EU crisis response currently is facing through five paradoxes that permeate these operations. While all five paradoxes are not equally present in all cases, they characterise EU crisis response efforts and demand more attention from research and policy. These paradoxes are (1) that the EU strives for local ownership, but often fails to achieve this beyond national government consent, (2) that it aims for conflict sensitivity but creates

Brussels-based designs that are rarely tailor-made to local contexts, (3) that it seeks demand-driven crisis response, but ends up with a supply-based one, (4) that it intends to do statebuilding, but in reality pursues much narrower security objectives, and (5) that it preaches long-term solutions, but practices short-term conflict management efforts. What this suggests is an EU that in its external crisis response operations is not necessarily as norm-oriented as much of the EU literature suggests, but has increasingly moved towards a more realist and securitised approach to conflict management (see Bøås and Rieker, 2019). What is happening on the ground is therefore more an attempt of conflict management driven to a large extent by external security concerns that make the EU states' ambitions of contributing to conflict resolution and transformation hard, if not impossible to achieve. The main reason for this is that the five paradoxes that permeate these operations create a lack of local ownership and conflict sensitivity that leads programming of EU crisis response to become supply-driven and focused on short-term security objectives. This trend is present in all these three cases, but its manifestation is not uniform. It is most present in Mali, where narrow European security concerns with regard to terrorism and migration is a lead narrative for an international operation that in practice is becoming increasingly focused on achieving state stability through conflict management. It is less present in Afghanistan, where at least at times the EU has taken a slightly different approach than the United States (e.g., in police reform that we highlight in this chapter), while in the case of Iraq, the EU has never had a really visible presence due to the role of the United States.

An important finding explored in this chapter is that many of the challenges that the EU is facing relate to the inner functioning of the Union, including its ability to act as a unitary actor. That these key obstacles are primarily internal barriers is at the same time both discouraging and promising, in that the EU struggles to practice what it preaches – for example, conflict resolution and eventual conflict transformation – but that the potential to enhance the effectiveness of its crisis responses is significant. However, for this to take place substantial changes to the way the EU works are necessary.

At the heart of the EU's crisis response in Afghanistan, Iraq and Mali lies the restoration of state authority, primarily through efforts related to SSR. In theory, SSR concerns crucial elements of conflict resolution and transformation through the provision of human and state security with appropriate democratic oversight and control (Hänggi, 2004). Sedra (2010) moreover, suggests SSR processes are people-centred, locally driven and includes civil society. The extent to which practice dovetails the formal objective of SSR is, however, very limited. SSR processes are frequently criticised for not being people-centred, to be externally imposed, and to exclude – beyond the political and security elite – local actors like civil society (Gordon, 2014: 129; Mobekk, 2010; Jennings and Bøås, 2015). Indeed, according to Sedra (2010: 201), successful examples of SSR are in short supply. While numerous handbooks and guidelines exist (most prominently OECD DAC, 2007), and many efforts have been made, three key factors render most SSR programmes unsuccessful: lack of adaptation to local contexts, the blurring of what SSR really is, and a short-term perspective (Sedra, 2010: 103). Moreover, SSR becomes increasingly difficult when a particular security sector in question is engaged in wars. This is very much the case of Afghanistan, Iraq and Mali, and as Loschi *et al.* (2018: 18) argue, such cases, 'which often have short-term perspectives and occur in the absence of a more all-encompassing SSR ..., may well lead to the unwarranted legitimisation, co-option and institutionalisation of highly controversial security actors'.

EU crisis response in the extended neighbourhood

The EU has over the last two decades deployed several missions in conflict theatres far beyond its immediate borders. Its missions in Afghanistan, Iraq and Mali all have elements of humanitarian aid and SSR, including provisions for a potential move from conflict management to conflict resolution and transformation, but this potential is by and large not reached and while important similarities exists between these cases, the missions and their mandate are particular to each.

Afghanistan

The EU's intervention in Afghanistan followed the US entrance in 2001 after the 9/11 attacks. Between 2002 and 2007, European countries were primarily engaged bilaterally, where Italy (rule of law), Germany (the police) and the UK (counter-narcotics) all had their individual responsibilities (Suroush, 2018: 7). Many other European countries were involved through the NATO-led International Security Assistance Force (ISAF). In the reform of the police, the key priority of the German Police Project Office (GPPO) was the Kabul Police Academy (KPA), where senior police officers were trained. The rationale for such a top-down approach was the belief that only with professional and well-trained senior officers would the reform be effective (see International Crisis Group, 2007).

In 2006, the London Conference on Afghanistan had provided a new framework for cooperation between the Afghan government and the international community. Following a joint assessment mission to assess the 'Afghan needs in the rule of law sector' at the fall of 2006 (see European Court of Auditors, 2015), another fact-finding mission suggested that the EU should establish a mission to rebuild the Afghan National Police (ANP) (see EU, 2007). A year later, the EU approved EUPOL in Afghanistan. It was based on the same 'train the trainer' approach of the German programme that preceded it and was supposed to coordinate and benefit from the contributions of all European countries, essentially drawing together 'all non-US efforts' (Larivé, 2012: 191).

The first EUPOL was to be a non-executive mission, primarily to monitor, mentor, advice and train (EU, 2007). The mission was mainly involved with Afghanistan's Ministry of Interior Affairs, Ministry of Justice and Office of the Attorney General. The EUPOL mission was extended two more times: first in May 2010 and in December 2014 (until December 2016). The EUPOL budget from 2007 to December 2015 was around €457 million (European Court of Auditors, 2015).

EUPOL was to serve as a potent symbol for the EU's stated ambition to become a global security provider aiming beyond conflict management and security narrowly defined to become a key provider of a comprehensive civilian approach (see Fescharek, 2015). Therefore, the EU prevented donation of equipment which could have dual use, for instance, walkie-talkies. EUPOL was designed for the formation of viable, sustainable and effective civilian policing arrangements, under Afghan ownership that would guarantee proper interaction with the wider criminal justice system (Echavez and Suroush, 2017: 5). The outcome is as we will see much more mixed and much closer to a narrow approach to conflict management.

Iraq

Prior to the ousting of Saddam's Ba'athist Regime in 2003, the EU had no political or contractual ties with Iraq besides adhering to UN sanction mandates and extending humanitarian aid in the aftermath of the 1991 Uprising. The EU was the second largest contributor of humanitarian aid behind the UNHCR.

The 2003 Iraq War unearthed faultlines within the EU since key EU member states failed to unify under one banner, thus calling into question the viability of having a common EU foreign policy (Spyer, 2007). Gradually, EU-Iraq relations warmed, underpinned by two agreements: Memorandum of Understanding on Energy Cooperation and Partnership; and a Cooperation Agreement. The former, signed in January 2010, pertains to developing energy ties and collaborating on mutually beneficial projects, while the latter, signed in 2012, deals with partnering on vital political, security, human rights and environmental issues, among others. Once the EU established a permanent presence in Iraq, its engagement there increasingly involved collaborating with international and national actors to enhance the nation's capacity in several realms, including rule of law, capacity-building, development assistance, and – most recently – SSR. Thus, initially the EU's aspirations in Iraq boiled down to two key interventions, namely the EUJUST LEX-Iraq and interventions on reconstruction, development and humanitarian aid.

EUJUST LEX-Iraq sought (a) to promote closer collaboration between the different actors across the criminal justice system, (b) strengthen the management capacity of senior and high-potential officials for the police, judiciary and penitentiary, and (c) improve skills and procedures in criminal investigation in full respect for the rule of law and human rights (Peters *et al.*, 2018).

The backdrop for the EU's work on reconstruction, development and humanitarian aid lies in the EU's emphasis on identifying a more comprehensive approach than purely conflict management to support political and economic reconstruction, which included development and humanitarian aid. The need for humanitarian aid was evident, as the EU pointed to the catastrophic humanitarian situation in Iraq, which was closely linked to the level of violence. The need for longer term development aid was clear too, which had the EU pledge support for improving basic state services to the people. In these efforts, the EU's projects were primarily directed at human rights and rule of law, capacity-building in primary and secondary education, and sustainable energy for all (see Peters et al., 2018).

Mali

While the EU has been active in Mali earlier, its most recent engagement with the security sector in Mali started in February 2013 with the establishment of the EUTM to Mali. Its engagement was expanded with the establishment of EUCAP Sahel Mali in 2015. These missions form part of the EU's efforts to restore state authority in Mali. While the EU, along with other donors, has long been present in Mali as a development partner, these programmes have a stronger emphasis on conflict management through security in their approach than previous ones, a result of increasing instability in Mali since 2012. Both EUTM and EUCAP arose from a request from the Malian Government and are based on the UN Security Council resolution 2085 of 2012.

EUTM Mali seeks to enhance the leadership skills within the Malian Army by providing 'legal and leadership skills education as well as on tactical and strategical education, training planning process, basic military principles and International Humanitarian Law' (EEAS, 2016:1). The EUTM's third mandate given in March 2016 expanded operations northwards towards the river Niger loop, and hence intended to expand trainings to the regions of Gao and Timbuktu. Per 2017, the EUTM consists of 575 officers, with participants from 27 countries (EUTM, 2018). In 2018, the EU Council almost doubled funding from €33.4 million in 2016–18 to €59.7 million for 2018–20 and amended the mission 'to include in its objectives the provision of advice and training support to the G5 Sahel Joint Force, as part of the EU's ongoing efforts to support the G5 Sahel process' (EUTM, 2018). Most of the EUTM personnel are stationed in the Koulikoro training camp 60 kilometres north-east of Bamako. EUTM Mali remains a non-executive mission and does, therefore, not participate in combat nor accompany the Malian army in operational zones (EEAS, 2016).

In 2015, the EU expanded its engagement in Mali with the establishment of EUCAP. This provides 'assistance and advice to the national police, the national gendarmerie and the national guard in the implementation of the security reform set out by the new government' (EUCAP, 2018: 1). It has, until October 2017, trained around 3,400 officers in, among other subjects, command structure, professional methods, human rights and gender issues (EUCAP, 2017). Its mandate was in January 2017 renewed until January 2019, with a budget of €29.7 million the first year of operations. In its second mandate, there is a greater emphasis on Mali's counter-terrorism services as well as support to Malian authorities concerning irregular migration, including trafficking, as well as border control (EUCAP, 2017).

Another component of the EU's efforts within the Malian security sector concerns borders and border management. The EU perceives the 'problem of porous borders' to be one of the key challenges in Mali, and in the Sahel region more broadly, and is therefore involved in a number of such projects. While border control became part of EUCAP's second mandate in 2017, the EU also funds mostly security-focused programmes through the newly established EUTF. One important programme is PARSEC, a EUTF programme that aims to support enhanced security and of the management of border areas in the Mopti and Gao regions. However, it is currently only focusing on Mopti and the border to Burkina Faso. This programme is working in coordination with EUCAP and EUTM but is also operating as a supporting component of a larger Malian plan for enhancing state forces and supporting local governors' capacity to protect and administer security.[1]

The five paradoxes that characterise EU crisis response

The red thread in the EU's performance in its crisis responses is the gap between intentions and implementations. While it wishes to conduct its operations based on principles close to conflict resolution and conflict transformation that many – per 2020 – believe are laudable (like local ownership and conflict sensitivity), it continuously fails to walk the talk, thus mainly remains a provider of attempts at crisis response through conflict management tools and approaches. This section analyses the five paradoxes the EU faces in Afghanistan, Iraq and Mali. These are analysed in a loosely defined chronological order – from ideas and intentions to implementation and results.

Lacking local ownership

Local ownership is generally seen as a precondition for effective third-party intervention (Osland, 2014), and therefore crucial for conflict resolution and transformation, but international institutions struggle to achieve this (Mac Ginty and Richmond, 2013; Bøås and Stig, 2010). This is also the case for the EU, which remains reluctant to get involved with local actors on the ground, and which struggles with balancing the interests and desires of local populations with those of its own.

Local ownership and conflict sensitivity are interlinked concepts and often analysed together. This concern, in short, is the extent to which local forces own and work to implement any programme, and the extent to which external actors tailor-make their response to a specific setting. In other words, while local ownership is here thought to create the framework within which actions and programmes are implemented, conflict sensitivity concerns more the content of those actions and programmes. For example, while an external actor may garner support from local governments and interest groups for a border management programme on the Mali-Niger border, it may – because it is not conflict-sensitive – serve to increase tension in the area and not contribute to resolving root causes, thus not only quite effectively preventing conflict resolution and transformation, but also highly likely being counterproductive for conflict management.

Local ownership concerns the extent to which actions and programmes are anchored in and driven by local forces, where the government typically plays a central role. The opposite of local ownership, then, is essentially the imposition of actions and programmes by external actors. The consequences of lacking local ownership include lacking political support and willingness to drive through these changes, a lack of actors and agents to implement any programme, and probably ill-adapted programmes which are – as we see in the next paradox – not intended to solve underlying issues but address one's own agenda.

In Mali, the EU policy has been to leave a 'light footprint' through building ownership with local partners and with people on the ground. However, the programme designs seem predominantly to arise from policy-makers in Brussels concerned with terrorism, trafficking and refugees. While there is significant interest in Mali in tackling both the issues of terrorism and migration, the relevance and local rooting of policies are limited. According to Peters *et al.* (2018: 82) there seems to be a 'lack of clear distinction between the different groups in Mali in the respective Council documents', suggesting a lack of grounded conflict sensitivity. This is likely partly a result of a tendency to develop policies in Brussels with limited consultations with local partners in Mali – sometimes even the EU delegation itself.[2] As the National Platform for Civil Society in Mali (an organisation that coordinates civil society in Mali) suggest: 'They ask our opinions, but then don't want to further engage with us. They ask us to comment about pre-conceived needs, not about our needs.'[3] Indeed, the EU has already acknowledged the need for local ownership of external assistance programmes, but this has rarely been employed in practice (Mac Ginty and Richmond, 2013; Bøås and Stig, 2010).

Similarly, in Iraq, the EU has proclaimed its desire for local ownership, but has ended up supporting international NGOs in their work. While, ideally, local NGOs with extensive knowledge, networks and belonging are hired for its humanitarian aid projects, international NGOs are the ones receiving most of the EU's support. The predominant logic is that local NGOs do not have the operational capacity to implement large projects, and – which often goes unstated – do not always have the trust of international actors to handle resources given with enough accountability.[4] However, there are exceptions, including the efforts of the Deutsche Gesellschaft für Internationale Zusammenarbeit (GIZ) to train local NGOs (Mohammed, 2018).

Finding the right actors to cooperate with is challenging in a polarised conflict zone like Iraq. However, to be effective, it is key to be cognisant of local power dynamics and the limited control of the central government in Baghdad (Mohammed et al., 2017).

In Afghanistan, the EU's police mission EUPOL was implemented with little local ownership, and with limited support even from the Afghan police officials themselves. Afghan officials were involved only to a limited extent with design and implementation and were often not aware of EUPOL activities. While there were significant efforts to include national stakeholders, confidentiality of, for example, documents prevented further cooperation and joint benchmarking (Suroush, 2018: 19). A Ministry of Interior official stated: 'It was not clear to us how much budget they had and how they were spending their budget.'[5] In general, police officials were unhappy with EUPOL's 'long and complicated procedures' of decision-making, including 'too much reliance' on individual member states.[6] Moreover, the EU was criticised for not having built any relationship with Afghan civil society organisations.[7]

Indeed, '[d]espite their rhetoric of national ownership, the US and other Western donors' control SSR processes on the ground' (Baranyi and Salahub, 2011: 50). The intervention in Afghanistan was, in general, largely externally driven, and the Afghan government was given little power to impact the designs. In Afghanistan, then, as in Iraq, 'hard' security priorities in line with a narrow conflict management – like training and equipping security forces – have displaced or undermined 'soft' justice and governance reforms (Baranyi and Salahub, 2011). While the US preference for a military approach largely dwarfed the EU's more civilian attempts, the EU also failed to cooperate extensively with local actors. While this is understandable given the dire security situation and the high levels of corruption, such an approach also has consequences. 'Western actors have not invested enough in understanding local complexities and have therefore made costly mistakes: the West is fuelling conflict by aligning itself to certain elites, ethnic groups and paramilitary forces in each society' (Baranyi and Salahub, 2011: 50). As has been alluded to earlier, SSR in post-authoritarian and post-conflict societies remains challenging (Hänggi, 2004) if not 'impossible' in cases of protracted wars like Afghanistan and Iraq (Wulf, 2004: 6), thus also suggesting the huge challenge of achieving much more than relatively benign conflict management at least in a short-term horizon.

Elusive conflict sensitivity

Conflict sensitivity is, in the literature, often lauded as key to success and an essential component of any crisis response. However, while 'recognised as an important priority from systemic and organizational perspectives, it nonetheless remains conceptually elusive' (Handschin *et al.*, 2016: 4). APFO *et al.* (2004: 1) has suggested a generic definition where conflict sensitivity is the ability of an organisation to understand the context in which it operates; to understand the interaction between its intervention and the context; and to act upon the understanding of this interaction, in order to minimise negative impacts and maximise positive impacts. The real challenge of conflict sensitivity, however, is to transform generic claims of being conflict-sensitive into concrete conflict-sensitive analyses and programming.

In Mali, the EU intends to be conflict-sensitive, but does not manage this in a coherent manner. While the minimal requirement – the government's consent – was obtained in Mali, the 'EU's output effectiveness has also been hampered by a low degree of conflict sensitivity and encountered problems in creating local ownership in qualitative terms, although the quantitative metrics show a more positive result' (Peters *et al.*, 2018: 83). Indeed, our summary of perception studies in Mali suggest that over half of the respondents found the EU to be conflict-sensitive. This probably implies that the respondents benefited from the EU's support, and that the support was needed. Perhaps it also mattered that interviews were conducted in the capital city Bamako only, where the conflict may not be felt as directly, and where many might in any case prefer the current situation over the highly tumultuous times in 2012–13 (Cissé *et al.*, 2017: 7). In other parts of Mali, however, where the security situation has made needs assessments impossible and where local beneficiaries are not consulted, projects often lack relevance.[8] Hence, we have reason to suggest that EU conflict sensitivity is limited, and thereby its potential for conflict resolution and transformation.

Indeed, the EU's real intentions to tailor-make policies to the Malian context was questioned by respondents. One informant with intimate knowledge about the EU in Mali suggested Mali may be a 'laboratory for EU crisis response policies'.[9] While the EU may wish to be conflict-sensitive, it seemed like the EU system left programme designs rushed and without the necessary (and ideally sought-after) local consultations. An example is the EU's border management efforts in the larger Sahel region, where the objective is to stop transnational terrorism and cross-border illicit trafficking while facilitating legal trade (Bøås *et al.*, 2018: 21). These efforts are curious, however. For example, 'terrorists and agents of organised crime' are already on Malian territory, and securing Mali's vast borders requires more personnel than Mali can provide – and EU personnel may hardly help, as they are restricted from much of the relevant areas due to security concerns. Moreover, these borders posts will be easy to tackle for smugglers who can bribe the officers – as they did in Niger (see Molenaar *et al.*, 2017) – or simply enter through less-protected and peripheral crossings. It is hard to believe, however, that half a day of human rights training or countercorruption training at EUCAP would counteract this livelihood strategy (see Bøås *et al.*, 2018: 21). Rather, this may lead to further securitisation, cross-border trafficking and smuggling (see Strazzari, 2015). Many interviewees were sceptical, noting that these projects were missing key smuggling routes,[10] saying that 'these projects are designed to fail'.[11]

While improved border management in the Sahel is a high priority for the EU, this may not necessarily be the case for local stakeholders and communities. In fact, for some local communities who depend on cross-border trade and other types of economic activities, it may seem more like a threat to their livelihoods than beneficial. This approach has also to take into consideration the ECOWAS protocol of free movement and trade (Raineri, 2018). Rather than seeking to accommodate local populations, the EU's approach seems more designed to solve its own potential problems, primarily migration, trafficking and terrorism.

Similar dynamics were identified in Iraq, where beneficiaries found the EU's crisis response conflict-sensitive, while key informants suggest the EU lacks this: indeed, judging by the results of perceptions studies conducted, 81.3 per cent of beneficiaries of EU humanitarian aid in Iraq say they find the EU's crisis response conflict-sensitive. The same beneficiaries also found that the EU's crisis response helped alleviate the crisis (82.4 per cent) (Mohammed *et al.*, 2017: 6). These data, most likely, suggest that at least some of these people's needs were met by the EU's crisis response. However, this may not be the case beyond the four Kurdish cities (Erbil, Sulaymaniyah, Dohuk, Kirkuk) in which the survey was carried out. Indeed, key informants interviewed were more critical, suggesting the EU considers 'Iraq as one unit, while on the ground such a thing does not exist. There is no reason to have a project on how to swim where there is no sea in that place', while a civil society activist explained that 'the EU has been influenced by their one Iraq policy. They cannot do any project in Kurdistan Region unless the same is done in Baghdad or another part of Iraq. Different governorates (provinces) may require different needs. But the EU does not have this approach' (Mohammed, 2018: 16–17).

Also, in Afghanistan we see several examples of a lack of conflict sensitivity. On the more fundamental level, the originally German approach of rebuilding the ANP was flawed, as police structures were for all practical purposes non-existent (Larivé, 2012). Later on, in Italy's lead efforts on judiciary reform (Larivé, 2012), they hardly understood the issue at hand, and its efforts faced a lack of political will in the Afghan government to reform (Burke, 2014: 1). Furthermore, few international advisors knew Islamic law well – critical in a justice system with large influence from this (Burke, 2014: 12). These examples illustrate how the EU seems very far away from building local ownership and making interventions conflict-sensitive, lowering any hope that it might achieve its higher ambitions of conflict resolution and transformation.

Demand or supply?

Some of the reasons for which local ownership, but primarily conflict sensitivity, remain elusive can be found in another paradox; while the EU's crisis response seeks to be demand-driven, it is rather supply-driven. While conflict sensitivity, per our definition above, asks interventions to minimise negative impact and maximise positive impact, interventions are seldom planned and designed around the interests of the local population. Rather, interventions arise from a complex web of reasons, many (or often most) of which are external to the conflict itself. Afghanistan, Iraq and Mali are certainly no exceptions.

Taking Afghanistan as an example, we see that external powers engaged in the first place as a US and consequently NATO response to the 9/11 attacks. The intervention, then, was driven by external actors' – notably US – efforts to fight terrorism. The interests of the United States, then, drove policy and the external intervention in Afghanistan, making Afghanistan the key example of the 'war on terror'. While on widely different scales, then, in Afghanistan the external interventions in SSR were either the US quick train-and-equip strategy, which prepared policemen also to conduct counter-insurgency, or the German (and later EU) approach of three year-long trainings but only for a few people (International Crisis Group, 2007).

Despite talk of the United States and its more militaristic approach undermining the EU's civilian ones, one should keep in mind the EU's intentions to – contrary to what they saw the United States doing – conflict resolution. The intention, in other words, seemed 'right', but the strategy to get there was – as we have seen – characterised by numerous flaws. Understanding the reasons for the EU's entrance, though, cannot be taken by their stated intentions. Their entry was – as often is the case – more based on their readiness to supply rather than meet Afghanistan's needs (Peters *et al.*, 2018). When the United States increased deployment around 2006, moreover, the EU faced a dilemma: not sending any forces (and damaging transatlantic relations) or launching a civilian EU mission (Peters *et al.*, 2018).

Member states' diverse interests explain the supply-based approach. France, for example, is key in many francophone countries, such as Mali. Such interests, however, are not necessarily of negative value, as it could also foster the necessary willingness to conduct important interventions. However, as with France in Mali, it enters with its own agenda, which in few ways corresponds with Malian priorities. However, the French success in generating sufficient support for international interventions in the country, also suggests the international community's interests were substantial, seeking to manage a conflict that security experts already in 2013 feared could spill over to neighbouring Burkina Faso and Niger (see Bøås *et al.*, 2020). It was indeed the UN Security Council resolution that laid the basis for the French and UN operations, which also formed the background for the EU mission. The EU, however, also entered with their agendas, which were heavily influenced by the French insistence, but also on the overall issues of migration, trafficking and terrorism (Bøås et al., 2018).

In Afghanistan, European countries engaged in the first place with the United States as a response to the 9/11 attacks. Later, it sought to carve out a different approach in Afghanistan. Its rhetoric was one of providing a more civilian approach to the US paramilitary approach, where policemen were supposed to engage in counter-insurgency efforts (Suroush, 2018: 11–12). While this has been hailed by some as necessary and important, others suggest that the EU's approach has made little impact given the massive military strength of the United States. Moreover, also within the theme of civilian policing in Afghanistan, the EU has supplied more of what it finds important, rather than basing their approach on the needs and requests of Afghans. The EU's two flagship initiatives in Afghanistan, for example – the Crime Management College and the Staff Management College in Kabul – were both funded through intense German pressure (Fescharek, 2015: 49). Indeed, the content of the EU's crisis response is very much based on the willingness of individual member states to provide funding and personnel.

The main implication being that the interests of EU member states, such as France in Mali, trump efforts to build local ownership and conflict sensitivity. Such constellations, showing the diverse interests of EU member states, also have operational challenges – for example, in Afghanistan, where member states are reluctant to merge or even cooperate their police missions with that of the EU one (see, e.g., Kaldor et al., 2018). This was also a key challenge for EUPOL in Afghanistan as key member countries decided to contribute to the NATO Training Mission-Afghanistan (NTM-A) instead of EUPOL (Peters et al., 2018). 'When push came to shove,' as Buckley phrases it, 'most countries prioritise their national interests' (Buckley, 2010: 3), making a narrow approach to conflict management the only likely outcome.

Securitisation v. statebuilding

Since 2015, the liberal peace agenda has been waning in importance and support, paving the way, rather, for a more realist and securitised approach to conflicts, focusing on state stability to conflict management. This development is illustrated by the UN's three so-called 'stabilisation' missions in the DR Congo, Central African Republic and Mali. Hence, Karlsrud (2018: 1) argues that 'Western states are shifting their strategy from liberal peacebuilding to stabilisation and counterterrorism'. The consequences, Karlsrud warns, is that 'by primarily providing military support to suppress what is defined as security threats, states like the United States and France are not addressing root causes like weak and corrupt governance, marginalisation and lack of social cohesion' (Karlsrud, 2018: 11).

The question is therefore whether the EU only is trying to manage conflicts without any real attempt at tackling root causes. We argue that the answer to this is not yes or no, but more blurred. On the one hand, the EU seeks to, more than the direct involvements of France in Mali and the United States in Afghanistan and Iraq, tackle root causes. On the other, however, while these intentions are good, its programming and implementation are not apt to achieve the intended impact. Rather, they seem more and more to follow a securitisation approach, where its own interests in combating terrorism, trafficking and tackling migration come first. Indeed, more than building the state and securing the people, the EU increasingly secure a disputed state with potentially counterproductive consequences for the people, but also in the long run for Europe's interests and security.

The EU recognises the importance of long-term capacity-building of the Malian security apparatus, and it recognises the importance of civilian policing in Afghanistan. Efforts to build capacities and a civilian police force seem, on paper, valuable, but several elements prevent an effective implementation. First, its efforts seem ill-adapted to building the state and seem rather to build up under a securitisation agenda which does not solve underlying efforts, making conflict resolution and transformation almost impossible to achieve given current approaches. In all the cases examined, the security apparatuses the EU seeks to contribute to building, are not strong and lacks legitimacy at least among segments of the populations. As has been argued in the case of Mali above, deep-rooted changes in the composition of the police force and military and in the management culture is necessary in the long run. As we elaborate on below, the EU's efforts seem hardly sustainable in the long run in Mali. In Afghanistan, the inclusion and support of women police is important, and may have planted some seeds for the development of a more civilian and women-friendly police in the future. However, the small-scale trainings – both in terms of length of training and number of policewomen trained – is small and can easily be reversed.

Second, there is already a tendency that the EU's and other external actors' own security agenda and securitised approach undermine Malian and the five neighbouring countries' own agendas. The G5 Sahel, it seems, is developing into an instrument that external actors use to get more boots on the ground (Bøås, 2018). Here, reducing migration flows and combating groups labelled jihadist terrorists seem key priorities over peace and development in the Sahel. Securitisation may not only be an ill-advised approach, it may also make a 'bad situation worse', and reflects a general lack of understanding of 'what these states are and how they work' (Bøås, 2018: 5). Indeed, both training an army and a police force with limited legitimacy on the ground and attempting to restore a state that did not work, may both have counterproductive effects (Bøås et al., 2018; Craven-Matthews and Englebert, 2017).

In Afghanistan, the external intervention was securitised from the beginning, where the United States put their own COIN agenda ahead of statebuilding. However, the EU is not necessarily providing what is necessary either – and is by some argued not to do enough (and not be able) to counteract the United States (Fescharek, 2015). Trainings, on the other hand, take too much time, which translates into few people actually trained, and hence limited impact in the short term. The EU has been commended for infusing 'some Afghan leaders with professional policing skills that a different Afghan regime may be able to draw upon in the future' (Burke, 2014: 16). However, these have also been found too cumbersome: indeed, there seems to be no middle option between the long-term civilian approach of Germany and (later) the EU, and the quick-fix COIN-approach of the United States (International Crisis Group, 2007: 8). Thus, as Friesendorf and Krempel argue (2011: i), 'militarisation cannot solve the problem of the weak legitimacy of the Afghan state.... The militarisation of the ANP is therefore at best ineffective and at worst counterproductive. Only a police force which the people trust can be effective'.

Long-term aspirations; short-term perspective

The securitisation v. statebuilding paradox can also be viewed as, respectively, short-term and long-term solutions to similar problems, while ambitions of conflict resolution and transformation at the same time requires a long-term perspective. While securitisation generally refers to actions that are needed now to tackle the symptom – the use of violence – statebuilding is what is needed to create a strong and legitimate state that can tackle these threats itself in the long run. Are the EU's efforts long-term or short-term in nature? And what are the differences between stated intentions and practice?

In Afghanistan, several authors argue (e.g., Kaldor *et al.*, 2018; Peters *et al.*, 2018) that the long-term approach of the Europeans – and Germany in particular – was victim of the United States' more short-term goals. As has been mentioned previously, the United States' more short-term and securitised approach, where the police would support the military in its COIN, did not merge well with the Europeans' civilian approach. Essentially, while here represented by the intervention of the United States, this brings us back to problems related to doing SSR in times of war. First, the conflicts themselves suggest that – in most cases – there is already an issue of legitimacy within the state security apparatus. Second, it implies that the police and soldiers one wants to train will often be occupied and in the field. Indeed, while long-term training is ideally what the Afghan police would need, it was also in need of the rapid training of many police officers, something the German approach (prior to the EUPOL-Afghanistan intervention) did not include (Gross, 2012: 116).

The EU has long-term aspirations in line with conflict resolution and transformation perspectives, but its interventions' design and implementation signal more a short-term approach. Several reasons across cases explain this. One reason why the EU's desire for long-term impact falters in practice is that while the EU approach of 'training the trainers' and training leaders (in, e.g., international humanitarian laws or gender issues) may be appealing and theoretically sound, changing the culture of management requires a long-term commitment, the training of larger numbers of personnel, and more local ownership. In Mali, the EUTM starts from 'our

[European] experience in needs assessment, acknowledges top-down approach, and only then attunes to Malians' feedback'.[12] Indeed, for a longer term SSR, one needs an inclusive Malian process that tackles deep-rooted problems in the security apparatus.

Another problem is that trainings have been found to be too short – from a couple of weeks for standard military training to the human rights and gender course to train the trainers that only lasts for three days. Moreover, as the police and armed forces are spread thin in general and are needed in combat, the time they have available for training is limited. According to a EUCAP staff member, this necessitates 'replacing a wheel while the car is going at full speed'.[13] Trainings are also found to be ineffective for other reasons, including limited ownership and high staff rotation. In Mali, in particular, the EU is not able to track the soldiers it trains in the field; hence it is unable to follow-up on their human rights approaches and other trainings. Here, rather than considering the necessary actions that a restoration of the Malian security apparatus implies, it fails to provide necessary follow-up, and its efforts, therefore, end up having little if any impact.

Also, in Afghanistan (Burke, 2014) and Iraq (Christova, 2013), the low number of trained officers is an issue. In Iraq, the 'EU had impacts on the individuals who benefited from the EU programmes, for example as the judges at individual or single institution level. These individuals, in most cases, have failed to impact their organisations and institutions'.[14] Especially faced with the inertia of post-authoritarian states, the influence of a low number of officers will remain limited (Hänggi, 2004). The challenges EUPOL has faced in Afghanistan speak to similar challenges, including the security concerns that come with operating in a theatre of war along with weak domestic institutions (Suroush, 2018: 18).

Lessons learned: SSR in theatres of war

From these paradoxes, several lessons learned arise. In this section we address some of the internal obstacles the EU faces, and which can – theoretically – be amended by the EU itself. However, it is important to keep in mind that many of these also concern external obstacles, including the challenges brought about by operating in theatres of war, with states with limited legitimacy and capacity.

While, in some ways, Afghanistan, Iraq and Mali are in the post-crisis phase, none of these contexts have a functioning peace agreement or extended ceasefire in place. This places considerable pressure on whatever intervention the EU has in place in these countries. Take the example of Mali: the current conflict started in 2012, but despite a huge international engagement the security situation is not improving. Rather, it is worsening with the spread of conflict not only from the North to the Central region, but also across borders to neighbouring Burkina Faso and Niger. This does not allow for much development work or make capacity-building of the security apparatus any easier.

Similarly, the non-fulfilment of key requirements put forth for effective reform of the security sector significantly complicates EU efforts in the cases. While a minimal capacity and size of the state and the security sector along with legitimacy within large parts of the population is required, this has not been the case in neither Afghanistan, Iraq nor Mali. This is a key trap into which the EU has fallen, and will likely continue to fall, as it attempts to do SSR in theatres of war: the strengthening of a security apparatus that is hardly legitimate and may participate in abuse and be characterised by impunity. In Afghanistan, the US paramilitary/militarised approach undermined the EU's intentions of contributing to a civilian police force (Kaldor *et al.*, 2018). Also, in Iraq, the EU contributed to security and justice sector reform without having much of an impact, and its efforts to solve root causes of conflict as corruption and impunity had limited effects. In Mali, finally, the EU struggles with a similar issue, where the security apparatus has been found implicated in several human rights abuse scandals (Amnesty International, 2018). While the EU cannot be blamed for these abuses, it must to a greater extent recognise these challenges, and consider changing its approach. For the moment, not being able to track the soldiers and police it trains, and hence not able to provide follow-up, critically diminishes the EU's ability to ensure sustainability in Mali. Indeed, while the EU did not create the conditions of these countries in crisis, it did make the decision to enter in the first place.

Another internal obstacle which has important consequences for the impact on the ground is the EU's risk averseness, a result of strong pressure at home to avoid casualties in far-away countries like Afghanistan, Iraq and Mali. In Mali, EU trainers are not allowed to follow their trainees in the field, while in Afghanistan, police officials were disgruntled by the security restrictions EUPOL took and their reluctance to move outside their camps.[15] Thus, without the ability to see if training has its desired effect, a drastic change in approach may have to follow.

Importantly, to have its desired impacts, coordination and stronger cooperation with other national and international actors is vital. On an overall level in Afghanistan, Iraq and Mali, the variety of efforts can both have a larger effect given greater cooperation, and is currently suffering from duplication, sometimes having counterproductive effects. In Afghanistan, results were severely limited by a lack of coordination and cooperation between international actors involved with police reform. A prominent example is the 2002 initiative that put five states in charge of five tasks in Afghanistan: Japan in charge of DDR, the United States of the army, Germany of the police, Italy of justice and the UK of narcotics. These were rarely linked sufficiently.

A key challenge the EU thus continuously must deal with, is the cacophony of Member State interests. These voices prevent a clear and strategic engagement in places such as Afghanistan, Iraq and Mali, and lead to a 'Brusselisation' of programme design, to the detriment of consultations with local actors. Others relate to the challenging theatres in which the EU chooses to operate. This includes a challenging security situation, weak and fragmented state institutions, and states with limited legitimacy. At the core of these two types of obstacles, then, lies the gap between what the EU seeks and intends to do and what it manages to implement, namely mainly conflict management. While the EU has the potential to tackle obstacles related to its inner functioning, it has – due to its size and the lack of large-scale impact of its crisis response itself – a limited potential impact on the situation itself. Then, one would ask if its aspirations are realistic, and if its approach is, really, sustainable.

Moreover, the EU still struggles with identifying strategic objectives, and to conduct coherent operations. In Afghanistan, for example, mandates remained like 'job descriptions' (Fescharek, 2015). Despite being a 'must win' mission (Larivé, 2012), no real comprehensive approach was formulated. Neither did it clearly and decisively counteract the US militarisation of the ANP, nor did it have clear goals for what it wanted to do. More than based on strategic objectives, its actions depended on what member states could provide of funding and personnel (Fescharek, 2015). Moreover, to point to technical problems – like payment systems – rather than how departments were running, and underlying issues of corrupt and partly criminal departments (as these issues) is considered too 'complicated and political' (Bolle, 2017). Overall, then, the EU quest for 'security autonomy' from the United States has remained elusive (Fescharek, 2015).

Conclusion

Drawing on our extensive empirical data, we argue that both a drastic change in EU approach and a re-consideration of the EU's added value is necessary. While similar to advice offered before, this is becoming more acute, specifically in Mali, where the EU is getting further committed to an approach that seems – eight years after its onset – not to have the desired impact.

This chapter has sought to point to some of the inner obstacles the EU faces in its crisis response. While they are internal obstacles, this do not make addressing them easy. In fact, a key one – its member states' diverse interests – is an integral part of the European idea. The key point made is that while the EU will never intervene based only on the interests of host states, its potential positive contribution suffers from minimalist concepts of conflict sensitivity and local ownership. This is further impacted on by the tendency of the EU's crisis response to prioritise securitisation as a supply-based and short-term process that leaves what the EU does in practice firmly in the conflict management sphere. The EU has, as we have shown, larger aspirations towards a more comprehensive approach that includes perspectives akin to conflict resolution and transformation, but so far this remains by and large a rhetorical stance. One important reason for this is the Union's inability to deal constructively with what we have identified and defined as the five paradoxes of EU crisis response. What this leads to is that in the internal balancing in the Union, the needs and interests of conflict resolution and transformation lose out against more narrow security concerns that favour conflict management.

In all cases examined here (Afghanistan, Iraq and Mali), the EU struggles with reconciling its intentions and abilities to satisfy these. The consequence is not only that bridging the gap between aspirations and performance is necessary, but also that addressing internal obstacles can enhance the impact of its crisis response on the ground and ultimately – perhaps – its aspiration to be a norm-based global security provider that privileges conflict resolution and transformation in its approach. If this remains a central objective of the Union, it clearly needs to rethink the current drive towards a more realist, narrow security approach and rethink an approach to conflict-sensitive conflict management that promotes grounded local ownership and a knowledge-based approach to conflict sensitivity that is mainstreamed throughout the Union's crisis response mechanisms.

Notes

1 Interview with EUCAP official, Bamako, 20 October 2017.
2 Interview with EU officials, Bamako, 26 October 2017.
3 Interview with National Platform for Civil Society, Bamako, 26 October 2017.
4 Interview with Republic of France representative in Erbil, Erbil, 31 July 2018.
5 Interview with a then Deputy Minister for MOI, Kabul, 20 December 2017.
6 Interview with a high-ranking police official, MOI, 13 December 2017.
7 Interview with the head of a leading civil society organisation, 18 November 2017.
8 Interview, Segdi Ag Rhally, ONG GARDL, Malian civil society from the region of Kidal (President of the CSO committee of the Region of Kidal), 22 October 2017.
9 Interview, EUCAP official, Bamako, 20 October 2017.
10 Interview with MNLA (Movement for the National Liberation of Azawad) member, Bamako, 25 October 2017.
11 Interview with GAITA (Groupe d'Autodéfense Touareg Imghad et Alliés) member, Bamako, 26 October 2017.

12 Interview EUTM officer, Bamako, 25 October 2017.
13 Interview EUCAP, Bamako, 26 October 2017.
14 Interview Iraqi scholar, Erbil, 30 July 2017.
15 Interview with a high-ranking Afghan police official, MOI, Kabul, 13 December 2017.

References

Amnesty International (2018) *Mali: 2017–2018* (London: Amnesty International), www.amnesty.org/en/countries/africa/mali/report-mali/ (accessed 20 August 2019).

APFO, CECORE, CHA, FEWER, International Alert, and Saferworld (2004) *Conflict-Sensitive Approaches to Development, Humanitarian Assistance and Peacebuilding: Resource Pack* (London: Saferworld).

Baranyi, S. and J.E. Salahub (2011) 'Police reform and democratic development in lower-profile fragile states', *Canadian Journal of Development Studies/Revue canadienne d'etudes du développement*, 32(1): 48–63.

Bolle, T.A. (2017) 'Bistandsmilliarder til omstridt politistyrke', *Bistandsaktuelt* 11/12/17, www.bistandsaktuelt.no/nyheter/2017/bistandsmilliarder-til-omstridt-politistyrke/ (accessed 4 September 2019).

Bøås, M. (2018) 'Rival priorities in the Sahel – Finding the balance between Security and development', Policy Brief No. 3 (Uppsala: Nordic Africa Institute).

Bøås, M. and P. Rieker (2019) *Executive Summary of the Final Report & Selected Policy Recommendations: A Conflict-Sensitive Unpacking of the EU Comprehensive Approach to Conflict and Crisis Mechanisms* (Brussels: Centre for European Policy Studies).

Bøås, M. and K. Stig (2010) 'Security sector reform in Liberia: An uneven partnership without local ownership', *Journal of Intervention and Statebuilding*, 4(3): 285–303.

Bøås, M., A.W. Cissé, A. Diallo, B. Drange, F. Kvamme and E. Stambøl (2018) 'The EU, security sector reform and border management in Mali', Working paper on the implementation of EU crisis response in Mali, EUNPACK Working Paper, D.7.4, EUNPACK project.

Bøås, M., A.W. Cissé and L. Mahamane (2020) 'Explaining violence in Tillabéri: Insurgent appropriation of local grievances?' *The International Spectator*, 55(4): 118–132.

Bøås, M., J.B. Bjørkheim and F. Kvamme (forthcoming) *The EUNPACK Data Set – Tabulation Report* (Oslo: NUPI).

Buckley, J. (2010) 'Can the EU be more effective in Afghanistan?', Policy Brief (London: Centre for European Reform), www.cer.eu/sites/default/files/publications/attachments/pdf/2011/pb_afhganistan_27apr10-223.pdf (accessed 1 June 2021).

Burke, E. (2014) 'Game over? The EU's legacy in Afghanistan', FRIDE Working Paper No. 122 (Madrid: FRIDE, February).

Christova, A. (2013) 'Seven years of EUJUST LEX: The challenge of rule of law in Iraq', *Journal of Contemporary European Research*, 9(3): 424–439.

Cissé, A.W., A. Dakouo, M. Bøås and F. Kvamme (2017) 'Perceptions about the EU Crisis response in Mali – a summary of perception studies', EUNPACK Policy Brief, D.7.7, EUNPACK project.

Craven-Matthews, C. and P. Englebert (2018) 'A Potemkin state in the Sahel? The empirical and the fictional in Malian state reconstruction', *African Security*, 11(1): 1–31.

Echavez, C.R. and Q. Suroush (2017) 'Assessment of EU's Response in Afghanistan: Did EU's conflict response through EUPOL deliver as it intended: A review of how EU in general and EUPOL in particular were received and perceived among Afghan stakeholders in Kabul', Policy Brief D.7.6, EUNPACK project.

EEAS (2016) 'Military and civilians missions and operations' (Brussels: EEAS), https://eeas.europa.eu/topics/military-and-civilian-missions-and-operations/430/military-and-civilian-missions-and-operations_en (accessed 15 June 2019).

EU (2007) 'Crisis management and response' (Brussels: EU), https://eeas.europa.eu/topics/crisis-response/412/crisis-response_en (accessed 16 June 2019).

EUCAP (2017) 'Factsheet, updated September 2017', www.consilium.europa.eu/en/press/press-releases/2017/01/11/eucap-sahel-mali/#:~:text=On%2011%20January%202017%2C%20the%20Council%20extended%20the,from%202015%20January%202017%20to%20 14%20January%202018 (accessed 15 June 2019).

EUCAP (2018) 'EUCAP Sahel Mali mandate', https://eucap-sahel-mali.eu/about_en.html (accessed 5 June 2019).

European Court of Auditors (2015) *The EU Police Mission in Afghanistan: Mixed Results*, Special Report No. 7/2015 (Luxembourg: Publications Office of the European Union).

EUTM (2018) 'EU training mission in Mali – Council extends mission for two years with broadened mandate to include support for G5 Sahel Joint force', Press release, www.consilium.europa.eu/en/press/press-releases/2018/05/14/eu-training-mission-in-mali-council-extends-mission-for-two-years-with-broadened-mandate-to-include-support-for-g5-sahel-joint-force/ (accessed 4 September 2019).

Fescharek, N. (2015) 'Forward procrastination? Afghanistan's lessons about Europe's role as a security provider', *International Spectator*, 50(3): 43–59.

Friesendorf, C. and J. Krempel (2011) *Militarised versus Civilian Policing: Problems of Reforming the Afghan National Police*. Report No. 102 (Frankfurt: Peace Research Institute Frankfurt).

Gordon, E. (2014) 'Security sector reform, statebuilding and local ownership: Securing the state or its people?' *Journal of Intervention and Statebuilding*, 8(2–3): 126–148.

Gross, E. (2012) 'The EU in Afghanistan', in R.G. Whitman and S. Wolff (eds), *The European Union as a Global Conflict Manager* (London: Routledge), 107–119.

Handschin, S., E. Abitbol and R. Alluri (2016) 'Conflict sensitivity: Taking it to the next level', Working Paper 2 (Geneva: Swiss Peace).

Hänggi, H. (2004) 'Conceptualising security sector reform and reconstruction', in A. Bryden and H. Hänggi (eds), *Reform and Reconstruction in the Security Sector*, No. 6 (Geneva: DCAF / Münster: LIT Verlag).

International Crisis Group (2007) *Reforming Afghanistan's Police*, Asia Report No. 138 (Brussels: IRG).

Jennings, K.M. and M. Bøås (2015) 'Transactions and interactions: Everyday life in the peacekeeping economy', *Journal of Intervention and Statebuilding*, 9(3): 281–295.

Kaldor, M., I. Rangelov and S. Selchow (eds) (2018) *EU Global Strategy and Human Security: Rethinking Approaches to Conflict* (London: Routledge).

Karlsrud, J. (2018) 'From liberal peacebuilding to stabilization and counterterrorism', *International Peacekeeping*, 26(1): 1–21.

Larivé, M.H.A. (2012) 'From speeches to actions: EU involvement in the war in Afghanistan through the EUPOL Afghanistan Mission', *European Security*, 21(2): 185–201.

Loschi, C., L. Raineri and F. Strazzari (2018) 'The implementation of EU crisis response in Libya: Bridging theory and practice', EUNPACK Working Paper, D.6.2, EUNPACK project.

Mac Ginty, R. and O.P. Richmond (2013) 'The local turn in peace-building: A critical agenda for peace', *Third World Quarterly*, 3(5): 763–783.

Mobekk, E. (2010) 'Security sector reform and the challenges of ownership', in M. Sedra (ed.), *The Future of Security Sector Reform* (Ontario: Centre for International Governance Innovation), 230–243.

Mohammed, K.W. (2018) 'The EU crisis response in Iraq: Awareness, local perception and reception', EUNPACK Working Paper D.7.2, EUNPACK project.

Mohammed, K.W., D. Ala'Aldeen and K.M. Palani (2017) 'Perceptions about the EU crisis response in Iraq – summary of perception studies', EUNPACK Policy Brief D.7.5, EUNPACK project.

Molenaar, F., A.E. Ursu and B.A. Tinni (2017) *Local Governance Opportunities for Sustainable Migration Management in Agadez* (The Hague: Clingendael).

OECD DAC (Organisation for Economic Co-operation and Development / Development Assistance Committee) (2007) *Handbook on Security System Reform* (Paris: OECD).

Osland, K.M. (2014) *Much Ado about Nothing? The Impact of International Assistance to Police Reform in Afghanistan, Bosnia and Herzegovina, Kosovo, Serbia and South Sudan: A Comparative Case Study and Developing a Model for Evaluating Democratic Policing* (Oslo: Faculty of Social Sciences, University of Oslo) (PhD dissertation).

Peters, I., E. Ferhatovic, R. Heinemann, S. Berger and S.M. Sturm (2018) 'The European Union's crisis response in the extended neighbourhood: Comparing the EU's output effectiveness in the cases of Afghanistan, Iraq and Mali', EUNPACK Working Paper D.7.1 (part 4), EUNPACK project.

Raineri, L. (2018) 'Human smuggling across Niger: state-sponsored protection rackets and contradictory security imperatives', *Journal of Modern African Studies*, 56(1): 63–86.

Sedra, M. (ed.) (2010) *The Future of Security Sector Reform* (Ontario: Centre for International Governance Innovation).

Spyer, J. (2007) 'Europe and Iraq: Test case for the Common Foreign and Security policy', *The Middle East Review of International Affairs*, 11: 94–106.

Strazzari, F. (2015) 'Azawad and the rights of passage: the role of illicit trade in the logic of armed groups formation in Northern Mali' (Oslo: Norwegian Centre for Conflict Resolution).

Suroush, Q. (2018) 'Assessing EUPOL impact on Afghan police reform (2007–2016)', EUNPACK Working Paper, D.7.3, EUNPACK project.

Wulf, H. (2004) *Security Sector Reform in Developing and Transitional Countries* (Berlin: Berghof Research Center for Constructive Conflict Management).

7

The effectiveness of EU crisis response in Afghanistan, Iraq and Mali

Ingo Peters, Enver Ferhatovic, Rabea Heinemann and Sofia Sturm

Introduction

How effective is the EU's crisis response policy in terms of its CSDP missions in Afghanistan, Iraq and Mali, that is, in the EU's self-defined extended neighbourhood? Are the crisis responses conservative and constrained (crisis management) or emancipatory and ambitious (crisis transformation)? These are pertinent questions guiding the social sciences discourse on EU foreign policy in general and on the appropriateness of EU crisis response policy in particular. To the first question, the debate has been focused for some years on the issues of the 'actorness and power' of the EU as an international actor. A salient part of this discourse has been the issue of foreign policy effectiveness, encompassing contributions varying between degrees of dismissal or praise of EU performance, also in comparison to other international actors.[1] The second question relates to the debate on EU peacebuilding in the wider sense and the prevalent empirical evidence suggesting 'that a shift from conflict management practices to critical forms of crisis transformation are required if the EU is to have a normative and legitimate foreign policy in conflict-affected societies around the world.'[2]

Empirical analyses from the three case studies point to a significant gap between EU ambitions in favour of an emancipatory 'crisis transformation' approach stressing the need for providing attention to the individual and the local, and the structural courses of conflict, on the one hand, and a constrained and conservative practice of EU policy-making geared, especially in the EU's extended neighbourhood, towards EU's interests rather than norms and human rights, on the other hand.

Following the breakdown of governance in parts of its neighbourhood in the 1990s, the EU has intervened by civilian, military or mixed CSDP missions in post-conflict areas.[3] The EU has linked its foreign policy objectives to the Treaty of Lisbon (TEU/Art.21, 2) which among other goals comprises to 'preserve peace, prevent conflicts and strengthen international security' and to 'foster the sustainable economic, social and environmental development of developing countries, with the primary aim of eradicating poverty' (European Union HR/VP, 2016: 14f). In this regard, SSR has been the preferred mode of intervention for the EU in crisis areas as it has been seen as a cornerstone of liberal state- and peacebuilding processes and a concept at the conjunction of security and development. These two dominant threads of EU foreign policy are envisaged to integrate development assistance into security-related fields (Sedra, 2013: 371).

Core challenges for EU crisis response policy in Afghanistan, Iraq and Mali were structurally similar concerning (a) governance deficits, (b) ethnic, religious, social and economic fragmentation, (c) embeddedness in regional instability and power struggles, combined with poorly managed borders and cross-border interventions, rendering all these cases 'areas of limited statehood' (Krasner and Risse, 2014: 548). However, pronounced differences across cases exist regarding individual histories (including colonial), political cultures, and the various legacies of war involving external powers. Moreover, the EU's operational environment is complex not least because of multiple simultaneous international interventions within each of our cases demanding international coordination. The United States has been the agenda-setter as much as the international gatekeeper in Afghanistan and Iraq. Organisations like ECOWAS and the G5 Sahel play a much bigger role in Mali than regional counterparts do in Iraq and Afghanistan. The UN has been a key actor across the three cases with its own country or regional missions as much as regarding UN Security Council mandates providing international legitimacy for military and civilian engagement.

EU SSR has followed a similar pattern in different conflict settings – one size fits all (Börzel and Risse, 2004): The end or pause of major hostilities is followed by the design of liberal reform programmes in Brussels and EU member states' capitals based on good governance principles. Our three cases, although varying in detail, were or are located in conflict and post-conflict contexts (Hänggi, 2004: 17). In each case, the fragmentation of security structures has been particularly challenging, leading to similar policies in response to the respective crises. This matters when it comes to initiating and conducting missions and other policies, raising questions of neo-colonialism (Nicolaïdis *et al.*, 2015) or 'soft imperialism' (Hettne and Söderbaum, 2005). Britain in Afghanistan and Iraq, and France in Mali acquired special roles in the respective countries and acted de facto as 'lead nations' inside the EU's policy-making machinery. However, the role and motivation of key member states have been varying across cases and over time. The EU Council as well as EC crisis response policies, have been marked by structurally similar problem definitions leading to the same strategic and operational objectives, grand and operational strategies as well as the application of common tools and funding instruments (Peters *et al.*, 2018: annex 6).

The research questions stated at the outset will guide and structure this analysis by utilising for the evaluation of policy effectiveness the standardised foreign policy cycle (output, outcome and impact effectiveness) (Peters, 2016: 27f, and Figure 2.1, this volume) focusing on respective CSDP missions. For assessing the characteristics of EU peacebuilding, the typology of conflict response will be used, differentiating conflict management, conflict resolution, and conflict transformation, or critical conflict

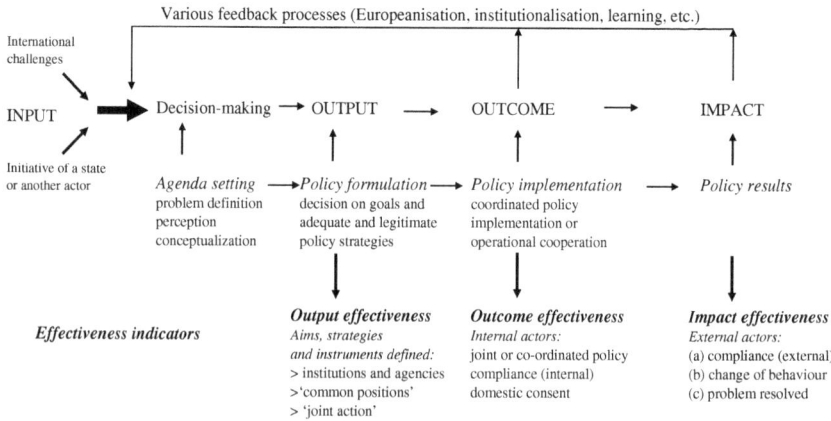

Figure 7.1: Categorising effectiveness: the example of CFSP
Source: Heider *et al.*, 2004; based on Underdal, 2004.

transformation (Table 7.1).⁴ Policy assessment is based on document analysis, background talks with actors of EU institutions and missions, public perceptions studies conducted in the framework of the EUNPACK project on-site, and implementation reports by the EU and experts' assessments. The EUNPACK perception surveys[5] covered the EU's beneficiaries in the case countries, coupled with key informant interviews from each case (Echavez and Suroush, 2017; Mohammed *et al.*, 2017; Cissé *et al.*, 2017). Additionally, key stakeholders from the Brussels institutions were interviewed.[6]

Effectiveness of the EU's crisis response policy in Afghanistan, Iraq, and Mali: evaluating the EU's crisis response *output* and *outcome* effectiveness

Effectiveness as actor coherence

Actor coherence, measured as actor unity (of voice)[7] on the output level and evolution of mandates on the outcome level, posed a major challenge for the EU in Afghanistan and Iraq while in Mali the challenges emerged primarily with policy implementation (policy outcome). In general, horizontal as well as vertical coherence was hampered by diverging member states' preferences. The often slowly emerging consensus and compromises among member states regarding strategic decisions in the EU Council in the early years of policy formulation for Afghanistan and Iraq retarded opportunities for Commission engagement, that is statebuilding via reforming and building pertinent (state) institutions (Burke, 2009: 8; Peters *et al.*, 2018: 12).

Actor unity on the *output level* is an indispensable precondition for any mission mandate. In the case of Afghanistan, the sluggish increase in EU mission staff and operationally limiting budgets resulted in the harmonisation of EU engagement only by 2012. Moreover, member states' bilateral policies in the realm of SSR, such as the German Police Project Team (GPPT), the Italian *carabinieri* regiment seconded to the NATO Training Mission-Afghanistan (NTM-A) or the UK's close-hold operations in Herat were not harmonised. Coordination with and between member states remained difficult within the International Police Coordination

Table 7.1 Classification of peacebuilding frameworks

	Hyper-conservative (political realism, top-down)	Conservative (top-down and bottom-up)	Orthodox (multilevel approach)	Emancipatory
Generation	First generation	First and second generation	Third generation	Fourth generation
Type	Crisis(Conflict) Management	Crisis(Conflict) Resolution	Crisis(Conflict) Transformation	Critical Crisis(Conflict) Transformation
Characteristics				
Premises	Conflicts are endemic to men; external actors as balancer. Meta-level: >>rational application of scientific knowledge >>order through international cooperation over coercion	Crystallised out of a critique of conflict management. >>Conflict as psychological, sociobiological or product of political, economic and social structures >>Conflict arises out of repression and deprivation of human needs which is a social and a psychological phenomenon	Lies at the heart of the liberal peacebuilding project. >> Emphasizes requirements and perceptions of policymakers, officials and actors involved in top-down and bottom-up visions of peace at first with local actors' consent and later also without.	Crisis Resolution and Transformation created conditionality between the agents and recipients. >>Pluralist, critical and self-reflective approach (all of society)

Table 7.1 (continued)

	Hyper-conservative (political realism, top-down)	Conservative (top-down and bottom-up)	Orthodox (multilevel approach)	Emancipatory
	>>windows of opportunity for conflict resolution can be settled through basic peace as ambitious peace cannot be achieved >>Limited peace is based upon a fragile equation of state interests, issues and resources often depending on external guarantors	>>Broke away from state-centric notions of conflict >>Human needs like identity, political participation, and security put over state security >>Conflict requires social, political and economic engineering >>Conflicts cannot be resolved unless concerns of civil society are met ('Cosmopolitan Turn').	>>Conflicts cannot be resolved unless concerns of civil society are met ('Cosmopolitan Turn') and liberal peace is dependent on a vibrant civil society. >>Liberal Concept of Peace revolves around the reform of governance, is highly interventionary and has a problem-solving character.	
Objectives	Reduction and management of (violent) conflict; CM as problem-solving process; Limited peace or acceptable level of violence	>>Win-win peace as an ambitious goal >>Social, Economic and Political Engineering by third-party interveners to remove events and conditions that create violence	Peace that is technically plausible to be constructed by external actors in cooperation with local actors	Institutions have to open up to cultural, customary dynamics on the local level >>Considers the long term effects of an intervention

(Continued)

Table 7.1 (continued)

	Hyper-conservative (political realism, top-down)	Conservative (top-down and bottom-up)	Orthodox (multilevel approach)	Emancipatory
Policy tools	Mediation, coercion, robust peacekeeping; military intervention	Multi-track diplomacy, peacebuilding and contingency approaches	Multiple forms of intervention: UN peace operations, mediation and negotiation, development, humanitarian relief and specialised reform of security, economy, borders, HR and RoL	Mediation between the local and international over peacebuilding practice and social, political and economic practices that both deem acceptable. \>\> Review and monitoring of measures
External agents	States, Individuals, institutions and IOs – as external guarantors	Peacekeepers, NGOs, donors and officials	International actors, UN, IFIs, NGOs	Regional and International actors
Agents addressed; addressees	State actors and political elites	Local (individual and civil society), state actors	Local, state and regional actors	Non-elite actors from the ground/bottom level

Source: Peters *et al.*, 2018; based on Richmond *et al.*, 2016.

Board (IPCB) and the Law and Order Trust Fund for Afghanistan (LOTFA) due to diverging national approaches (European Court of Auditors 2015: 15–17). In the case of Iraq, after the US-led war in 2003, a profound split between the war-opposing and war-supporting member states preceded and significantly influenced the EU internal decision-making processes regarding EU engagement in general and the deployment of a CSDP rule of law mission in particular (Council of the European Union, 2012: 3; 2016: 3f). For example, initiatives for creating the post of an EU special envoy or representative to Iraq and opening an EU office in Baghdad were temporarily blocked not least by France, since Paris confined institution-building in Iraq to the UN (Youngs, 2004: 8). In contrast, the EU engagement in Mali was from the very beginning characterised by a largely unitary and swift reaction in the face of the unfolding crises (Council of the European Union, 2012a: 5; Council of the European Union, 2012b: 3).

Regarding actor coherence on the *policy output level in response to lessons learned during policy implementation*, evolving mandates were a feature of EU crisis response policy across cases.[8] A chief example of changing contexts and adjustment of policy priorities was the shift of EU concerns towards containing migration which gradually emerged following the 'Arab Spring' of 2011. The inclusion of migration also in Council documents indicates a shift towards securitisation of the migration issue (in terms of perceiving it a security threat rather than a humanitarian challenge) and signifies a strong nexus between the EU's and its member states' internal and external policy agenda. This shift was also observable concerning the EU's neighbourhood – for example, in Libya (Council of the European Union, 2015). CSDP missions' mandates were changed in Afghanistan four times in nine years (2007–16), in Iraq twice in eight years (2005–13), and in Mali three times in seven years (2013–20). The evolution of mandates, however, also illustrates the EU's ability to find a common response to changing contexts. In Afghanistan, for example, the mission's initial focus on capacity-building (mentoring and training) was progressively replaced by an advisory approach. In Mali, with its third mandate, the EUTM broadened its narrow focus from training and advice towards, inter alia, a geographical extension and the intensification of regional cooperation with the G5 Sahel (Council of the European Union,

2016: 3f). In consequence, the EU policy-making on the output level of policy rhetoric and ambitions has de facto been meandering between the crisis response types of conflict resolution, conflict transformation and critical conflict transformation.

Effectiveness as process coherence

Besides actor coherence, process coherence impacts effectiveness of EU policies in terms of changing actors' behaviour and resolving political problems defined at the outset. The criteria for assessing process coherence encompass *coherence of policy features, institutional coherence, continuity of core concepts* (Peters et al., 2018: annex 7) and *resonance of EU output with implementation* (equipment, personnel, training, monitoring). Concerning the first criterion, the core strategic, as well as intermediate objectives of the EU, have been continuously visible in EU policy formulation. EU strategic objectives in essence covered improving 'security', 'stability' and 'prosperity'.[9] On the operational level, problem definitions, objectives and strategies, as indicated in mission mandates and other core EU documents displayed a high degree of continuity and visibility, indicating policy output effectiveness. Operational strategies (transformative mechanisms) like socialisation (by dialogue and partnership) and capacity-building (by empowering state institutions, personnel and civil society) are well embedded in EU 'grand strategies'. Good governance norms like democracy, human rights and rule of law have been guiding mandate formulations across the cases, resembling dominantly the third generation of crisis response policy that is crisis transformation.

When it comes to *institutional coherence* – across EU institutions, between EU institutions and member states, in Brussels as well as in the field – empirical evidence points at discontinuity of horizontal and vertical coherence. For example, the lack of prioritisation and coordination of policies between the Commission and EUPOL-Afghanistan rendered capacity-building efforts like training and the oversight function within LOTFA and the IPCB ineffective (European Court of Auditors, 2015: 18f, 30f). Although the Multiannual Indicative Programme states that 'the EU can build on the groundwork established by the CSDP Mission (EUPOL Afghanistan)' (European Commission and EEAS, 2014: 8), the 'proposed result indicators were not related to EUPOL's civilian policing outcomes' (European Court of Auditors, 2015: 30). Thus, the institutional coherence in the field remained a challenge, as the EU Delegation/EUSR had no clear objectives beyond support for the Trust Fund, while the member states' policies and CSDP Mission lacked coordination and sustainable long-term planning (European Court of Auditors, 2015: 18). In Mali, coordination of policies between the EEAS and the Commission remained challenging. To add to the complexity at hand with the latest European Defence Fund (EDF) review, the Commission identified security as a priority concern, marking a departure for an institution primarily responsible for development.[10]

EU crisis management policy across our three cases has been shaped by intergovernmental policy-making with national approaches often diverging also during policy *implementation*. In Afghanistan, the lack of coordination between the member states, EUPOL, the EUSR and the EC was detrimental to the SSR efforts. Yet, an agreement to jointly set up the Professional Training Board for the development and accreditation of police training curricula was accomplished (European Court of Auditors, 2015: 19). In the Iraq case, the empirical investigation of EU documents also revealed issues with policy and institutional coherence for the implementation of the EUJUST LEX mandate. During Javier Solana's term, tensions reportedly existed between the role of the HR/VP and the Political and Security Committee (PSC) regarding coordination with other key players (Korski, 2010: 236). As indicated by background talks, coordination between EUTM Mali and other EU instruments has reportedly worked well on the ground.[11]

However, insufficient external EU cooperation and coordination (or competition) with domestic authorities and international actors was detrimental across all three cases. In Iraq, for example, the gradual increase of the EU Commission's assistance for reconstruction and development rendered coordination with the UN and the World Bank indispensable, which both acquired through a growing role in the Donor Committee of the International Reconstruction Fund Facility for Iraq (IRFFI). The EU Commission's dissatisfaction with the IRFFI performance due to its technical approach led to policy adjustments when the EU shifted funds directly towards civil society groups (Youngs, 2004: 12f). In Mali, Malian government representatives complained that international partners follow their agenda without consulting domestic authorities' which leads to accusations of international tutelage or loss of national sovereignty (Tull, 2017). Cooperation with ECOWAS and the UN has been considered crucial for an effective training mission.

Effective policy implementation is about the resonance of EU policy output with policy practice. In all three cases, shortages of material and equipment due to slow procurement and limited budgets curtailed the quality of the training and operational readiness (Council of the European Union, 2013: 5; Barea, 2013). EUPOL-Afghanistan throughout its lifecycle had problems with the procurement of equipment for the mission (European Court of Auditors, 2015: 46). In Mali, a lack of communication equipment prevented FAMa from protecting the population in the north (Bøås et al., 2018: 17; EEAS, 2015: 4, 9).

Similar problems marked our three cases regarding mission personnel. Pledges made in terms of staff deployment were mostly not followed up in practice, thus undermining the legitimacy and effectiveness of the missions. In Afghanistan, EUPOL's impact was limited partly due to low levels of staff seconded by the EU member states. The mission strength authorised was 400 staff, but never exceeded 340 (in 2012) (European Court of Auditors, 2015: 12f). For EUJUST LEX – implemented mostly outside Iraq until 2009 – merely four staff members were deployed inside Iraq (Korski, 2010: 237). Only with the amended mandate of 2009, the number of staff in Baghdad rose to eight in 2010 and ultimately 66 (including 13 locals and 40% female) until the end of the mission in December 2013 (EEAS, 2014a). With over 580 personnel by 2016, EUTM Mali is a relatively big mission. However, compared to a mission strength of 4,000 French personnel deployed in the context of its military intervention force Opération Barkhane in the Sahel, the relevance of EU numbers is modest and its possible impact may be questionable (EEAS, 2016: 2).

CSDP capacity-building has been implemented through advising, mentoring, monitoring and training of relevant ministries' personnel, police officers, judiciary, prison services and military personnel. These policy features convey a governance-focused approach targeting key state actors and resemble a hybrid between conflict resolution and conflict transformation. Across cases, the EU missions delivered notable results, although to varying degrees. In Afghanistan, capacity-building was implemented through the establishment of the Police Staff College, the Criminal Investigation College and train-the-trainer courses. Moreover, civilian norms were promoted through institutional capacity-building inside the Ministries of Interior and Justice and the Attorney General's Office. However, incoherence existed regarding understandings of civilian policing, mostly rooted in the diversity of EU security cultures and practices, and quality of EU personnel. EUPOL learned at an early stage that it was crucial to agree on a mission-wide common understanding as incoming experts often expected to convey their ideas known from their home countries.[12] Similarly in Iraq, member states failed to implement one of the key recommendations of the Iraq Expert Team: 'to develop a common and detailed curriculum that all the training had to follow' (Korski, 2010: 238).

Another indicator of the crisis transformation approach focusing on key governance institutions, is the EU engagement in building up local Civil Justice Systems, police and military. In all three cases the EU did not foresee a critical evidence-based evaluation of mandate implementation, quality assurance and objective monitoring of mandate implementation. This can be explained mostly due to security concerns, risk aversion and lack of deployed resources but ultimately the lack of delivery by EU member states. In Afghanistan, due to the security constraints, monitoring of trained police was never an option. For Iraq, lessons learned could only partially be developed due to security restrictions on travel. Hence, evaluation seminars happened, but until 2010/11, the effectiveness of the training could not systematically be assessed.[13] Additionally, political constraints undermined the EU's ability to deliver. For instance, the EU did not get access to Iraqi training establishments (Christova, 2013: 435) while in Mali, training an army at war but not monitoring and tracking the trained soldiers due to security reasons limited the possibilities for follow-up training.

The fourth criterion for *process coherence* is *continuity of core concepts* marking EU policy output and outcome, primarily meaning the *comprehensive approach*, *conflict sensitivity*, and *local ownership*. The comprehensive approach[14] is inherent in the policy features identified as 'grand strategies' of EU crisis response documents. The high aspirations formulated on the level of general objectives by respective operational strategies and mission mandates suffered significantly from the changing security situation on the ground in Afghanistan and Iraq during policy implementation.

In Afghanistan, the application of the comprehensive approach was problematic due to the deteriorating security situation on the ground, and the lack of SSR expertise within the EU Delegation/EUSR. In Iraq, EU Commission policies became re-oriented from an 'agenda for change' to an 'agenda for consolidating'. This de facto entailed a farewell to the ambitions of a comprehensive approach in favour of pragmatic adjustments resembling conflict resolution at best despite more ambitious rhetoric; simultaneously, this corresponded with the end of the EUJUST-LEX Iraq mission in December 2013 (European Commission, 2014: 6–12, n52). Commission problem definitions for Mali have been witnessing a gradual shift towards stability and security, which was manifest in the EU's approach to MENA countries after the Arab Spring of 2011 and the respective EUNPACK case study on Libya. With this shift, a strong security–development nexus became emphasised also indicating the EU's ambitions towards a comprehensive approach (European Commission, 2015). As in Afghanistan, there was however a mismatch between the skills of EU delegation staff with development backgrounds on the one side and the security expertise needed when collaborating with the Ministry of Interior and Police on the other side (Bøås et al., 2018: 17).

The concept of *conflict sensitivity*[15] based on the 'do-no-harm' approach has consistently been part of pertinent documents on EU crisis response, signifying a critical conflict transformation approach. However, the actual *continuity* and *visibility* of the concept have increased over time, with most references in policy documents regarding Mali (Peters, 2017: annex 3). This evolution of reference to the concept shows its increasing significance for policy-making and its relevance for policy implementation. However, in the daily work of EU practitioners, the concept of *conflict sensitivity* tends to be merely sullenly accepted.[16] In general, EU normative principles of crisis response policy match the EU's identity. On the ground the lack of conflict sensitivity has led to civilian policing standards being prioritised within an open conflict setting in Afghanistan. In Iraq, conflict sensitivity was insufficient concerning the EU's awareness and equal treatment of minority groups (Bapir, 2010). Furthermore, a proper understanding of the legal systems of the countries of concern was missing (Korski, 2010: 237). In Mali, the EU has not acted in conflict-sensitive ways when training an army that does not include all ethnicities, has low legitimacy among the Malian population and supports a partly illegitimate state (Bøås et al., 2018: 15). Hence, the EU supports structures that are root causes for the conflict in Mali and might therefore even increase the prevalent fragmentation in the society. Another challenge for a conflict-sensitive EU engagement in any unstable country is being caught in the 'counter-insurgency logic' (Vermeij, 2015: 3): The focused support for primarily central government actors to enhance stability remains an ambiguous practice, typical for conflict management practices (as opposed to the concepts of conflict resolution or transformation) since it leads to preserving the conflict-prone status quo.

The EU's performance concerning *local ownership*[17] has been identified as one of the pertinent features of the EU crisis response on the level of policy formulation and implementation, signifying the concept of conflict transformation. Of all EU normative premises, the concept of local ownership appeared most often across EU policy documents concerning our three cases (Peters et al., 2018: annex 3). In practical terms, in Afghanistan, for example, mainstreaming human rights in training modules, and developing a female policing component within the ANP ran counter to Afghan priorities. In Iraq, the mission was responsive to local concerns by continuous amendments of course curricula and design. Likewise, the incorporation of 'Work Experience Secondments' as an element of EU police training occurred reportedly 'in response to the Iraqi request for more practical learning experiences' (Dari et al., 2012: 56; Troszczynska-van Genderen, 2010: 19). In Mali, domestic stakeholders criticised that the European trainers and experts delivered courses too abstract for daily practice, indicating a lack of knowledge of the reality on the ground (Bøås et al., 2018). The Malian government further laments shortages in weaponry and an overall tactical approach of EUTM training procedures, while the EUTM mandate explicitly stresses the non-combat character of the mission (Malijet, 2017; Skeppström et al., 2015: 357). This example illustrates, far more than only a material deficiency, a political mismatch between Malian authorities and the EU.[18] Policy responsiveness to changing circumstances as much as to priorities identified by domestic authorities hence link conflict sensitivity and local ownership, and so EU ambitions were translated into political practice, but more in terms of managing the conflict then transforming it.

Evaluating the EU's crisis response impact effectiveness

Ultimately, the EU's crisis response policy aims at 'making a difference' that is changing actors' behaviour and solving problems on the ground according to the EU's definitions of issues and inferred policy objectives. This dominantly leads to a rhetoric of the third generation of crisis response policy that aims at conflict transformation, while EU policy practice remained at best in the realm of conflict resolution if not crisis management. Therefore, the impact effectiveness of the three CSDP missions is measured against the respective mandates and concerning, first, EU strategic and intermediate objectives, second, *EU* operational objectives, and third, the core policy concept of local ownership based on domestic perceptions of EU policy-making. This evaluation is indicating overall policy features and causal factors regarding EU crisis response policy at large (Bøås and Rieker, 2019).

In sum, the EU's ambitious programmatic statements (Peters *et al*., 2018: annex 6) on its (a) strategic objectives to contribute to peace, security, sustainability, prosperity, peace and stability, (b) intermediate aims of democratisation, internationalisation, statebuilding and promotion of human rights/gender, and (c) operational objectives to contribute to the establishment of effective civilian policing in Afghanistan, to strengthen the rule of law and promote human rights in Iraq and to strengthen and contribute to the restoration of military capacity to restore Malian territorial integrity, were coherent regarding policy formulation but lacked local ownership and legitimacy. Once more, the EU's emancipatory ambitions became visible but were not matched by its policy implementation.

Impact of EU policy: strategic and intermediate objectives

Our three cases from the extended neighbourhood have been beset by similar challenges of weak statehood preceding EU engagement.

Hence, progress made regarding EU objectives of supporting peace, stability and prosperity and good governance in Afghanistan, Iraq and Mali may become discernible by pertinent indices.[19] In Afghanistan, support to the MoI, the ANP and judicial authorities focused on key institution-building elements. The Democracy Index score for Afghanistan has even slightly deteriorated from 3.06 in 2006 to 2.85 in 2019, though with an upward trend over the past three years (The Economist Intelligence Unit, 2019: 13). However, the Worldwide Governance Indicators show a positive tendency,[20] and the Corruption Perception Index has considerably improved from 1.8 in 2007 to 15 in 2017, though this rank is still one of the lowest (177 out of 180) (Transparency International, 2018).

Iraq has been categorised as a 'chronically fragile state' since 2008 (OECD, 2018: 26), and the perceived level of public sector corruption remained high during the mission. Currently, Iraq still ranks 169 out of 180 countries (Transparency International, 2018). Similarly, the Democracy Index score stuck around 4 (on a scale of 0 to 10) (The Economist Intelligence Unit 2018: 16). Although Mali's governance has improved since the crisis in 2012,[21] the scores are lagging behind those before the crisis and it has lost its status as one of the few at least 'flawed democracies' in sub-Saharan Africa (The Economist Intelligence Unit, 2017). Mali has remained 'extremely fragile' since 2014 and continues to perform poorly regarding security and corruption indicators (OECD, 2018: 86).

Human Rights and Gender are, according to EU policy premises, falling somewhere between the concepts of conflict transformation and critical conflict transformation, mainstreamed throughout SSR activities in the three cases. However, such a policy remains controversial since all case countries are marked by diverse religious and ethnic communities with traditions not resonating with Western normative standards. In Afghanistan, EU commitment in protecting human rights and gender was mirrored in extensive training of the Afghan police to respect human rights as a key element of EUPOL engagement. Yet, allegations that 'the national police has been responsible for incommunicado detention, enforced disappearances, mass arbitrary detention and extrajudicial killings during counter-insurgency operations' (UN, 2017: 4) persisted. According to EU self-assessment, EUJUST LEX accomplished significant improvements regarding prison management, prison security and prisoners' human rights as well as local capacities for fighting domestic violence and trafficking in persons (EEAS, 2014b). However, the Commission at a later stage concluded more critically that Iraq still lacked a stable system of rule of law, as demonstrated by human rights violations against civilians committed by Iraqi Security Forces and affiliated armed groups in their efforts to defeat ISIL (European Commission, 2014: 7; UN, 2015). EUTM Mali has provided training to all ranks in the Malian military forces, including courses on the humanitarian situation, human rights, protection of women, children and displaced persons and the return of refugees (Carrasco *et al.*, 2016). Nevertheless, severe human rights violations by Malian military *counter-terrorism operations* as well as sexual and gender-based violence committed by members of the military in conflict-affected areas were reported (Human Rights Watch, 2017; UN, 2016).

In sum, the impact effectiveness of EU efforts on the level of strategic and intermediate objectives across cases are overshadowed by poor results when looking at general governance indices and pertinent human rights reports. Causally, this can be ascribed to the EU's focus, despite its more ambitious policy objectives, on narrow security concerns and stabilisation strategies rather than addressing underlying structural issues thus resembling conflict resolution or at best conflict transformation, but hardly critical conflict transformation (see EU crisis response paradoxes 4 and 5 in Bøås and Rieker, 2019: 15–16).

Impact of EU policy: operational objectives

On the operational level, capacity-building refers to the training of respective police (Afghanistan and Iraq) and armed forces (Mali) as well as institutional reforms contributing to political stability in the respective country overwhelmingly reflecting a statist model of conflict resolution.

By 2016, approximately 7,300 Afghan police officers had attended the various higher education courses offered by the Police Staff College facilitated by EUPOL-Afghanistan. The mission moreover supported the build-up of the Female Police within the ANP starting with 180 in 2007 to reach 3,200 by 2016 (Suroush and Ferhatovic, 2017: 16). After seven years, according to official EU figures and self-assessment, 5,000 Iraqi Criminal Justice System (CJS) personnel and more than 7,000 Iraqi officials were trained (EEAS, 2014b). However, concerning the overall number of police (about 400,000), the possible impact of EU efforts remained modest at best (Christova, 2013: 427). In Afghanistan, the high attrition rates of up to 75 per cent in 2011 (House of Lords, 2011: 19) and lack of monitoring in the field limited the impact of training. Moreover, CJS personnel faced violent attacks and suffered significant losses between 2003 and 2011, with figures varying from 9,000 to 12,000 (Christova, 2013: 430; Korski, 2010: 238). The EU's post-training monitoring data was limited on 'how many of the course-goers are alive, remain in their jobs or have been promoted, let alone whether they are applying their skills' (Korski, 2010: 239). As of July 2018, EUTM Mali trained 12,000 FAMa trainees in total (EUTM, 2018). Even taken at the highest estimation of the total number of Malian security forces (estimated numbers to 20,000),[22] EUTM Mali has trained a remarkable number of soldiers in five years, and hence accomplished its operational goal to contribute to the restoration of FAMa's military capacity. However, the education and training level of Malian soldiers within a course vary and therefore affect the effectiveness of training by EUTM Mali (Fuhrmann, 2016).

In sum, concerning the overall number of police in Iraq and Afghanistan, the dominance of the NTM-A, the United States/United Kingdom in Iraq and France in Mali, the possible impact of EU efforts unavoidably remained modest at best. These achievements on the operational level sound impressive, however, high numbers do not reflect the qualitative standards of police or military training. Moreover, the significance of these numbers is questionable given the lack of EU's engagement with underlying structural issues and root causes of the conflict resulting in conflict transformation at best (see paradox 4 in Bøås and Rieker, 2019: 15).

Impact of EU policy: local ownership

In its documents and policy statements, the EU has persistently conveyed its ambitions to facilitate social and political reforms but not to impose its policy preferences on the partner country. In consequence, local ownership has continuously been a declared intermediate goal to empower the people and the country to take care of its concerns autonomously and hence to foster the legitimacy and sustainability of EU policies. From an EU perspective, 'ownership' basically refers to recipient countries and actors sharing or embracing EU premises concerning SSR, including basic policy norms of good governance. This chapter analyses ownership along its inherently relational dimension, taking into account that EU priorities are often diverging or difficult-to-align with local understandings and practices, hence laying bare once more the mismatch between conflict-transformation action and critical conflict-transformation rhetoric.

In Afghanistan, local ownership was a key principle within EUPOL's stated objectives and strategies to contribute to the establishment of sustainable and effective civilian policing arrangements (Council of the European Union, 2007). However, ownership and conflict sensitivity have not always been tangible, as Islamic law and native customs were not covered by training curricula (European Court of Auditors, 2015: 25). According to EU self-assessment, EUJUST LEX-Iraq had excellent relations with both domestic and international counterparts, and Iraqi experts participated in the design of curricula for training courses. Still, it remained uncertain whether EU training practice was adopted by the Iraqi police's training plan. Besides, EU police professionals allegedly did not grasp the specifics of Iraq's political system in general and the legal system in particular (Korski, 2010: 238). EUTM Mali's regionalisation efforts, by extending its training to the G5 Sahel Joint Force, could be an avenue towards a 'long-desired Africanization of international efforts' (Lebovich, 2017), with the G5 Joint Force representing another level of the 'local'. Moreover, favouring one regional actor (G5) instead of or even at the expense of another (ECOWAS) could trigger (unintended) consequences in terms of conflict sensitivity (Lebovich, 2017).

As a complement to ownership, the respective perceptions of EU conflict and crisis engagement by conflict-affected societies and international actors matter if taking the premise of critical conflict transformation as a prerequisite for legitimate and effective crisis response policy seriously. In practice, lack of local ownership tends to impair the EU's legitimacy and lead to unsustainable policies.

The focus of the EUPOL mission on civilian policing was criticised by the Afghan MOI as well as by major international actors like the US and NATO Training Mission between 2009 and 2011 (Bayer Tygesen, 2013). NTM-A's dominance of the international training effort, its focus on fighting the insurgency coupled with the lack of civilian police trainers led to poorly-trained police, which in consequence was seen as 'corrupt, brutal and predatory … [and] … feared and mistrusted' by Afghan citizens.[23] 'The EU approach to rolling out a civilian police training programme and it's subsequent failure to gain the support of the local stakeholders fighting the insurgency thus served to symbolize its ineffectiveness' (House of Lords, 2011: 3). The lack of involvement of Afghan police officials in the implementation of the EUPOL Operational Plan further hampered local buy-in (Suroush and Ferhatovic, 2017: 19).

Perception studies conducted within the EUNPACK project show that a general sense of awareness about international actors involved in crisis response could be detected. Specific knowledge of EUPOL engagement among local communities was lacking with over half of the respondents of communities with EUPOL-trained staff not being aware of the mission. Even more, among those aware of EU crisis response, respondents said either they had a neutral attitude regarding their satisfaction with EU support or criticised that it would disproportionately benefit EU officials, state officials and the military while it would not extend to the marginalised parts of communities (Echavez and Suroush, 2017: 8f).

In Iraq, successive governments evaluated EUJUST LEX primarily as a political symbol for Europe's overall Iraq engagement. EUNPACK perception studies (Mohammed et al., 2017: 3) indicate, however, that the majority of interviewed domestic actors are aware of the EU's engagement in crisis response in Iraq albeit a comparatively low awareness became tangible regarding specific CSDP activities, while the awareness of other EU-funded agencies and projects (UNDP, NGOs) and international actors (UN, US) was remarkably higher. The highest number of respondents, 87.5%, was aware of the EU's engagement in the humanitarian field and the second-highest number, 77%, was reported in the capacity development field (Mohammed et al., 2017: 3). While the overall attitude of participants towards EU crisis response engagement in Iraq received a considerable positive score (39% partially satisfied, 30%

satisfied), the EU assistance was considered 'well-targeted' (75%) and of the 'right type' (70%) (Mohammed *et al.*, 2017: 6).

Training courses by EUTM Mali have been perceived as too short or concepts being too abstract for the local reality (Djiré *et al.*, 2017: 42). Furthermore, the lack of knowledge about the content of EU engagement among the Malian population indicates a lack of effort to achieve ownership through a proper communication strategy by the EU. And yet, respondents in Bamako – to which interviews were confined – still had a rather positive view of the EU being conflict-sensitive (58%) and helping to mitigate the crisis (72%) (Cissé *et al.*, 2017).

In sum, our findings support the overall results of the EUNPACK project regarding those paradoxes flagging ownership issues. EU interventions display across the three cases a tendency of lacking thorough understandings of root causes of the conflicts they try to tackle as much as the often visible mismatch of EU and local populations preferences (see paradoxes 1–3 in Bøås and Rieker, 2019: 15).

Conclusions: the politics of peacebuilding, SSR and CSDP missions

In this concluding section, we focus on the most salient dimension of EU crisis response policies: the *politics* dimension of EU efforts. It covers[24] collective preference formation and decision-making across policy-making in and between the member states, between member states and EU institutions, between and inside EU institutions, among different representations of the EU on-site, as well as between the EU and domestic actors ('locals').

The politics dimension on the intergovernmental level

Crisis response policy is more than formulating and implementing functionally appropriate strategies – 'it is politics, stupid!', regarding preferences of member states and the challenge of reaching viable compromises. Interestingly, though not surprisingly because of the principal–agent relationship (Kassim and Menon, 2003; Hawkins *et al.*, 2006), the EU policy is mostly turning a blind eye towards the *politics* of crisis response policy and instead focuses on coordination problems and institutional challenges of policy-making. Nevertheless, EU lessons-learned documents 'go political in disguise' when criticising an incoherent statebuilding strategy not systematically related to SSR. Likewise, the criticism of the project-based approach for lacking flexibility due to its short-term nature, or the depreciation and lack of a long-term strategic approach and the limitation of measures on the operational/technical level ignoring governance as a cross-cutting issue are indeed political issues (European Commission and HR/VP, 2016: 11, 3; Bøås and Rieker, 2019: 11f).

EU lessons learned hence entail a tendency of *de-politicisation*, in terms of a functional understanding of underlying challenges, which often comes at the expense of a proper diagnosis and therapy for operational challenges identified.[25] Likewise, this *de-politicisation* is fostered by the comprehensive approach, which insinuates that peacebuilding is foremost about 'functional' 'social engineering'. However, without political settlements among conflicting parties in any given state or society, 'functional' SSR policies will mostly be in vain, as – among others – the cases of Afghanistan and Iraq show (Mac Ginty, 2010).

Another political dimension is the 'securitisation' of peace- and statebuilding of EU missions and SSR efforts since these responses are conceived as efforts at fending off security risks if not threats. Domestic concerns about migration have drastically shifted policy concerns and preferences. This transformed conflict response policy from fostering reforms and good governance to enhancing stability and functioning state administrations able to cut 'migration flows' for EU-internal security concerns, possibly aggravating credibility and legitimacy deficits of EU foreign policy.[26] This internal–external nexus comes with issues of governments' legitimacy *inside* the EU and member states. Domestic discourses and concerns thus shape foreign policy preferences adding another politics dimension to EU crisis response policy. However, when analysing strategies and tools matching to EU problem definitions, some pitfalls can be seen. For example, EUTM Mali has no capabilities when it comes to 'fighting' migration, which is currently on top of the EU member state problem definitions regarding Mali, thus EUTM as a mission cannot be expected to address this issue.[27] Overall, *de-politisation* and *securitisation* identified as 'meta-features' of EU crisis response policy are parallel but contradictory policy features with securitisation indicating a strong politicisation tendency spilling over from one to the other policy field.[28]

Achieving actor unity among member states as much as across EU institutions is a major factor for successfully formulating a swift policy response to conflicts and crises – as a necessary but not sufficient precondition for policy effectiveness (Thomas, 2012). Converging or diverging preferences will ultimately define the coherence of both Council and Commission foreign policy. Our case studies show that the quality of compromises among EU institutions or member states does not just define the quality of policy output but also significantly effects the quality of common policy implementation. Partly diverging preferences represent manifest cooperation and coordination problems, which – according to institutionalist writings (Martin, 1993; Zürn, 1993) – may gradually be overcome by adjustments of institutional forms and practices.

Political leadership is one mechanism for facilitating intergovernmental foreign policy-making and EU SSR and CSDP missions – exemplified by, France's role as the 'lead nation' in Mali embedding its national engagement in EU crisis response policy (Janning, 2005). Colonial ties of EU member states may provide a comparative advantage concerning country and language expertise. However, this may render those member states more immediate stakeholders than the EU. This in turn may infringe on the EU's legitimacy via negative impact on 'local ownership' due to reservations regarding post/neo-colonial engagement. In consequence, an inherent tension exists between greater effectiveness due to political leadership by individual EU member states and the representation of the EU as a whole (Okemuo, 2013).

The politics dimension on the institutional level

The overlap of EU instruments and action leads to frequent misinterpretations in the field on the roles of EU Delegations and CSDP missions in regards to representation, reporting and donor coordination (European Court of Auditors, 2015: 18). The EU's institutional complexity implies 'political deals', a system of political checks and balances impeding effectiveness and efficiency of individual policies. Hence, 'turf wars' within CFSP, CSDP and SSR policies leading to delays and inefficiency are not just a coordination problem but are also about competencies, resources, relative influence and hierarchy inside the EU that is about lower-level politics. This also applies to other international actors, not least the UN, and even to state actors like the United States concerning its inter-agency policy coordination in the realm of conflict and crisis management.[29] Hence, the aforementioned feature can hardly be ascribed to the sui generis character of the EU polity – at least not in principle (Øhrgaard, 2004). Mere coordination challenges based on political disagreements on policy goals and strategies – viewed again through the lenses of institutionalist research – could be overcome by respective institutional adjustments. In the cases of Afghanistan (after 2011) and Mali (early established through the EUSR in 2014), for example, coordination mechanisms under the auspices of the EUSR supported a comprehensive analysis of the crisis environment and enhanced policy coordination, which had a positive impact on the delivery of respective mandates.

The politics dimension on the local level

Guiding principles of EU foreign policy in general and conflict response policy in particular – like conflict sensitivity, local ownership and a comprehensive approach – have been continuous features of EU policy documents and practices across our three cases, hence underpinning the EU's critical conflict transformation ambitions. As deeply ingrained *causal beliefs* (George, 1979), these principles are constitutive for EU foreign policy. By emphasising its constitutive set of social and political norms and practices, the EU in the cases at hand promoted itself as a role model in terms of externalising its norms and 'institutions' to the cases in question (Schimmelfennig and Sedelmeier, 2005; Bøås and Rieker, 2019: 11–15). However, these identity-related causal beliefs are highly political for establishing the EU as an international actor on the global level.

Hence, a final dimension of politics regards the very motivation behind CSDP efforts. Krasner and Risse (2014: 547) require certain preconditions for state-building at the domestic level of the partner country and society to be effective: a solid institutional design, cooperation and coordination (task complexity) and a high level of local political ownership on the structure, content and direction of the reform process (legitimacy). Local ownership poses a particularly challenging international–domestic nexus (mirroring the domestic–international nexus inside the EU). If ownership is not ensured from the outset but has to be 'produced' or enhanced through peacebuilding and SSR, a long-term engagement to socialise local partners in favour of EU norms and values to generate legitimacy for EU engagement on the partner side is needed (European Commission and HR/VP, 2016: 12).

Unless building on a solid national peace agreement and conflict settlement, the EU will have to choose local partners and will be challenged by international partners engaged in local conflicts by the question of legitimacy (Mac Ginty and Richmond, 2013; Ejdus and Juncos, 2018). This is visible in all our three cases, and results in problematic political deals, especially since in all our cases the necessity to build up hard security capacity of the central government was considered necessary but undermined civilian approaches to SSR and run counter to the premises of critical conflict transformation. The indispensable choice of local partners is likely to challenge existing 'local' power structures across all levels of government (see paradox 1 in Bøås and Rieker, 2019: 15). Involving local stakeholders in terms of an inclusive approach to a continuous reform process may foster resistance of locals due to infringements on their 'traditional' political influence and power and, in consequence, question the effectiveness of reform efforts and EU efforts.[30]

In sum, policy evaluations of SSR efforts and specifically CSDP missions reveal several strengths, weaknesses but also challenges. Factors constraining EU policy effectiveness are located on all levels of policy-making, the output and outcome levels of policy formulation by member states and EU institutions as much as the level of implementation in the field. However, ultimately political responsibility and accountability in a democratic polity like the EU reside with the 'government' and ultimately in the realms of intergovernmental foreign policy-making of member states.

A critical reflection provides good reasons to question whether the EU's SSR interventions are indeed primarily meant to solve political conflicts and social violence in the extended neighbourhood. On the politics level, the EU and member states are raising suspicion that they are more interested in a demonstration of a global role for the Union, rendering '(h)oisting the EU colours and gaining in profile as an international actor … often more important than immediate problem-solving!' (Peters, 2016: 265; see European Parliament, 2015: 7f). Starting with formulating elusive policy goals – from the strategic to the operational level – continuing with missing or flexible benchmarks for success, and lacking an organisational approach to learning leads us to doubt whether EU crisis response policy is capable to deliver beyond political lip-services. Defining mandates and strategy broadly and abstractly enables the EU to construct success narratives for the public. Whether in arms control matters, environmental standards, the fulfilment of the Copenhagen criteria for accession to the EU, or in EU in crisis response policy, monitoring may be done collectively and from diverse (external) agencies, but the 'certification of compliance' or effectiveness so far, unfortunately, remains a prerogative of politics and thus of political expediency. The interventionary character of CSDP missions pursuing mostly EU-centric reforms, the lack of conflict sensitivity and understanding of the root causes of conflicts it seeks to solve and the incoherence of its comprehensive approach in sum lead to, the EU's crisis response policy in practice being stuck between conflict transformation and conflict resolution approaches. The EU's rhetorical awareness and ambition that legitimate, effective and sustainable conflict response policies ought to be geared towards critical crisis transformation require a critical practice turn.

Notes

1 See literature review in Peters, 2016: 6–25.
2 See, for details, Chapter 2, this volume, and the section, 'Theory and concepts'.
3 See Beswick and Jackson, 2011: 251. As of April 2019, the EU has launched 34 missions and operations (see EEAS, 2019).
4 These categories and their specific characteristics are established in Chapter 2, this volume.

5 The perception studies, following a close to identical design, were all carried out in 2017. The questionnaire was adapted to local contexts, including local languages. In Afghanistan in 2017 a total of three hundred respondents from three categories with a hundred each, namely: people in the community with EUPOL-trained police assigned in the area, stakeholders from implementing ministries, and police officers involved or who were mentored/trained by EUPOL were interviewed and filled out the questionnaires. In Iraq in 2017, 295 questionnaires were answered across four governorates: Erbil, Sulaimaniah, Dohuk and Kirkuk covering proportionally refugees, internally displaced persons, local governments and civil society organisations (CSOs) with 50.5 per cent being direct beneficiaries of the EU's involvement, and 35 per cent were female. In Mali in 2017, 105 participants with 24 per cent being female with police and gendarmerie and local beneficiaries of CSDP missions as respondents.
6 Between 2016 and 2019, interviews were conducted with staff of the European Parliament, EC, the EEAS and mission members as well as EU Member State representatives in the Committee for Civilian Aspects of Crisis Management.
7 For the operationalisation of categories, criteria and indicators see Peters *et al.*, 2018: annex 7.
8 See for the same EU practice, for example, regarding the EU Police Mission in Bosnia and Herzegovina (EUPM BiH) and EUPOL Proxima (Tolksdorf, 2014: 68).
9 For an overview on EU policy features see Peters *et al.*, 2018: annex 6.
10 Interview with EU officials in Brussels, 6–8 March 2017.
11 Several projects relate to the framework of the 'Sahel Window' of the European Trust Fund. See Boutillier, 2017: 190.
12 Interview with former EUPOL mission member, 2018.
13 For a more critical assessment see Korski, 2010: 237; Troszczynska-van Genderen, 2010: 17f.
14 For a detailed conceptualisation of the *comprehensive approach*, see Bátora *et al.*, 2016: 6.
15 *Conflict sensitivity* in the context of EU crisis response implies recognising the complexity and multilayeredness of conflict, and that different groups in conflict have differing perceptions of the root causes of conflict and legitimate actions and agents. For details, see Bátora *et al.*, 2016: 31f.
16 Interview with EU officials in Brussels, 7 March 2017.
17 For details variants of ownership as defined in EU documents, see Heinemann, 2017: annex 4.6.
18 For another example for such a discrepancy between EU delivery and local expectations in the field of training and equipment in the case of Libya, see Loschi *et al.*, 2018: 6.

19 Like statistics, indices have to be used with care, see Munck and Verkuilen, 2002; Davis et al., 2015.
20 See World Bank Group, 2018. This index comprises six dimensions of governance: voice and accountability, political stability and absence of violence/ terrorism, government effectiveness, regulatory quality, rule of law, and control of corruption.
21 The country has increased its score in *Voice and Accountability*, *Political Stability and Absence of Violence/Terrorism* and *Control of Corruption*. See World Bank Group, 2018.
22 At the beginning of EUTM engagement, FAMa consisted of around 10,000 soldiers. In January 2016, the president announced that due to the additional recruitment of 10,000 voluntary soldiers, this number is aimed to increase to 20,000 until 2019. See Malijet, 2017.
23 NTM-A encompassed about 558 mentor teams with up to 4,000 trainers and an annual budget of US$3.5 billion in 2011 (House of Lords, 2011: 15).
24 'Politics' is here ultimately defined with David Easton as the process of decision-making within a political system authoritatively allocating values for society (here the EU). See Easton, 1965: 96.
25 For overlaps with other expert literature see, for example, Peters, 2016: 265; Dari et al., 2012: 52; Gross, 2013: 23f; Oksamytna, 2011: 10.
26 For the controversy on the impact of external shocks on securitisation processes see, for example, Boswell, 2007: 590–8.
27 Interview with EEAS official in Brussels, 6 March 2017; Bøås and Rieker, 2019: 13, and paradoxes 4 and 5.
28 See also EUNPACK findings in Raineri and Rossi, 2018.
29 See, for example, Belo and Koenig, 2011 on the UN's lack of achievements in Timor-Leste.
30 This has been a long-time concern of peacebuilding and SSR literature. See Schroeder et al., 2014; Stedman, 1997.

References

Bapir, M.A. (2010) 'Iraq: a deeply divided polity and challenges to democracy-building', *Information, Society and Justice Journal*, 3(2): 117–125.

Barea, J.C.C. (2013) *The Malian Armed Forces Reform and the Future of EUTM. Opinion Document.* Vol. 93/2013 (Madrid: Instituto Español de Estudios Estratégicos).

Bátora, J., S. Blockmans, E. Ferhatovic, I. Peters, P. Rieker and E. Stambøl (2016) 'Understanding the EU's crisis response toolbox and

decision-making processes', EUNPACK Working Paper D.4.1, EUNPACK project.
Bayer Tygesen, C. (2013) 'A cloud over EU's legacy in Afghanistan?' The Europe Center (TEC), https://tec.fsi.stanford.edu/news/a_cloud_over_eus_legacy_in_afghanistan_20130219 (accessed 26 September 2018).
Belo, N. De Sousa and M.R. Koenig (2011) *Institutionalizing community policing in Timor-Leste: Exploring the politics of police reform, Occasional Paper 9* (San Francisco: Asia Foundation).
Beswick, D. and P. Jackson (2011) *Conflict, Security and Development: An Introduction* (Oxford: Routledge).
Bøås, M. and P. Rieker (2019) *EUNPACK Executive Summary of the Final Report & Selected Policy Recomendations: A Conflict-Sensitive Unpacking of the EU Comprehensive Approach to Conflict and Crisis Mechanisms* (Brussels: Centre for European Policy Studies).
Bøås, M., A.W. Cissé, A. Diallo, B. Drange, F. Kvamme and E. Stambøl (2018) 'The EU, security sector reform and border management in Mali', Working paper on implementation of EU crisis response in Mali, EUNPACK Working Paper D.7.4, EUNPACK project.
Börzel, T.A. and T. Risse (2004) 'One size fits all! EU policies for the promotion of human rights, democracy and rule of law', paper prepared for the *Workshop on Democracy Promotion,* 4–5 October, Center for Development, Democracy, and the Rule of Law, Stanford University.
Boswell, C. (2007) 'Migration control in Europe after 9/11: Explaining the absence of securitization', *JCMS: Journal of Common Market Studies*, 45(3): 589–610, doi: https://doi.org/10.1111/j.1468-5965.2007.00722.x.
Boutillier, C. (2017) 'The security and development nexus', in J. Rehrl (ed.), *Handbook CSDP. The Common Security and Defence Policy of the European Union*, 3rd edn (Vienna: Federal Ministry of Defence and Sports of the Republic of Austria), 184–192.
Burke, E. (2009) 'The case for a new European engagement in Iraq', FRIDE Working Paper 74 (Madrid: FRIDE).
Carrasco, C. Márquez, C. Churruca Muguruza, and R. Alamillos Sánchez (2016) *Case Study: Common Security and Defence Policy (CSDP), Fostering Human Rights among European Policies* (FRAME, EU Commission FP7/2007–2013, project no. 320000, Work Package D.10.3) (Leuven: KU Leuven Centre for Global Governance Studies (KUL-GGS)).
Christova, A. (2013) 'Seven years of EUJUST LEX: The Challenge of Rule of Law in Iraq', *Journal of Contemporary European Research*, 9(3): 424–439.
Cissé, A.W., A. Dakouo, M. Bøås and F. Kvamme (2017) 'Perceptions about the EU crisis response in Mali – a summary of perception studies', EUNPACK Policy Brief D.7.7, EUNPACK project.

Council of the European Union (2007) Council Joint Action 2007/369/CFSP of 30 May 2007 on establishment of the European Union Police Mission in Afghanistan (EUPOL Afghanistan), Brussels: Council Secretariat, https://op.europa.eu/en/publication-detail/-/publication/80f4fc25-d232-4bd2-88a1-42abfd88e823/language-en (accessed 13 March 2020).

Council of the European Union (2012a) Council Conclusions on the Situation in Mali, Brussels: Council Secretariat (14926/12).

Council of the European Union (2012b) Council Conclusions on the Situation in Mali, Brussels: Council Secretariat (17535/12).

Council of the European Union (2013) EU Council Conclusion Iraq, Brussels: Council Secretariat (8680/13), http://eeas.europa.eu/archives/docs/iraq/docs/iraq_council_2004-08_en.pdf (accessed 10 February 2017).

Council of the European Union (2015) Council Conclusions on the Sahel Regional Action Plan 2015–2020, Brussels: Council Secretariat (7823/15).

Council of the European Union (2016) Council Decision amending and extending Council Decision 2013/34/CFSP on a European Union military mission to contribute to the training of the Malian Armed Forces (EUTM Mali), Brussels: Council Secretariat (6375/16).

Dari, E., M. Price, J. van der Wal, M. Gottwald and N. Koenig (2012) *CSDP Missions and Operations: Lessons Learned Processes* (Brussels: European Parliament).

Davis, K.E., B. Kingsbury and S.E. Merry (2015) 'Introduction: The local-global life of indicators: Law, power, and resistance', in S.E. Merry, K.E. Davis and B. Kingsbury (eds), *The Quiet Power of Indicators – Measuring Governance, Corruption, and Rule of Law* (New York: Cambridge University Press), 1–24.

Djiré, M., D. Sow, K. Gakou, and B. Camara (2017) *Assessing the EU's Conflict Prevention and Peacebuilding Interventions in Mali* (Bamako: Université de Sciences Juridiques et Politiques de Bamako).

Easton, D. (1965) *A Framework for Political Analysis* (Englewood Cliffs, NJ: Prentice-Hall, Inc).

Echavez, C. and Q. Suroush (2017) 'Assessment of EU's Response in Afghanistan: Did EU's conflict response through EUPOL deliver as it intended: A review of how EU in general and EUPOL in particular were received and perceived among Afghan stakeholders in Kabul', EUNPACK Policy Brief D.7.6, EUNPACK project.

Ejdus, F. and A.E. Juncos (2018). 'Reclaiming the local in EU peacebuilding: Effectiveness, ownership, and resistance', *Contemporary Security Policy*, 39(1): 4–27, doi: 10.1080/13523260.2017.1407176.

EEAS (2014a) 'Common Security and Defence Policy: EU Integrated Rule of Law Mission for Iraq (EUJUST LEX-Iraq)' (Brussels: EEAS),

www.eeas.europa.eu/archives/csdp/missions-and-operations/eujust-lex-iraq/pdf/facsheet_eujust-lex_iraq_en.pdf (accessed 6 October 2016).
EEAS (2014b) 'Strengthening the efficiency and credibility of the criminal justice system and enhancing the rule of law' (Delegation of the European Union to Iraq, 26 May).
EEAS (2015) 'Annual 2014 CSDP Lessons Report' (Brusssels: EEAS).
EEAS (2016) 'EU Training Mission in Mali' (Brussels: EEAS).
EEAS (2019) EU Missions and Operations. As part of the EU's Common Security and Defence Policy (CSDP) (Brussels: EEAS).
European Commission (2014) 'Multiannual Indicative Programme for Iraq 2014–2017', Brussels (20726919).
European Commission (2015) 'European Union – West Africa – Regional Indicative Programme 2014–2020'.
European Commission and EEAS (2014) 'Multi-Annual Indicative Programme 2014–2020', Brussels.
European Commission and HR/VP (2016) Joint Communication to the European Parliament and the Council. Elements for an EU-wide strategic framework to support security sector reform, (JOIN2016/31 final) (Brussels: European Commission).
European Court of Auditors (2015) *The EU Police Mission in Afghanistan: Mixed Results*, Special Report No. 7/2015 (Luxembourg: Publications Office of the European Union).
European Parliament (2015) 'Report on the implementation of the Common Security and Defence Policy (based on the Annual Report from the Council to the European Parliament on the Common Foreign and Security Policy)' (Brussels: European Parliament (A8–0054/2015)).
European Union HR/VP (2016) *Shared Vision, Common Action: A Stronger Europe. A Global Strategy for the European Union's Foreign and Security Policy* (Brussels: EU).
EU Training Mission in Mali (EUTM) (2018) 'Factsheet' (July) (Brussels: EUTM), https://eutmmali.eu/wp-content/uploads/2018/07/EUTM_Mission_Factsheet_31July18_EN.pdf (accessed 7 August 2019).
Fuhrmann, J. (2016) 'The response has been very positive', 13 January, www.deutschland.de/en/topic/politics/peace-security/the-response-has-been-very-positive (accessed 4 September 2018).
George, A.L. (1979) 'The causal nexus between cognitive beliefs and decision-making behavior: The "Operational Code" belief system', in L.S. Falkowski (ed.), *Psychological Models in International Politics* (Boulder, CO: Westview Press), 95–124.
Gross, E. (2013) *Assessing the EUs Approach to Security Sector Reform (SSR)* (Brussels: European Parliament).

Hänggi, H. (2004) 'Conceptualising security sector reform and reconstruction', in A. Bryden and H. Hänggi (eds), *Conceptualising Security Sector Reform and Reconstruction* (DCAF Geneva / Münster: LIT Verlag).

Hawkins, D.G., D.A. Lake, D.L. Nielson and M.J. Tierney (2006) 'Delegation under anarchy: states, international organizations, and principal-agent theory', in D.G. Hawkins, D.A. Lake, D.L. Nielson and M.J. Tierney (eds), *Delegation and Agency in International Organizations* (New York: Cambridge University Press), 3–38.

Heider, T., M. Kleine and I. Peters (2004) 'Discussion paper: Options for evaluating CFSP effectiveness' (unpublished manuscript).

Heinemann, R. (2017) 'The European Union's crisis response in the extended neighbourhood: The EU's output effectiveness in the case of Mali', EUNPACK Working Paper D.7.1, EUNPACK project.

Hettne, B. and F. Söderbaum (2005) 'Civilian power or soft imperialism? The EU as a global actor and the role of interregionalism', *European Foreign Affairs Review*, 10(4): 535–552.

House of Lords (2011) European Union Committee. The EU's Afghan Police Mission, London, https://publications.parliament.uk/pa/ld201011/ldselect/ldeucom/87/8704.htm (accessed 14 February 2020).

Human Rights Watch (2017) 'Mali: Unchecked abuses in military operations', 8 September, www.hrw.org/news/2017/09/08/mali-unchecked-abuses-military-operations (accessed 12 March 2018).

Janning, J. (2005) 'Leadership coalitions and change: The role of states in the European Union', *International Affairs*, 81(4): 821–833.

Kassim, H. and A. Menon (2003) 'The principal-agent approach and the study of the European Union: Promise unfulfilled?' *Journal of European Public Policy*, 10(1): 121–139.

Korski, D. (2010) 'EUJUST LEX (Iraq)', in G. Grevi, D. Helly and D. Keohane (eds), *European Security and Defence Policy: The First 10 Years (1999–2009)* (Paris: EU Institute for Security Studies), 231–242.

Krasner, S.D. and T. Risse (2014) 'External actors, state-building, and service provision in areas of limited statehood: Introduction', *Governance*, 27(4): 545–567, doi: 10.1111/gove.12065.

Lebovich, A. (2017) 'Serious questions remain over G5 Sahel military force', European Council on Foreign Relations, Commentary, 16 June, www.ecfr.eu/article/commentary_serious_questions_remain_over_g5_sahel_military_force_7300 (accessed 11 March 2018).

Loschi, C., L. Raineri and F. Strazzari (2018) 'The implementation of EU crisis response in Libya: Bridging theory and practice', EUNPACK Working Paper D.6.2, EUNPACK project.

Mac Ginty, R. (2010) 'Hybrid peace: The interaction between top-down and bottom-up peace', *Security Dialogue*, 41(4): 391–412, doi: 10.1177/0967010610374312.

Mac Ginty, R. and O.P. Richmond (2013) 'The local turn in peace building: A critical agenda for peace', *Third World Quarterly*, 34(5): 763–783, doi: 10.1080/01436597.2013.800750.

Malijet (2017) 'Les forces armées maliennes aujourd'hui', http://malijet.com/a_la_une_du_mali/187481-les-forces-arm%C3%A9es-maliennes-aujourd%E2%80%99hui.html (accessed 18 September 2018).

Martin, L. (1993) 'The rational state choice of multilateralism', in J.G. Ruggie (ed.), *Multilateralism Matters: The Theory and Praxis of an Institutional Form* (New York: Columbia University Press), 91–121.

Mohammed, K., D. Ala'Aldeen and K.M. Palani (2017) 'Perceptions about EU crisis response in Iraq – a summary of perception studies', EUNPACK Policy Brief D.7.5, EUNPACK project.

Munck, G.L. and J. Verkuilen (2002) 'Conceptualizing and measuring democracy: Evaluating alternative indices', *Comparative Political Studies*, 35(1): 5–34, doi: https://doi.org/10.1017/S1537592711000880.

Nicolaïdis, K., B. Sébe and G. Maas (eds) (2015) *Echoes of Empire. Memory, Identity and Colonial Legacies* (London: I.B. Tauris Publishers).

OECD (2018) *States of Fragility 2018* (Paris: OECD Publishing).

Øhrgaard, J.C. (2004) 'International relations or European integration: Is the CFSP sui generis?', in B. Tonra and T. Christiensen (eds), *Rethinking European Union Foreign Policy* (Manchester: Manchester University Press): 26–44.

Okemuo, G. (2013). 'The EU or France? The CSDP Mission in Mali the Consistency of the EU Africa policy', *Liverpool Law Review*, 34(3): 217–240.

Oksamytna, K. (2011) 'The European Union Training Mission in Somalia: Lessons learnt for EU Security Sector Reform', Istituto Affari Internazionali. IAI Working Papers, 11(16): 1–16.

Peters, I. (ed.) (2016) *The European Union's Foreign Policy in Comparative Perspective: Beyond the 'Actorness and Power' Debate* (London and New York: Routledge).

Peters, I. (2017) 'The European Union's crisis response in the extended neighbourhood: The EU's output effectiveness in the case of Iraq', EUNPACK Working Paper D.7.1, EUNPACK project..

Peters, I., E. Ferhatovic, R. Heinemann, S. Berger and S.M. Sturm (2018) 'European Union's crisis response in the extended neighbourhood: Comparing the EU's output effectiveness in the cases of Afghanistan, Iraq and Mali, EUNPACK Working Paper D.7.1 (part 4), EUNPACK project.

Raineri, L. and A. Rossi (2018) 'The security–migration–development nexus in the Sahel: A reality check', in B. Venturi (ed.), *The Security–Migration–Development Nexus Revised: A Perspective from the Sahel* (Rome: Istituto Affari Internazionali), 13–34.

Richmond, O., S. Pogodda and R. Mac Ginty (2016) 'Towards critical crisis transformation', EUNPACK Working Paper D.3.2, EUNPACK project.

Schimmelfennig, F. and U. Sedelmeier (eds) (2005) *The Europeanization of Central and Eastern Europe* (Ithaca, NY and London: Cornell University Press).

Schroeder, U.C., F. Chappuis and D. Kocak (2014) 'Security sector reform and the emergence of hybrid security governance', *International Peacekeeping*, 21(2): 214–230, doi: 10.1080/13533312.2014.910405.

Sedra, M. (2013) 'The hollowing-out of the liberal peace project in Afghanistan: The case of security sector reform', *Central Asian Survey*, 32(3): 371–387, doi: 10.1080/02634937.2013.843387.

Skeppström, E., C. Hull Wiklund and M. Jonsson (2015) 'European Union Training Missions: Security sector reform (SSR) or counter-insurgency by proxy?', *European Security*, 24(2): 353–367, doi: 10.1080/09662839.2014.972382.

Stedman, S.J. (1997) 'Spoiler problems in peace processes', *International Security*, 22(2): 5–53, doi: 10.2307/2539366.

Suroush, Q. and E. Ferhatovic (2017) 'Assessing EUPOL Impact on Afghan Police Reform (2007–2016)', EUNPACK Working Paper D.7.3, EUNPACK project.

The Economist Intelligence Unit (2017) *Mali: Country Report* (London, New York, Hong Kong).

The Economist Intelligence Unit (2018) *Democracy Index 2017. Free speech under attack* (London).

The Economist Intelligence Unit (2019) *Democracy Index 2019* (London).

Thomas, D.C. (2012) 'Still punching below its weight? Coherence and effectiveness in European Union foreign policy', *JCMS: Journal of Common Market Studies*, 50(3): 457–474, doi: https://doi.org/10.1111/j.1468-5965.2011.02244.x.

Tolksdorf, D. (2014) 'Incoherent peacebuilding: The European Union's support for the police sector in Bosnia and Herzegovina, 2002–8', *International Peacekeeping*, 21(1): 56–73, doi: 10.1080/13533312.2014.885710.

Transparency International (2018) 'Corruption Perceptions Index 2017', www.transparency.org/news/feature/corruption_perceptions_index_2017 (accessed 14 August 2018).

Troszczynska-van Genderen, W. (2010) *Human rights challenges in EU civilian crisis management: The cases of EUPOL and EUJUST LEX*, Occasional Paper 84 (Paris: EU Institute for Security Studies).

Tull, D.M. (2017) *Mali und G5: Ertüchtigung des Sicherheitssektors. Politische Hindernisse für eine effektive Kooperation der Regierung und ihrer Partner*, SWP-Aktuell 76 (Berlin: SWP).

Underdal, A. (2004) 'Methodological challenges in the study of regime effectiveness', in A. Underdal and O.R. Young (eds), *Regime Consequences: Methodological Challenges and Research Strategies* (London: Kluwer Academic), 27–48.

United Nations (2015) 'Concluding observations on the fifth periodic report of Iraq' (New York: UNHRC (CCPR/C/IRQ/CO/5)).

United Nations (2016) 'Concluding observations on the combined sixth and seventh periodic reports of Mali' (New York: UNHRHC Committee on the Elimination of Discrimination against Women (CEDAW/C/MLI/CO/6–7 MALI)).

United Nations (2017) 'Concluding observations on the second periodic report of Afghanistan' (New York: Office of the UNHCHR, Committee against Torture (CAT/C/AFG/CO/2)).

Vermeij, L. (2015) 'MINUSMA: Challenges on the ground,' Policy Brief 19 (Oslo: NUPI).

World Bank Group (2018) 'Worldwide Governance Indicators', http://info.worldbank.org/governance/wgi/#reports (accessed 12 March 2018).

Youngs, R. (2004) 'Europe and Iraq: From stand-off to engagement?', CEPS Working Documents 216 (Brussels: Centre for European Policy Studies).

Zürn, M. (1993) 'Problematic social situations and international institutions – on the use of game theory in international politics', in F.R. Pfetsch (ed.), *Inaugural Pan-European Conference: International Relations and Pan-Europe* (Münster and Hamburg: LIT-Verlag), 63–84.

8

Dissecting the EU response to the 'migration crisis'

Luca Raineri and Francesco Strazzari

Introduction

Europe has long been the destination of mixed-migration flows.[1] Since the early 2000s, the regulation of these flows has been at the core of EU policies vis-à-vis neighbouring countries. The ENP promoted regional economic integration and institutional convergence alongside the hardening of its external borders and more stringent provisions tackling irregular migration. Coupled with the adoption of bilateral border cooperation treaties – especially between southern EU member states and southern EU neighbours – these measures have contributed considerably to keeping irregular migration to the EU under control (UNODC, 2011).

From 2011 onwards, the disruptive reconfiguration of the EU's southern neighbourhood brought about by the so-called 'Arab Springs' and their aftermath first challenged and eventually destabilised this framework. In particular, uncertain political transitions and the violent conflicts that flared up in Syria and Libya resulted in increased border porosity and large displacement numbers. The EU became a target for mixed migratory flows on an unprecedented scale: the peak was reached in 2015, when more than one million migrants, asylum-seekers and refugees reached the EU irregularly across the Mediterranean Sea and the Balkan Peninsula. In overall terms these figures are bigger than those of refugees that reached Europe in the mid 1990s, at the apex of the wars in the former Yugoslavia, which was often depicted as Europe's worst refugee crisis since World War II.

The most conspicuous stream of this flow was observed across the Aegean Sea between Turkey and Greece, where more than

850,000 migrants – largely of Syrian, Iraqi and Afghan origin – transited in 2015. However, from March 2016 the passing of a controversial EU-Turkey 'Deal'[2] helped drastically reduce mixed migration across South-Eastern Europe. Along the so-called Central Mediterranean Route (CMR), instead, mixed migratory flows proved steadier and more resilient: between 2013 and the first half of 2017, more than half a million people crossed the Mediterranean Sea from Libya to Italy. These migrants and asylum-seekers came largely from sub-Saharan Africa, including an overall amount of more than 100,000 Eritreans,[3] 85,000 Nigerians and 30,000 Gambians. Throughout the same five-year period, the requests for international protection filed in Italy boomed to 427,000, dwarfing the total of 317,000 in the preceding twenty-seven years between 1985 and 2012 (Geddes, 2018).

The drastic scale-up of mixed migratory flows from the southern neighbourhood into the EU put a considerable strain on EU member states' capacity of coping and absorption. Capturing European audiences' growing concern for a phenomenon that appeared as spiralling out of control, in a period that was marked by a series of jihadist terror attacks perpetrated on European soil, the German Chancellor Angela Merkel alerted that the 'asylum issue … would preoccupy Europe much, much more than the issue of Greece and the stability of the euro' (Westcott, 2015). At the same time, the quantitative change – that is, 'large numbers' and fears of their impact – brought about a qualitative shift in how the phenomenon came to be imagined and apprehended. Media and policy discourses have increasingly addressed these dynamics in terms of a European 'migration' and/or 'asylum' 'crisis' (Berry *et al.*, 2015). This framing, albeit contested (Jeandesboz and Pallister-Wilkins, 2016), proved performative in shaping perceptions and prompting demands of swift responses by European leaders. Though, the multifaceted nature of the 'migration crisis' – and the polysemy of a designation that encompasses humanitarian, security, economic and identity concerns – made the identification of the most appropriate response strategy a highly divisive question across Europe.

Taking this inherent ambiguity as a starting point for our investigation, our contribution re-traces the processes that have led to the framing of an 'EU migration crisis' and to the adoption of the specific 'crisis response' measures. To this end, the first part of the chapter incorporates the methodological insights of securitisation studies (Buzan et al., 1998) and process-tracing (Bennett and Checkel, 2014) to unearth the complex combination of interests and concerns allegedly threatened by the rapid escalation of Europe-bound mixed migration according to different stakeholders.

The second part examines the specific crisis response approach that underpins the variety of tools and measures adopted by the EU to cope with the 'migration crisis'. To do so, we build on recent developments in peace studies (Mac Ginty et al., 2016; Richmond et al., 2016). We outline three approaches to crisis response, inspired by different traditions of social science: a realist response (i.e., crisis management), a structuralist response (i.e., crisis resolution) and a liberal response (i.e., crisis transformation). We define crisis management as primarily concerned with the stabilisation or containment of a crisis. It 'regards the state with its border regimes and defence mechanisms as a bulwark against negative effects of security interdependence' with the aim to 'prevent crises from spreading, destabilising regions or inflicting harmful repercussions on the EU. Crisis management works through short-term interventions, but rejects long-term engagement with the underlying causes of the crisis' (Richmond et al., 2016: 13–14). For its part, crisis resolution purports the ambition to resolve the crisis by tackling its root causes. These are typically found in the structural constraints that stifle individual needs and jeopardise the achievement of a positive peace (Galtung, 1969), such as economic marginalisation, bad governance and different forms of insecurity. Lastly, crisis transformation is focused less on tackling the conditions that made the crisis possible than on considering the long-term impact of the crisis and seeking to accommodate those new realities while at the same time addressing the crisis 'conditions of possibility' at structural level. Crisis transformation thus aims to cultivate resources such as resilience, recognition, ownership and legitimacy, that help a society cope with stressors and disruptions even when technocratic aid from abroad fades away, in order to ward off negative long-term effects of short-term crisis response measures.

The broader strategic framework of the EU provides little – and somewhat contradictory – indications about the actual orientation of the EU crisis response. On the one hand, the general guiding principles of EU crisis response – such as conflict and context sensitivity, local ownership, human rights and humanitarian obligations, comprehensive approach to security, etc. (Pirozzi, 2013) – are more in line with crisis transformation. On the other hand, the review of the ENP – that the crises in the Mediterranean contributed to prompting (Ivashchenko-Stadnik et al., 2017) – acknowledges the trade-offs between the promotion of democratic norms and the pursuit of stability: the new ENP's (European Commission and HR/VP, 2015) manifest leaning towards the latter demonstrates the toning down of the EU normative engagement and a realist shift favourable to a crisis management approach (Raineri and Strazzari, 2019). Half-way between the two, the 2016 EU Global Strategy for Foreign and Security Policy (EEAS, 2016a) purports to uphold both stabilisation and societal resilience.

These observations bring to the fore the hypothesis that the actual crisis response approach favoured by the EU may stand out more clearly within narrower policy sectors. The EU response to the migration crisis provides a valuable case study, owing to both its specificity and wide-ranging, cross-cutting influence. The tripartite analytical framework herein outlined provides the basis to ascertain whether a shift to crisis management, stabilisation and containment can be observed in the EU's dealing with its neighbourhood (Pomorska and Noutcheva, 2017) in the domain of migration policies, too.

We choose to narrow down our empirical analysis to the 'migration crisis' unfolding along the CMR so as to better illuminate the connections and contradictions between EU migration policies and the responses to the Libyan security crisis, a scenario in which – unlike elsewhere – for example, Syria – the EU did and does play a significant role. The analysis of policy documents is compounded by the qualitative evidence collected through 60-plus interviews with EU officers, UN staff, members of international organisations and NGOs, as well as Libyan, Malian and Nigerian state officials and civil society representatives. Interviews were conducted in Tunis, Libya (remotely), Bamako, Niamey, Agadez and Brussels between February 2017 and November 2018, also in the framework of the EUNPACK project.

Framing the 'EU migration crisis'

On 19 April 2015, a boat ferrying migrants and asylum-seekers from Libya to Italy shipwrecked off the shore of the island of Lampedusa, killing more than eight hundred people in what the UNHCR later defined 'the gravest humanitarian disaster in recent times' (Bonomolo and Kirchgaessner, 2015). While political concern about cross-Mediterranean migratory flows had been brewing for some time, this tragic event became the trigger that brought the EU to seize cross-Mediterranean migrations as a priority issue and devise a coordinated response. Given the swift pace of the events that followed, one can conjecture that the EU response had been at least partly planned in advance, and that the tragic fatality provided an opportunity for it to gain steam.

The day after the Lampedusa shipwreck, on 20 April 2015, a joint Foreign and Home Affairs Council was convened to discuss the event. In a joint statement, EU HR/VP Federica Mogherini and the Migration and Home Affairs Commissioner Dimitris Avramopoulos defined the situation a 'crisis' requiring urgent reaction, and introduced a ten-point plan to tackle it (the so-called Mogherini Plan, see European Commission, 2015a). Implicitly drawing on the Council's decision to foster a comprehensive approach to security (Council of the European Union, 2013), the plan called for a coordinated and enhanced mobilisation of all relevant EU instruments and resources, including Frontex (European Border and Coast Guard Agency), EASO, EUROPOL, EUROJUST, EEAS Delegations and CSDP missions.

A few days later, on 23 April 2015, a Special Meeting of the EU Council elaborated on the Mogherini Plan and committed to a number of measures to 'increase search and rescue possibilities', 'combat the smuggling and trafficking of human beings', 'tackle the root causes of illegal migration', and 'reinforce internal solidarity' and burden-sharing with frontline EU member states. Noteworthy, the Council took a more cautious attitude, and qualified the situation in the Mediterranean as 'a tragedy', and 'an emergency', but never as 'a crisis' nor as 'a threat'. The word security was never mentioned in the Council's conclusions, which nevertheless noted that 'instability in Libya create[d] an ideal environment for the criminal activities of traffickers' (Council of the European Union,

2015a). The martial tone, however, immediately resurfaced in the remarks that Avramopoulos addressed to the Council: the commissioner claimed that 'Europe is declaring war on smugglers' (European Commission, 2015b).

The concern for comprehensiveness prompted the Council's invitation to systematise the approach endorsed for the CMR on a broader scale. As a result, the Commission issued a renewed EU Agenda on Migration on 13 May 2015: this new release updated and replaced the overarching framework governing EU external migration and asylum policy since 2005 (i.e., the Global Approach to Migration and Mobility – also known as GAMM). The new Agenda introduced a number of detailed measures to meet the ambitious objectives spelt out in the conclusions of the April Special Meeting of the EU Council: among them, military and police naval operations, external interventions to tackle migration flows upstream in the countries of origin and transit, the strengthening of EU external border controls and data collection systems, the so-called 'hotspot' approach, the review of the Dublin system for asylum applications processing, schemes for asylum-seekers' relocation, resettlement or return, and the promotion of legal migration pathways (Geddes, 2018). At the same time, the EU Agenda on Migration also moved the securitisation of migration one step further. The Agenda repeatedly defined the situation in the Mediterranean as a 'crisis' affecting European border security and to be dealt with through security means, first and foremost CSDP missions (European Commission, 2015c). It also added that 'every crisis will be different, but the EU needs to heed the lesson and be prepared to act in anticipation of a crisis, not just in reaction' (European Commission, 2015c: 11).

Building on the indications of the Council, the Commission and the Agenda on Migration, the HR/VP immediately requested the *Crisis* Management and Planning Directorate (CMPD, emphasis added) of the EEAS to develop a *Crisis* Management Concept (CMC, emphasis added) putting forward some options for a possible CSDP mission to fight migrant smuggling in the Mediterranean (EEAS, 2015). While the crisis-jargon was gaining momentum, it is worth noting that CMCs should theoretically have drawn on a respective PFCA issued by the EEAS Political and Security Committee. Since no PFCA on migration existed then, the rule was circumvented by relying on the 2014 PFCA for Libya (EEAS, 2014). This move ensured a little noticed – albeit crucial – attention shift: from a Libyan crisis to a migration crisis. This, however, remained implicit and was never clearly spelt out: the new crisis management concept did not qualify migration as 'a crisis', but only as 'a situation with very serious implications for the EU [which] requires urgent action' (EEAS, 2014: 3), also because of the 'need to prevent links between criminal networks and terrorist organisations' (EEAS, 2014: 6).

The fear of a crime–terror nexus therein articulated, however, seemed to rely on poor empirical evidence (Toaldo, 2015), and in fact it was entirely absent in the Libya PFCA (EEAS, 2014). EEAS officials subsequently acknowledged that 'migration and terrorism were amalgamated a bit too quickly', and admitted that they could not 'be sure whether there are actual links between terrorism and migrant trafficking' (quoted in Ivashchenko-Stadnik *et al.*, 2017: 29). Whenever asking themselves whether the nexus existed, they concluded that the answer is not easy to find. Nonetheless, assuming the existence of a crime–terror connection eased the resort to emergency measures for responding to security 'crises' in the face of a migration 'issue'. The decision-making process was thus streamlined, and the naval CSDP mission EUNAVFOR MED – Operation Sophia was approved in the record time of a couple of months from the Lampedusa shipwreck, on 22 June 2015. Its mandate revolved around the primary goals 'to disrupt the business model of human smuggling and trafficking networks in the Southern Central Mediterranean and prevent the further loss of life at sea' (EEAS, 2017).

One week after the launching of Operation Sophia, the Council issued a note in view of the preparation of the Valletta Summit on Migration. Announced in the Agenda on Migration, the Summit was designed to gather European and African leaders in Malta to coordinate the implementation of EU migration policies' external dimension. In the note, the Council studiously avoided mentions of 'crisis' and 'security', while the situation of migrants in the Mediterranean was repeatedly defined 'a tragedy' (Council of the European Union, 2015b). Similar circumspection can be found in the phrasing of the main concluding documents which were issued a few months later at the Valletta Summit – that is, the Political Declaration and the Action Plan.[4] Here, the notions of 'crisis' and 'in/security' were not referred to in relation to the phenomenon of large-scale migration per se, but to its root causes. In the outputs of the Valletta Summit, security is present in terms of human security (of migrants, to be preserved), food security (and lack thereof as one of the root causes of migration) and rule of law, while the commitment to the respect of human rights and humanitarian obligations is emphasised upfront. The Summit also decided to set up a new aid instrument aimed to provide a rapid, flexible and effective response to the migration issue, now described as an 'emergency': the EUTF 'for stability and addressing root causes of irregular migration and displaced persons in Africa' (European Commission, 2015d: 1).

The strategy outlined at the Summit can be considered the last step of the intense policy-making season inaugurated by the Lampedusa shipwreck of April 2015. The subsequent months were largely devoted to the implementation of the measures announced, with few unexpected additions. The process-tracing of these developments highlights that the scale-up of mixed migratory flows across the Mediterranean Sea triggered a proliferation of policies, strategies and new instruments by the EU in mid 2015. However, the subject matter was subject to considerable oscillation: the phenomenon to be addressed was qualified as a 'crisis', a 'tragedy', and an 'emergency'. As a preliminary observation, the Commission seemed to be more eager than the Council to securitise the migration issue, and it did so by tying it to notions of crisis, security and threat. Exploratory explanations for this may include the Commission's determination to emphasise the salience of the Mediterranean issue in order to elicit action by more recalcitrant member states; the Council's inherent collective action problem which tends to rule out radical options (Hampshire, 2016); or perhaps, more trivially, the Commissioners' national affiliation to countries more directly exposed to the rise of trans-Mediterranean mixed migration.

Be it as it may, the mobilisation of the concept of crisis was soon subsumed into a field of political struggle, stirring controversies. UN agencies working on migration questioned the appropriateness of labelling the EU migration issue a 'crisis', noting that in the same years several countries less resourced than the EU had been targeted by much larger flows of migrants and asylum-seekers (Miles, 2018). Some human rights organisations accused European leaders of cynically 'manufacturing' the so-called 'migration crisis' for political gain, urging them to speak instead of a *political* crisis prompted by large-scale migratory flows (de Bellis, 2019). Even the European Commission eagerly embraced the 'crisis' framing around 2015–16, only to denounce that enduring perceptions of a 'migration crisis' in 2018–19 were fuelled by 'fake news' and 'misinformation' (Rankin, 2019).

One could argue that this very polarisation, underpinned by calls for radical changes in EU migration policy, is in itself indicative that the migration issue fuelled a veritable crisis in the EU. According to peace studies scholarship, in fact, a crisis can be defined as 'a serious incident or set of incidents that culminates in socio-economic and/or political instability, generating strong political pressure for a radical change.... Crises do not need to involve opposing military forces, but are bound to polarise political environments by unleashing political opposition to the intended crisis response' (Mac Ginty *et al.*, 2016: 10). Transnational in nature, the 'migration crisis' seemed qualitatively different compared to other crises which were looming at the horizon of the EU at the same time, because of its inherent capacity to transcend the domestic–international dichotomy and generate tangible manifestations affecting Europeans' communities and daily lives.

While the framing of the migration issue as a crisis gradually made its way in political and security discourses, however, the specific nature and object of the crisis – that is, the referent object in the securitisation jargon – remained largely underspecified. Very often the iterations of the 'migration crisis' trope failed to specify *what* the crisis actually threatened, and therefore *what* crisis response mechanisms should protect. In some instantiations, the 'migration crisis' seemed to be articulated in humanitarian terms, eliciting the response to 'save lives at sea'. In other cases, and especially in iterations by the Commission, the crisis seemed to refer primarily to the escalation of transnational security threats such as smuggling networks, organised crime and terrorism. From this point of view, the crisis seemed to require a more muscular response including hardened border security, CSDP missions, and the fight (or 'war', in Avramopoulos's ineloquent wording) against migrant smugglers. Furthermore, soaring mixed migration flows prompted fears that the migration crisis would exacerbate the enduring economic crisis, overburdening the already stretched welfare system of southern European countries. It was also argued that the migration crisis, and the politicisation thereof, foreshadowed a deeper normative crack involving an existential crisis, whereby the rise of populist and xenophobic parties on the extreme right of the political spectrum fuelled nationalist sentiments and identity politics which, in turn, threatened the multilateralist orientation, if not the very survival of the EU (Hampshire, 2016). In a country like Italy, at the forefront of arrivals along the CMR, the Minister of Interior went as far as to express fear for the survival of democracy (*La Repubblica*, 2017). From this perspective, EU leaders may have favoured crisis response approaches primarily aimed to do as little harm as possible to election results, pursuing quick-fix solutions more attuned to the anxieties of their constituencies than to the needs of vulnerable groups (Loschi et al., 2018). These developments highlighted in unprecedented ways the rising tensions between the interests of national political elites, and the EU institutional architecture.

The use of the concept of 'crisis' with reference to the large-scale mixed migration in the Mediterranean can therefore be seen as clear illustration of how analytically loose the public debate was. This circumstance may be seen as convenient, in as much as the considerable – albeit implicit – spectrum of variation of the crisis's referent object could contribute to bridging consensus gaps among actors that are otherwise driven by diverging interests and concerns. From this perspective, the framing of migration policies in terms of crisis response could be said to amount to a case of 'constructive ambiguity', so common in EU policy-making (see, for instance, Jegen and Merand, 2014; Cusumano and Hofmaier, 2019). In this light, one should probably shift the analytical focus away from discursive framings, and consider instead how crisis response measures were implemented in practice. The investigation of the crisis at the response level can in fact provide valuable indications about the changing nature of the EU's actorness in crisis situations.

Responding to the crisis

On paper, the responses to the 'migration crisis' adopted by the EU entailed a variety of measures in pursuit of different objectives, including enhanced humanitarian action to save lives at sea; the strengthening of EU external borders to contain cross-border threats; the stepping-up of security coordination to disrupt migrant smuggling; the development efforts to tackle the root causes of migration; and the review of EU asylum policies to help frontline member states address the high volume of arrivals. Subsequent reports noted however that some of these measures have been implemented only poorly, if at all. Beyond the realm of discourses, then, the analysis of how EU migration policies have been implemented in practice can help illuminate the specific modalities and inherent tensions of the EU response to a migration issue framed as a crisis.

The different approaches to crisis response outlined in the introduction – crisis management, crisis resolution and crisis transformation – provide a valuable framework to drive the observations and categorise the cacophonic field of security practices. Crisis management arguably encompasses a variety of interrelated security practices aimed at stepping-up border security, promoting stabilisation operations, fighting cross-border networks such as – in this case – migrant smugglers, and ensuring humanitarian protection at home – with a limited commitment to the spreading of such norms abroad. On the other hand, responses to the migration crisis addressing primarily the needs of migrants and asylum-seekers who are forced to leave their countries of origin should be categorised as empirical manifestations of a crisis resolution approach. These may include measures to foster job creation, socio-economic development, good governance, accountability, rule of law and conflict resolution. Lastly, the strengthening of legal guarantees, the adoption of multilateral burden-sharing measures ensuring long-term sustainability, the promotion of civil society, and the fostering of capacity-building incorporating bottom-up perspectives and local knowledges, all exhibit a transformative approach in responding to migration.

These three approaches are not necessarily incompatible with each other. At first sight, the actual EU response to the migration crisis may seem adherent to all of them, at least in part. With a view to providing a fine-grained assessment of the different response approaches' relative weight in the overall EU response to the migration crisis, we analytically disentangle three distinct domains in our analysis: migration and development, humanitarian action, and border policing.

Migration and development

The focus on the nexus between migration and development is a longstanding feature of EU policy-making (see, for instance, Sinatti and Horst, 2015). In light of the expanding range and scope of policies and instruments designed to tackle the root causes of migration through enhanced development efforts, one may be tempted to conclude that a crisis resolution type of approach inspired the EU response to the migration crisis. A closer look, however, reveals some important inconsistencies between the crisis resolution template and the post-2015 articulation of the migration–development nexus by the EU.

One notices a marked shift in the aims pursued by the EU external action in these domains, which has turned the alleged nexus upside-down. Strategic documents issued before the migration crisis used to emphasise how migration could be beneficial to the achievement of development goals. For instance, the 2006 European Consensus on Development set out to 'make migration a positive factor for development, through the promotion of concrete measures aimed at reinforcing their contribution to poverty reduction, including facilitating remittances and limiting the "brain drain" of qualified people' (European Commission, 2006: 24). Similarly, the 2005 Commission's Communication on Migration and Development stressed the EU ambition to 'improv[e] the impact of migration on development' (European Commission, 2005: 3). Both documents, alongside the GAMM and the Lisbon Treaty issued in those same years, recalled the importance of fostering policy coherence for development. More recent strategies, by contrast, overturn the nexus, and exhort to make development aid functional to EU migration goals, first and foremost the curbing of irregular migration. For instance, the 2016 Partnership Framework on Migration – which builds on the Agenda on Migration and shapes the New European Consensus on Development (European Commission, 2017) – states plainly that

> coherence between migration and development policy is important to ensure that development assistance helps partner countries manage migration more effectively.… Positive and negative incentives should be integrated in the EU's development policy, rewarding those countries that fulfil their international obligation to readmit their own nationals, and those that cooperate in managing the flows of irregular migrants. (European Commission, 2016: 9)

This shift indicates a clear departure from the needs-based perspective of crisis resolution.

The EUTF provides another eloquent illustration of these trends. The EUTF is usually presented as the EU signature tool to tackle the root causes of migration through development assistance. However, it has been noted that the largest share of EUTF resources are not added to, but diverted from more traditional EU aid budgets, such as the European Development Fund and the Development Cooperation Instrument. The main change in the process is that the EUTF largely derogates from OECD best practices, most notably in terms of management transparency, alignment with national development strategies, local ownership, civil society involvement and needs-based assessment. As a result, beneficiaries of EUTF-sponsored projects are frequently identified based on their migratory status, rather than on their needs (Oxfam, 2017).

The actual allocation of development funds follows the same orientation. This is most visible in partner countries deemed strategic for the external governance of mixed migratory flows. In Libya, out of an overall EU budget for bilateral assistance amounting in early 2018 to €354 million, pooled from different instruments (EEAS, 2018), the largest share was devoted to programmes of migrants' repatriation and border management (Loschi et al., 2018). In Niger, where in the same years the overall EU development aid exceeded €900 million (Zandonini, 2018), representing 45 per cent of the country's whole national budget (Bergamaschi, 2017), the largest share of EU funds supported socio-economic development (Molenaar et al., 2018). However, it is noteworthy that it is only after the adoption of the Partnership Framework by the EU that Niger started to fight migrant smuggling, an activity that was otherwise locally seen as legitimate and beneficial (Raineri, 2018). In the same vein, the broader EU engagement in the Sahel adjusted its priority from development, as enshrined in the 2011 EU Security and Development Strategy in the Sahel, to migration and border controls, 'following the EU mobilisation against irregular migration and related trafficking' (EEAS, 2016b).

Overall, this analysis suggests that EU response to the migration crisis through development aligns poorly with the requirements of a crisis resolution type of approach. This is illustrated most clearly by the de-priorisation of migrants' and asylum-seekers' needs in the decisions over budget allocations. Similarly, the top-down direction of development strategies and the curtailment of local ownership and civil society's role is conflicting with crisis transformation. Instead, the transfer and/or subjection of resources earmarked for development to the implementation of border protection measures is more consistent with a realist-inspired approach to crisis response – that is, crisis management.

Humanitarian action

While the Mediterranean Sea hit the headlines of journalistic and scholarly reports as the deadliest border to cross for migrants worldwide (International Organization for Migration, 2017), many of the EU post-2015 migration policies purported the ambition to 'save lives at sea'. This suggests the importance of humanitarian concerns in the framing of the EU's overall response to the migration crisis. At the same time, critical scholarship has stressed the ambiguity of such humanitarian commitment, which can contribute not only to 'sav[ing] lives', but also to the entrenchment of exclusionary regimes and of bordering practices (Pallister-Wilkins, 2015; Cuttitta, 2018). Mirroring this ambivalence, the focus on humanitarian action shares some key features with all the approaches to crisis response detailed above. An in-depth analysis of EU humanitarian response is therefore required to ascertain whether this was more intended to manage the consequence of the migration crisis, address its root causes in situations of emergency, or build resilience by extending humanitarian guarantees.

One notices that the fight against migrant smuggling has generally taken precedence over humanitarian concerns in EU crisis response. In the countries crossed by mixed migratory flows, the criminalisation of irregular migration encouraged by the EU has reportedly jeopardised the capacity of EU-sponsored humanitarian organisations to gain access to migrants and asylum-seekers, and to provide assistance to those in need (Molenaar *et al.*, 2018). Even more explicitly, the CSDP-mission Operation Sophia was deliberately designed to minimise deployment in humanitarian operations, in spite of its mandate to 'to disrupt the business model of human smuggling' *and* 'prevent the further loss of life at sea'. On several occasions, EUNAVFOR MED strategic documents (EEAS, 2015,

2018) reiterated that SAR activities were not part of Operation Sophia's core mandate, while the mission's crisis management concept seemed to imply that EUNAVFOR MED's subjection to humanitarian (and human rights) obligations would be only contingent (Ivashchenko-Stadnik *et al.*, 2017).

By contrast, the EU and its member states progressively outsourced SAR activities to the Libyan authorities. Since the second half of 2016, the Political and Security Committee authorised EUNAVFOR MED to engage in the capacity-building of the Libyan coastguard, with increasing EUTF resources made available to this end. In June 2017 the Commission invited the Italian coastguard to help the Libyan authorities set up a Maritime Rescue Coordination Centre in Libya (EEAS, 2017). In the meantime, humanitarian NGOs who had stepped in to address the growing needs in rescue operations were subjected to increasing pressures by frontline member states – with the steady backing of Brussels – conceivably meant to deter SAR activities by non-state actors (Loschi *et al.*, 2018).

The strategy of externalising SAR operations was arguably a compromise between, on the one hand, the fear that Europe-bound rescue operations could incentivise irregular migrants to undertake dangerous sea-crossings and, on the other hand, the illegality under EU human rights law of returning rescued migrants and asylum-seekers to Libya by European actors, be they public or private. This approach, however, proved inconsistent with the humanitarian imperative of saving lives. The number of migrants reported dead in the attempt of crossing the CMR increased markedly between 2015 and 2016, from 3,149 to 4,581. The absolute decline observed in the subsequent years – to 2,853 in 2017 and 1,314 in 2018 – was compounded by a drastic rise in the proportion of deaths over the attempted crossing, peaking to approximately 1 in 10 in 2018.[5] This was a rate far higher than had been observed at any point during the crisis, prompting scholars to condemn EU humanitarian engagement as hypocritical (Cusumano, 2019). Although more difficult to quantify, the fatality rates appeared to soar also in the downstream segment of the migratory routes targeted by EU anti-smuggling measures, stirring the concerns of humanitarian actors (Danish Refugee Council, 2016).

At the same time, through the externalisation of SAR and humanitarian action to Libyan actors, the EU has indirectly promoted the massive resort to unsafe detention schemes for the management of irregular migration. The systematic abuses perpetrated on migrants and asylum-seekers documented in Libyan detention centres offer a clear illustration of this (UNSMIL and OHCHR, 2016), that the EU has been embarrassingly reluctant to acknowledge and condemn. This brought a variety of actors, including human rights organisations (Amnesty International, 2017), humanitarian NGOs (Liu, 2017) and UN agencies (OHCHR, 2017), to denounce the EU's perceived eagerness to compromise on its normative principles, exposing EU crisis response to unprecedented levels of criticism. Since late 2017, the EU has sponsored the humanitarian evacuations of vulnerable migrants trapped in Libyan detention centres. These, however, proved too limited in scope to offer more than a palliative response to a much more encompassing problem, especially as long as the underlying issue of migrants' legal status in the countries of transit is not adequately addressed (Molenaar and Ezzedine, 2018).

Overall, these observations highlight that, in spite of magniloquent claims, the humanitarian imperative to save lives within the EU response to the migration crisis was at best auxiliary to, if not contingent on, the fulfilment of other priorities. From this perspective, in isolation from a stronger determination to tackle broader insecurities and rule of law issues in third countries, EU humanitarian action cannot be seen as conducive to a resolution of the migration crisis. This is also because – by problematically equating migrant smuggling not to a means but to a root cause of irregular migration – the EU has appeared to neglect the needs of migrants and asylum-seekers. Furthermore, the deliberate curtailment of the role of civil society, the short-term temporality of the interventions, and the failure to extend the migrants' and asylum-seekers legal guarantees – whether in the EU or in third countries – suggest that EU-sponsored humanitarianism has had little to do with a transformative approach to the migration crisis. True, the emphasis on capacity-building may suggest otherwise. However, it should be noted that while this was frequently justified with humanitarian arguments, *de facto* capacity-building predominantly targeted law enforcement actors, with the purpose of supporting border management and containing the spill-over of the crisis. In conclusion, then, EU humanitarian action seemed more attuned with the (limited) ambition of a crisis management agenda than anything else.

Border policing

The stepping-up of border policing measures represents one of the most prominent domains of the crisis response by the EU. The migration crisis prompted in fact a massive escalation of EU investments in this domain, both at EU external borders and in third countries of transit of mixed migratory flows to Europe. Frontex, for instance, saw a sevenfold increase in its budget as a direct result of the migration crisis, from €15.7 million in its first full year of operation in 2006 to €114 million in 2015 (Hampshire, 2015: 549), and the Agenda on Migration prospected a further inflation to more than €300 million in 2020. The external dimension of border policing has expanded concomitantly. One report found that the ENP budget earmarked for border externalisation has boomed from €59 million in 2003, to €15.4 billion in 2014–20 (Akkermann, 2018). If one looks even further afield along migratory routes, the estimated costs of EU efforts to tighten border controls and deter irregular migration in third countries have reportedly exceeded €15 billion only in the eighteen months that followed the declaration of the migration emergency (Overseas Development Institute, 2016).

Prima facie, such a focus on border policing lends credibility to the hypothesis that the EU response was primarily shaped by a crisis management agenda, with its focus on state security and threat containment. Corroborating this interpretation, a considerable emphasis on the fight against migrant smuggling and trafficking (often conflated without further specification) through police and security means is a common thread tying together the Mogherini Plan, the conclusions of the Special Meeting on migration of the EU Council, the Agenda on Migration, the very deployment of EUNAVFOR MED – Operation Sophia, as well as a remarkable share of the EUTF allocations. One could even argue that, through the Agenda on Migration and the Partnership Framework, the fight against migrant smuggling was not only streamlined, but it also came to subsume and reconfigure the overall EU engagement with third countries in North Africa and the Sahel, as for instance the case of Niger illustrates.

At the same time, though, border policing is not necessarily incompatible with alternative approaches, as long as it integrates the needs of vulnerable groups and the knowledge of local actors, and it is designed to contribute primarily to good governance and/or societal resilience. Available studies however suggest that these ambitions were only marginally integrated in EU's growing focus on border policing. The genesis of Operation Sophia is particularly telling in this sense: at the peak of the crisis, the transformative ambition to foster an integrated border management in Libya was (provisionally) set aside to give priority to more muscular containment measures in order to prevent the spill-over of the crisis through the strengthening of the maritime border (Ivashchenko-Stadnik et al., 2017). In the extended neighbourhood, the EU has urged Sahelian countries to adopt anti-smuggling strategies before more encompassing migration strategies, and border security strategies before more comprehensive national security strategies. The precedence of the particular (security-oriented) over the general suggests a turning of the logic of a coherent support to good-governance upside-down. Furthermore, the EU has in many cases demonstrated its eagerness to turn a blind eye on the authoritarian and/or criminal drift of third countries' authorities in exchange for their cooperation on migration and border policing. From this perspective, EU crisis response may have contributed to empowering unaccountable rulers and cementing predatory practices stretching from capital cities to remote border outposts of partner countries. The cases of Mali (Lebovich, 2018), Niger (Raineri, 2018), Sudan (Molenaar et al., 2018), Turkey (Pierini, 2018) and Libya (Micallef et al., 2019) provide ample illustration of how the stress-test of a migration crisis (or perception thereof) has diluted the EU ambitions to promote good governance and liberal statebuilding.

Internally, the EU has by and large failed to adopt the reform needed to ensure the EU's own greater resilience through a more sustainable system of integrated border management, asylum applications processing, and burden-sharing. Owing to the reluctance of some EU member states, the relocation scheme enshrined in the Agenda on Migration was only poorly implemented, in spite of its rather limited ambitions (Geddes, 2018), while the reform of the Dublin regulation governing the asylum applications examination and processing has lagged behind. As the stalemate on these issues

Dissecting the EU response to the 'migration crisis' 219

fuelled mutual distrust and suspicions across the EU, the strengthening of EU external border policing soon emerged as one of the few domains where a modicum level of agreement and progress could be reached.

All in all, these observations suggest that border policing measures have provided one of the most enduring, consistent and expanding domains of the EU response to the migration crisis. However, it is only the interpretation and implementation of these measures in the rather conservative terms of crisis management – rather than crisis resolution or crisis transformation – that secured the needed levels of convergence among the disparate interests of EU institutions, EU member states and third countries' elites. The inability to address the more structural issues and longer term impacts of border protection, though, may be self-defeating and unsustainable as critics pointed out (Lebovich, 2018).

Concluding observations

With the reshuffling of the Mediterranean politics that followed the Arab Springs, the rapid surge of mixed migratory flows to Europe has tested the coping capacity of the EU and its member states. However, the very framing of this situation as a 'crisis', and the securitisation thereof, has not been straightforward, but uneven and contested. Re-tracing the discursive steps underpinning the mobilisation of the 'migration crisis' narrative has led us to note the considerable degree of analytical looseness of this framing (what the crisis is about) and of its referent object (what the crisis is threatening). We have argued that this could be seen as a case of 'constructive ambiguity' to bridge consensus gaps across different configurations of interests and concerns.

The ambiguity of the discursive framing has prompted the shift of the analytical focus to crisis response practices. We have therefore investigated in depth the specific strategies and measures put in place by the EU to respond to a migration issue defined as a crisis, looking in particular at the domains of migration and development, humanitarian action, and border policing. EU migration-related measures in these domains have been compared and contrasted with the policy prescriptions of crisis management, crisis resolution and crisis transformation templates, in order to ascertain the relative weight of different approaches to crisis response in EU actorness. Our analysis suggests that, while on paper, EU crisis response appears to combine insights from the three approaches, in practice the EU has invested much more in the management of the migration crisis. In all the three domains analysed, the focus is predominantly on the containment of irregular migration flows rather than on addressing their structural causes or on building societal resilience vis-à-vis their long-term impacts.

As a realist approach to crisis response inspires crisis management, this finding corroborates the conclusion of recent scholarship on the overall trend of EU security posture in the last decade or so (Pomorska and Noutcheva, 2017; Belloni *et al.*, 2019). Yet this is not merely pleonastic. Building on recent scholarship (Richmond *et al.*, 2016), in fact, one could have expected a greater geographic differentiation of EU crisis response, whereby structuralist and transformative approaches would prevail in the EU neighbourhood, in line with the normative ambitions of the ENP, while a realist strategy focused on security, borders and centralised states would rather fit EU action in the extended neighbourhood. Our analysis highlights instead that, in the context of the 'migration crisis', the realist approach to crisis response is cross-cutting, suggesting that such a discernment between different recipients of EU crisis response is waning. Interestingly, then, uniformity between EU neighbours and neighbours' neighbours is being achieved less by spreading norms from close to distant neighbours (i.e., crisis resolution and transformation) than by generalising the approach that was originally meant for distant neighbours only (i.e., crisis management) to all third countries. This suggests that the model of crisis response that is emerging through the 'migration crisis' is underpinned by a strong process of estrangement and othering, which widens the gap between the security approaches and normative standards accepted for the EU, and for 'the rest'. Bordering, thus, manifests itself not only as a material process, but also as a symbolic one, in which analytical distinctions that are sharp and essentialised are favoured to the ones which are more nuanced and tailored.

This dissonance, however, could contribute to fading the image of the EU as a reliable supporter of the demands of democracy, good governance and accountability. As outlined in this chapter, such shift may involve high reputational costs for the EU. At the same time, the potential for political and security costs, too, should not be underestimated. Alternative allies may become tempting for those in the EU neighbourhood bearing demands for change, and who feel constrained between the rock of local authoritarian rulers and the hard place of EU's self-absorbed attitude. One could argue that the increasing influence of Gulf states and Russia in the EU southern neighbourhood already provides an illustration of these ongoing dynamics. Similarly, unmet demands for social and physical mobility could find an expression through transnational radical ideologies that provide a formidable challenge to both the status quo and EU values.

In other words, by indulging in the realist drift of contemporary international politics, the EU may find itself obliged to play a game it is not equipped to play, a game in which the normative weapons of the EU constitutive arsenal become dull instruments. The South-Eastern EU borderlands were crossed in the 1990s by hundreds of thousands of refugees fleeing the Yugoslav wars, a tragedy that unfolded from the Maastricht summit of 1991 onwards, marking the beginning of the EU and its foreign projection. Today, we have seen in those very same corners of Europe, thousands of Syrian refugees who were rejected, detained and abused. An ill-thought crisis response to an ill-defined migration crisis makes the need for crisis management a self-fulfilling prophecy.

Notes

1 The term 'mixed migration' is more comprehensive than that of 'migrant' or 'refugee', as it encompasses the mobility of individuals with different legal statuses. According to the 2016 UN Declaration for Refugees and Migrants, the only internationally adopted document on both refugees and migrants, mixed migration refers to cross-border 'mixed flows of people, whether refugees or migrants, who move for different reasons but who may use similar routes' (UNGA, 2016).
2 Based on the Joint Action Plan to fight irregular migration, the 'deal' passed on 18 March 2016 between the EU and Turkey has raised significant legal controversies, both vis-à-vis its legal nature – whether an international legally binding agreement or a political statement – and

vis-à-vis its compatibility with international human rights and refugee law (Lehner, 2018).
3 It has been argued that many of those self-identified as Eritreans may in fact be Ethiopian nationals who purport an Eritrean identity to increase their chances of obtaining a refugee status in Europe (Reitano and Tinti, 2015).
4 Documents at www.consilium.europa.eu/it/meetings/international-summit/2015/11/11–12/ (accessed 1 February 2020).
5 Data at https://missingmigrants.iom.int/region/mediterranean?migrant_route%5B%5D=1376 (accessed 1 February 2020).

References

Akkerman, M. (2018, May) *Expanding the Fortress: The Policies, the Profiteers and the People Shaped by the EU's Border Externalisation Programme* (Amsterdam: Transnational Institute).

Amnesty International (2017) *Libya's Dark Web of Collusion: Abuses against Europe-Bound Refugees and Migrants* (London: Amnesty International, December).

Belloni, R., V. Della Sala and P. Viotti (eds) (2019) *Fear and Uncertainty in Europe: The Return to Realism?* (London: Palgrave Macmillan).

Bennett, A. and J.T. Checkel (eds) (2014) *Process Tracing: From Metaphor to Analytic Tool* (Cambridge: Cambridge University Press).

Bergamaschi, I. (2017) 'Aid in the Sahel in the 2000s: Tales of dependence and appropriation', Conference Paper, www.academia.edu/34241179/ (accessed 1 February 2020).

Berry, M., I. Garcia-Blanco and K. Moore (2015) *Press Coverage of the Refugee and Migrant Crisis in the EU: A Content Analysis of Five European Countries. Report prepared for the UNHCR* (UNHCR, December).

Bonomolo, A. and S. Kirchgaessner (2015) 'UN says 800 migrants dead in boat disaster as Italy launches rescue of two more vessels', *Guardian*, 20 April.

Buzan, B., O. Wæver and J. de Wilde (1998) *Security: A New Framework for Analysis* (London: Lynne Rienner Publishers).

Council of the European Union (2013) Joint Communication to the European Parliament and the Council – The EU's comprehensive approach to external conflicts and crises (Brussels: 12 December).

Council of the European Union (2015a) Special meeting of the European Council – Statement (Brussels: 23 April).

Council of the European Union (2015b) *Valletta Conference on Migration* (Malta, 11–12 November) – Orientation Debate (Brussels: 30 June).

Cusumano, E. (2019) 'Migrant rescue as organized hypocrisy: EU maritime missions offshore Libya between humanitarianism and border control', *Cooperation and Conflict*, 54(1): 3–24.

Cusumano, E. and S. Hofmaier (eds) (2019) *Projecting Resilience Across the Mediterranean* (London: Palgrave Macmillan).

Cuttitta, P. (2018) 'Delocalization, humanitarianism and human rights: The Mediterranean border between exclusion and inclusion', *Antipode: A Radical Journal of Geography*, 50(3): 783–803.

Danish Refugee Council (2016) 'Forgotten fatalities: The number of migrants' deaths before reaching the Mediterranean', Mixed Migration Monitoring Mechanism Initiative (Geneva: DRC, June).

de Bellis, M. (2019) 'European leaders are manufacturing a "migration crisis" for political gain', *Amnesty International Blog*, 18 January.

EEAS (2014) 'Libya, a Political Framework for a Crisis Approach' (Brussels: EEAS, 1 October).

EEAS (2015) *Working document – Crisis Management Concept* (Brussels: EEAS, May).

EEAS (2016a) *Shared Vision, Common Action: A Stronger Europe. A Global Strategy for the European Union's Foreign and Security Policy* (Brussels: EEAS, June).

EEAS (2016b) *Annual Report on the Sahel Regional Action Plan 2015/2016* (Brussels: EEAS, 23 December).

EEAS (2017) 'European Union Naval Force – Mediterranean Operation Sophia' (Rome: EEAS, 31 March).

EEAS (2018) 'Strategic Review on EUNAVFOR MED Operation Sophia, EUBAM Libya & EU Liaison and Planning Cell' (Brussels: EEAS, 27 July).

European Commission (2006) Communication to the Council, the European Parliament, the European Economic and Social Committee and the Committee of Regions: Migration and Development: Some concrete orientations (Brussels: European Commission, 1 September).

European Commission (2006) *The European Consensus on Development* (Brussels: European Commission, June).

European Commission (2015a) 'Joint Foreign and Home Affairs Council: Ten point action plan on migration', Press release (Luxembourg: European Commission, 20 April).

European Commission (2015b) *Speech: Remarks by Commissioner Avramopoulos at the press conference in Castille Place, Malta* (Valletta, 23 April).

European Commission (2015c) Communication to the European Parliament, the Council, the European Economic and Social Committee and the Committee of the Regions: A European Agenda on Migration (Brussels: European Commission, 13 May).

European Commission (2015d) 'Agreement establishing the European Union Emergency Trust Fund for stability and addressing root causes of irregular migration and displaced persons in Africa, and its internal rules' (Brussels: European Commission, 20 October).

European Commission and HR/VP (2015) Joint Communication to the European Parliament, the Council, the European Economic and Social Committee and the Committee of the Regions: Review of the European Neighbourhood Policy (Brussels: European Commission, 18 November).

European Commission (2016) Communication to the European Parliament, the Council and the European Investment Bank on establishing a new Partnership Framework with third countries under the European Agenda on Migration (Strasbourg: European Commission, 7 June).

European Commission (2017) *The New European Consensus on Development. 'Our World, Our Dignity, Our Future'* (Brussels: European Commission, June).

Galtung, J. (1969) 'Violence, peace, and peace research', *Journal of Peace Research*, 6(3): 167–191.

Geddes, A. (2018) 'The politics of European Union migration governance', *JCMS: Journal of Common Market Studies*, 56(S1): 120–130.

Hampshire, J. (2015) 'European migration governance since the Lisbon treaty: Introduction to the special issue', *Journal of Ethnic and Migration Studies*, 42(4): 537–553, doi: 10.1080/1369183X.2015.1103033.

Hampshire, J. (2016) 'Speaking with one voice? The European Union's global approach to migration and mobility and the limits of international migration cooperation', *Journal of Ethnic and Migration Studies*, 42(4): 571–586.

International Organization for Migration (2017) *Four Decades of Cross-Mediterranean Undocumented Migration to Europe* (Geneva: IOM, November).

Ivashchenko-Stadnik, K., R. Petrov, L. Raineri, P. Rieker, A. Russo and F. Strazzari (2017) 'How the EU is facing crises in its neighbourhood: Evidence from Libya and Ukraine', EUNPACK Working Paper D.6.1, EUNPACK project.

Jeandesboz, J. and P. Pallister-Wilkins (2016) 'Crisis, routine, consolidation: The politics of the Mediterranean migration crisis', *Mediterranean Politics*, 21(2): 316–320.

Jegen, M. and F. Mérand (2014) 'Constructive ambiguity: Comparing the EU's energy and defence policies', *West European Politics*, 37(1): 182–203.
La Repubblica (2017) 'Minniti: "Sui migranti ho temuto per la tenuta democratica Paese"', *La Repubblica*, 29 August.
Lebovich, A. (2018) 'Halting ambition: EU migration and security policy in the Sahel'. European Council on Foreign Relations (ECFR) Policy Brief (London: ECFR, September).
Lehner, R. (2018) 'The EU–Turkey "deal": Legal challenges and pitfalls', *International Migration*, 57(2): 176–185.
Liu, J. (2017) 'Europe is feeding a criminal system of abuse in Libya', *Doctors Without Borders Blog*, 7 September.
Loschi, C., L. Raineri and F. Strazzari (2018) 'The implementation of EU Crisis Response in Libya: Bridging theory and practice', EUNPACK Working Paper D.6.2, EUNPACK project.
Mac Ginty, R., S. Pogodda and O.P. Richmond (2016) 'Crises and concepts', EUNPACK Working Paper D.3.1, EUNPACK project.
Micallef, M., R. Horsley and A. Bish (2019) *The Human Conveyor Belt Broken: Assessing the Collapse of the Human-Smuggling Industry in Libya and the Central Sahel*. The Global Initiative Against Transnational Organized Crime and Clingendael (Geneva, March).
Miles, T. (2018) 'U.N. view on the European migrant crisis? There isn't one', *Reuters*, 6 July.
Molenaar, F. and N. Ezzedinne (2018) *Southbound Mixed Movement to Niger: An Analysis of Changing Dynamics and Policy Responses*. Clingendael CRU Report (The Hague: Clingendael Institute, December).
Molenaar, F., J. Tubiana and C. Warin (2018) *Caught in the Middle: A Human Rights and Peace-Building Approach to Migration Governance in the Sahel*. Clingendael CRU Report (The Hague: Clingendael Institute, December).
OHCHR (2017) 'EU "trying to move border to Libya" using policy that breaches rights – UN experts' (Geneva: OHCR, 17 August).
Overseas Development Institute (2016) *Europe's Refugees and Migrants: Hidden Flows, Tightened Borders and Spiralling Costs* (London: ODI, 14 September).
Oxfam (2017) 'An emergency for whom? The EU Emergency Trust Fund for Africa: Migratory routes and development aid in Africa', Oxfam Briefing Note (Brussels: Oxfam, 15 November).
Pallister-Wilkins, P. (2015) 'The humanitarian politics of European border policing: Frontex and border police in Evros', *International Political Sociology*, 9(1): 53–69.

Pierini, M. (2018) 'The 2018 Turkey Regress Report', Carnegie Article (London, 14 March).

Pirozzi, N. (2013) 'The EU's comprehensive approach to crisis management' (Brussels: DCAF, June).

Pomorska, K. and G. Noutcheva (2017) 'Europe as a regional actor: Waning influence in an unstable and authoritarian neighbourhood', *JCMS: Journal of Common Market Studies*, 55(S1): 165–176.

Raineri, L. (2018) 'Human smuggling across Niger: State-sponsored protection rackets and contradictory security imperatives', *Journal of Modern African Studies*, 56(1): 63–86.

Raineri, L. and F. Strazzari (2019) '(B)ordering hybrid security? EU stabilisation practices in the Sahara-Sahel Region', *Ethnopolitics*, 18(5): 544–559.

Rankin, J. (2019) 'EU declares migration crisis over as it hits out at "fake news"', *Guardian*, 6 March.

Reitano, T. and P. Tinti (2015) 'Survive and advance: The economics of smuggling refugees and migrants into Europe' ISS Paper 289 (Dakar: Institute for Security Studies, November).

Richmond, O.P., S. Pogodda and R. Mac Ginty (2016) 'Towards critical crisis transformation', EUNPACK Working Paper D.3.2, EUNPACK project.

Sinatti, G. and C. Horst (2015) 'Migrants as agents of development: Diaspora engagement discourse and practice in Europe', *Ethnicities*, 15(1): 134–152.

Toaldo, M. (2015) 'Migrations through and from Libya: A Mediterranean Challenge', IAI Working Paper 15 (Rome: Istituto Affari Internazionali, 14 May).

UNGA, Resolution 71/1 (2016) 'New York Declaration for Refugees and Migrants' (New York, 10 September).

UNODC (UN Office on Drugs and Crime) (2011) *The Role of Organized Crime in the Smuggling of Migrants from West Africa to the European Union* (Vienna: UNODC, January).

UNSMIL and OHCHR (2016) *'Detained and Dehumanised': Report on Human Rights Abuses against Migrants in Libya* (Geneva: UNSMIL, 13 December).

Westcott, L. (2015) 'Merkel: Refugees could be bigger challenge than Greek debt crisis', *Newsweek*, 17 August.

Zandonini, G. (2018) 'Niger: il perno instabile della politica UE nel Sahel', ISPI Commentary, 1 August.

Index

Afghanistan 75–77, 97, 98, 99, 102, 104, 140, 141–143, 148, 151, 152, 153, 154–155, 156, 158–160, 166–191, 202
agency 16, 41, 50, 54
Arab Spring 70, 173, 178

Balkans 46, 66, 67, 115–133, 202

civil society 35, 40, 43, 44, 46, 70, 119, 124, 127, 174
Common Foreign and Security Policy 70
Common Security and Defence Policy 29, 70, 105, 125, 166, 173, 175, 176, 181, 190, 207
conflict management 1, 12–13, 19, 21, 26, 28, 33–35, 54, 117–120, 128–133, 161, 166, 176, 204
conflict resolution 12–13, 21, 26, 33, 35–36, 65, 90, 145, 161, 176
conflict sensitivity 18, 21, 22, 23, 53, 67, 75, 101–102, 139–140, 148–151, 160, 177, 178–179
conflict transformation 12–13, 19, 21, 26, 28, 33, 36–39, 53, 65, 87, 116, 117–120, 128–133, 166
corruption 48, 127, 131, 181
crisis management 2, 3, 6, 18, 22, 23, 26, 41–43, 52, 53, 82, 86, 91, 175, 202

crisis resolution 2, 26, 43–44, 202, 212
crisis transformation 2, 26, 45–46, 82, 109, 202

democracy 22, 30, 67, 70, 130

enlargement 20, 65–66, 128
European Commission (EC) 20, 188, 208, 209, 212
European Council 20, 32, 61, 65, 168, 188, 208
European External Action Service (EEAS) 30, 46, 89, 102, 175
extended neighbourhood 12, 19, 21, 30, 60, 69, 81, 141–145, 204

fieldwork 16–17, 52, 65, 117, 139, 149, 169, 177, 192, 204
France 168, 173, 188

gender 53
Germany 6, 202

humanitarianism 41, 52, 90, 99, 150, 204, 209, 211
human rights 10, 13, 21, 22, 53, 121, 132, 181–182, 204, 208–209
hybridity 14, 33, 40, 41, 46, 47, 48, 50, 53, 119, 176

integrated approach 9, 86–110
integration 31, 42, 53, 66, 87
Iraq 6, 77–79, 98, 102, 140, 143–144, 147–148, 150, 158, 166–191
Italy 202

Kosovo 19, 66, 97, 100, 116, 117, 121–133

legitimacy 4, 10, 14, 26, 29, 44, 47, 52, 54, 102, 119, 158, 176, 184, 188, 190, 202
liberal peace 12, 21, 31, 37–39, 119–128, 153, 167, 203
Libya 15, 42, 44, 46, 52, 72–75, 99, 101–102, 105–107, 201, 207
local turn 3, 5, 14, 17, 32, 45, 48, 54, 87, 102–104, 117, 119, 125, 139–140, 146–148, 151, 160, 176, 177, 179–180, 183–186, 188, 189–191

Maastricht Treaty 7
Mali 15, 42, 44, 79–81, 98, 101, 102, 107–108, 140–141, 144–145, 147, 149–150, 152–153, 154, 156–157, 158–159, 166–191
migration 11, 14, 19, 30, 42, 43, 45, 48, 50, 53, 70, 72–75, 103–104, 104–108, 154, 155, 187, 201–221

NATO 7, 86, 95–96, 98, 99, 101, 153
neighbourhood 21, 30, 60, 69–70, 81, 201
Northern Ireland 40

Organisational Studies 4
Organization for Security and Co-operation in Europe (OSCE) 93–95

Palestine 52
Peace and Conflict Studies 2, 3, 4, 5, 12, 26, 33, 46
peacebuilding, 1, 3, 18, 21, 23, 32, 39, 115, 119–128, 166, 168
peacekeeping 23, 34, 38, 91–93
power 5, 10, 41–42, 60, 102, 148

recognition 44
resilience 52
Responsibility to Protect (R2P) 7
Russia 43, 72, 128

sanctions 43
security and securitisation 5, 9, 19–21, 22, 42, 44, 49, 66, 68, 83, 88, 98, 115–133, 153–155, 203
Security Sector Reform (SSR) 20, 140–141, 148, 152, 157–58, 168, 175, 178, 186–187, 188, 190
sovereignty 7
stability and stabilisation 2, 8, 10, 20, 23, 29, 31, 41, 54, 70–83, 90, 91, 119, 211
statebuilding 44, 50, 98, 117, 119, 153–155
Syria 32, 45, 201

terrorism 11, 52, 70–72, 152, 207
trade 30–31, 44, 150

Ukraine 43, 45, 70–72, 98–99, 100, 107
United Kingdom 12, 168
United Nations 1, 7, 18, 21, 43, 91–93, 119, 167
United States 86, 133, 152, 154, 156, 160, 173, 189

EU authorised representative for GPSR:
Easy Access System Europe, Mustamäe tee 50,
10621 Tallinn, Estonia
gpsr.requests@easproject.com

www.ingramcontent.com/pod-product-compliance
Ingram Content Group UK Ltd.
Pitfield, Milton Keynes, MK11 3LW, UK
UKHW021840140426
5217IPUK00022B/1533